Teaching and Learning in
Higher Education

MSc

Education at SAGE

SAGE is a leading international publisher of journals, books, and electronic media for academic, educational, and professional markets.

Our education publishing includes:

- accessible and comprehensive texts for aspiring education professionals and practitioners looking to further their careers through continuing professional development

- inspirational advice and guidance for the classroom

- authoritative state of the art reference from the leading authors in the field

Find out more at: **www.sagepub.co.uk/education**

Teaching and Learning in
Higher Education

Disciplinary Approaches to Educational Enquiry

Elizabeth Cleaver, Maxine Lintern and **Mike McLinden**

Los Angeles | London | New Delhi
Singapore | Washington DC

Los Angeles | London | New Delhi
Singapore | Washington DC

SAGE Publications Ltd
1 Oliver's Yard
55 City Road
London EC1Y 1SP

SAGE Publications Inc.
2455 Teller Road
Thousand Oaks, California 91320

SAGE Publications India Pvt Ltd
B 1/I 1 Mohan Cooperative Industrial Area
Mathura Road
New Delhi 110 044

SAGE Publications Asia-Pacific Pte Ltd
3 Church Street
#10-04 Samsung Hub
Singapore 049483

Editor: James Clark
Editorial assistant: Rachael Plant
Production editor: Thea Watson
Copyeditor: Jill Birch
Proofreader: Rose James
Indexer: Martin Hargreaves
Marketing manager: Catherine Slinn
Cover design: Naomi Robinson
Typeset by: C&M Digitals (P) Ltd, Chennai, India
Printed and bound by CPI Group (UK) Ltd,
Croydon CR0 4YY

MIX
Paper from
responsible sources
FSC
www.fsc.org   FSC® C013604

First published 2014

Library of Congress Control Number: 2013948044

British Library Cataloguing in Publication data

A catalogue record for this book is available from
the British Library

ISBN 978-1446-2-4622-2
ISBN 978-1446-2-5463-9 (pbk)

To our families who, through their support and patience,
have made this book possible.

CONTENTS

LIST OF FIGURES

LIST OF CASE STUDIES

ACKNOWLEDGEMENTS

Our grateful thanks go to Alexander Agathanggelou for his work formatting final drafts and corralling the various figures and case studies into a sensible system. Thanks also to Carole Craven for her final proof read of the chapters in full. For her valuable comments on an early draft of Chapter 4 our thanks go to Paula McGee. We are also extremely grateful to Tom Barker, Jon Harrison, Louise Hunt, Chris Willmott and Lindsay Yardley who kindly allowed us to embed their experiences and work into the text's chapters and case studies. We are indebted to the editorial team at SAGE for their support and helpful comments throughout. Last, but not least, we would like to extend our grateful thanks to our chapter authors without whom Part Two of this book would have been impossible to realise.

Chapter acknowledgements

Chapter 10 – Susan Orr and Julian McDougall:
  Julian McDougall would like to extend his thanks to Elizabeth Cleaver for facilitating the collaboration with Susan Orr that began with the co-authored

chapter in this collection and has developed into a range of other highly beneficial activities.

Chapter 12 – Sharon Buckley and Patricia Fell
We are indebted to Professors Marilyn Hammick and Nick Ross for their valuable comments on an early draft of this manuscript.

Chapter 13 – Rob Clucas and Gerry Johnstone
We are grateful to Elizabeth Cleaver for the invitation to contribute to this book and for helpful suggestions on an earlier draft and to those who participated in the research we have drawn upon in this chapter.

ABOUT THE AUTHORS

Dr Elizabeth Cleaver is Director of Learning Enhancement and Academic Practice at the University of Hull, UK where she leads work in the areas of teaching development, technology enhanced learning and quality enhancement. She returned to the HE sector in 2008 after six years as a senior researcher undertaking policy research and evaluation at the National Foundation for Educational Research (NFER). Her early academic career was in the discipline of sociology where she gained her PhD and taught and researched youth transitions to adulthood (early works are published under the name Kenyon). It was during this period that her interest in disciplinary approaches to teaching began. While studying for her Postgraduate Certificate in Teaching and Learning at the University of Portsmouth, UK, she became aware of the importance of *teaching sociologically* alongside thinking and researching sociologically. This has profoundly influenced her current work at the University of Hull where she is supporting academic teams to explore and develop their own disciplinary pedagogies.

Professor Maxine Lintern is Associate Dean for Learning Teaching, Research and Scholarship for the Faculty of Health at Birmingham City

University. She is the Director of Research and founder of the Centre for Health and Social Care Research. Her background is in biochemistry and neurophysiology and she has always been profoundly interested in the links and interfaces between research and teaching – hence her unusual portfolio of responsibility! The research strategy she has developed for the Faculty overtly links all research activity back into the development of innovative teaching environments and the curriculum leading to the generation of better healthcare professionals. Prior to her post at Birmingham City she was Director of Learning and Teaching at the University of Birmingham where she worked closely with staff from a wide range of subject areas as they undertook formal training in teaching as part of their PGCert. The challenge of helping them to see links back to their own research environment and how that could inspire educational development is one of the drivers for producing this book. She was awarded a personal chair in Biomedical Science in 2011.

Professor Mike McLinden is a programme tutor and Director of Education in the School of Education at the University of Birmingham. He is Senior Academic Advisor to the University's Centre for Learning and Academic Development (CLAD) and has recently completed a secondment as 'Director of Educational Development' within the Centre. Prior to commencing his role at the University Mike was a teacher of children with special educational needs. Since 2001 he has been co-director of the *Visual Impairment Centre for Teaching and Research* (VICTAR) and until May 2012 was co-editor of the *British Journal of Visual Impairment*. Mike has wide experience of curriculum design, delivery and evaluation across different academic disciplines, and has a broad research interest in educational enhancement within higher education. His current research activities include developing and promoting 'research-informed' pedagogical practice within higher education with a particular focus on cultivating staff and student expectations. Mike was conferred the status of Principal Fellow of the Higher Education Academy (PFHEA) in June 2013.

ABOUT THE CONTRIBUTORS

Dr Helen Barefoot is the Deputy Head of the Learning and Teaching Institute and a Senior Lecturer in Neuroscience at the University of Hertfordshire, UK. Helen leads continuing professional development (CPD) for academic staff at the University which includes managing the Postgraduate Certificate in Higher Education, coordinating a workshop and seminar series and organising the annual learning and teaching conference. Her research interests include: ensuring inclusive teaching and equality of opportunity for all learners; understanding the enablers and barriers to academic staff in terms of quality enhancement; plus research into how to improve assessment and feedback practice. Helen has developed her own educational enquiry work within her discipline through her interests in assessment and feedback and also provides support for staff across her institution in their enquiry activities. In July 2013 Helen became a Principal Fellow of the Higher Education Academy (PFHEA).

Dr Sharon Buckley is a Senior Lecturer in Medical Education at the University of Birmingham, UK. Having completed her PhD on the bioenergetics of antibiotic uptake, Sharon began her career in education in the North of Scotland. Before joining the University of Birmingham in 2003, she held various posts in secondary and post-16 education. Committed to evidence-based education, Sharon has published aspects of her work, including a Best

Evidence Medical Education (BEME) systematic review of the evidence for the educational effects of portfolios in undergraduate student learning. She is currently undertaking a second BEME review on aspects of the effectiveness of patient safety curricula. Sharon is an Associate Tutor for the University of Birmingham's Centre for Learning and Academic Development (CLAD), contributing to the Postgraduate Certificate in Academic Practice, and undertaking project work. In 2010, the Higher Education Academy awarded Sharon a National Teaching Fellowship in recognition of her work.

Dr Rob Clucas is a Lecturer in Law at the University of Hull, UK. Interested in teaching and learning since studying for the Postgraduate Certificate in Higher Education at the University of Sheffield in 1998, Rob has contributed to a number of teaching-related publications and continues to engage in reflective teaching practice. Rob's current research and teaching interests are in the field of sexuality, gender and the law, with a particular focus on church equality issues. As B. Clucas, Rob published articles and book chapters on jurisprudence (philosophy of law); medical ethics, particularly conjoined twins; human rights, and children's rights and welfare, and with G. Johnstone and T. Ward, co-edited the Nomos collection *Torture: Moral Absolutes and Ambiguities.*

Dr Patricia Fell is a Senior Academic in Health Sciences at Birmingham City University, UK. After obtaining a PhD in pharmacology, she spent a brief spell in Further Education before moving to higher education where she has been involved in teaching biosciences to both pre- and post-registration student nurses and allied health professions for over twelve years. Patricia became actively involved in the field of educational development and research in 2006 when she was seconded to the stakeholder partnerships BCU Centre of Excellence in Teaching and Learning (CETL) team. During this period she led an initiative which supported staff across the Faculty of Health and local NHS Trusts in the development and evaluation of small-scale teaching innovation projects. Patricia now leads several initiatives that support and research student learning of biosciences in healthcare education including two HEA funded Teaching Development projects. She is chair and founder of the Bioscience in Nursing Education (BiNE) national network.

Dr Elaine Fulton is Senior Lecturer in Modern History and Director of Undergraduate Studies for History at the University of Birmingham, UK. Elaine is heavily involved in curriculum design, developments in technology enhanced learning and the training and mentoring of new staff including postgraduate teaching assistants within her disciplinary area. From 2006 she was a member of the Advisory Panel for the Higher Education Academy's Subject Centre for History, Classics and Archaeology and was appointed National Co-ordinator for History Postgraduates and Postdoctoral Researchers from 2006 to 2007. The opportunity to be involved in the creation of this particular volume fitted well both with her ongoing interest in early career academic development and with her interests in educational enquiry. Elaine's forthcoming publications include *The Search for Authority in the Reformation* (edited with Helen Parish and Peter Webster, Ashgate, 2014).

Dr Michael Grove is inaugural Director of the STEM Education Centre at the University of Birmingham, UK, and former Director of the National HE STEM Programme, a three-year initiative across England and Wales which included a remit to enhance HE learning and teaching practices within Science, Technology, Engineering and Mathematics disciplines. He was also Assistant Director of the former Higher Education Academy Subject Centre for Mathematics Statistics and Operational Research. A physicist by background, Michael works on issues relating to learning and teaching within higher education and teaches mathematics to undergraduate students from a range of disciplines; he is also responsible for the University's Mathematics Support Centre. His teaching interests include supporting students in their transition to university, particularly in relation to non-specialist learning of mathematics, and supporting the professional development of early career academic staff. He has recently established, with Tina Overton, a national programme of activity to promote and encourage scholarship, evaluation and research in learning and teaching within HE STEM disciplines.

Professor Gerry Johnstone is Professor of Law at the University of Hull, UK. He is the author and editor of six books which examine innovations in penal policy, including *Restorative Justice: Ideas, Values, Debates* (2nd edition published by Routledge in 2011). His works are used on courses about restorative justice around the world and have been translated into Chinese, Japanese and Russian. He is the founding director of the University of Hull's unique online MA in Restorative Justice. In addition to writing about penal policy, for over two decades Gerry has been an active participant in national debates about nature and purposes of legal education in universities. His paper 'Liberal Ideals and Vocational Aims in University Legal Education' (*Web Journal of Current Legal Issues*, 1999) is frequently cited and discussed in the growing field of legal education studies.

Dr Helen King is Head of Academic Staff Development at the University of Bath, UK, with responsibility for both educational and researcher development. She has previously held leadership roles in discipline-based, UK-wide educational development projects and initiatives (including Assistant Director of the HEA Subject Centre for Geography, Earth & Environmental Sciences), and worked as an independent consultant based in the USA with a particular focus on geoscience education. She has been an active member of the Staff & Educational Development Associate (SEDA) since 1996, and holds a Senior Fellowship of SEDA, a National Teaching

Fellowship and is a Fellow of the Higher Education Academy. She has presented and published widely in the field of educational development, and is currently a member of SEDA's Scholarship & Research Committee and on the *Innovations in Education & Teaching International* journal editorial board. Her professional interests are in linking teaching and research, and disciplinary ways of thinking and practising, and how these themes can be explored through academic development: http://www.drhelenking.com.

Dr Joe Kyle was formerly Director of Undergraduate Studies for the School of Mathematics at the University of Birmingham and is currently acting as an Advisor in Mathematics to the newly established STEM Education Centre. He is also an Academic Associate in Mathematics, Statistics and Operational Research (MSOR) with the Higher Education Academy. He is Editor in Chief for the Higher Education Academy Journal *MSOR Connections* and sits on the Editorial Board of the Oxford University Press Journal *Teaching Mathematics and its Applications*. A pure mathematician by background, Joe also works for the Open University. Joe has recently written a *Guide for External Examiners in MSOR* and, in partnership with Peter Kahn, edited *Effective Learning and Teaching in Mathematics and its Applications*. Joe is regularly invited to contribute to national and international conferences and delivers (with others) workshops on teaching and learning for new and experienced UK academics. Current interests include problem solving in MSOR, flexible learning, and working with students as partners.

Dr Julian McDougall is Associate Professor in Media & Education in the Centre for Excellence in Media Practice, Bournemouth University, UK. He is editor of the *Media Education Research Journal* and author of *After the Media: Culture and Identity in the 21st Century* (Routledge); *The Media Teacher's Book* (Hodder); *Barthes' Mythologies Today: Readings of Contemporary Culture* (Routledge); *Studying Videogames* (Auteur) and a range of Media Studies course textbooks, journal articles and book chapters in the fields of Education, Media & Cultural Studies and teacher training resources. At Bournemouth, he is Programme Leader for the Educational Doctorate in Creative and Media. In recent years, he has completed research and pedagogy projects funded by the AHRC, European Union and Higher Education Academy.

Dr Rebecca O'Loughlin is an Educational Developer at York St John University. She has previously worked as a Learning and Assessment Developer at the University of Manchester, UK and as Academic Coordinator for Theology at the Higher Education Academy Subject Centre for Philosophical and Religious Studies, supporting teachers and learners in Theological and Religious Studies higher education throughout the UK. In this role, she was a member of the editorial board of *Discourse: Learning and Teaching in Philosophical and Religious Studies*. Formerly, she was employed as a Researcher at the Subject Centre, leading its pedagogic research programme. She has published on pedagogic research, enquiry-based learning, and theology and sustainable development, and has taught at the Universities of Leeds and Manchester.

Professor Susan Orr is Dean of Learning, Teaching and Enhancement at the University of the Arts London, UK. Susan is a National Teaching Fellow whose research explores art and design pedagogy. She has published a range of articles that explore Art and Design assessment practices, the Crit, reflective writing practices, creative group work and NSS. She is on the Editorial Board for the *Journal in Writing in Creative Practice* and the *Journal of Art Design and Communication in Higher Education*. Susan is on the Executive Board for the Council for Higher Education in Art & Design (CHEAD) and the Group for Learning in Art & Design (GLAD). She has taught on academic practice courses for new lecturers in the post-'92 sector as well as within the specialist arts HE sector.

Professor Tina Overton is Professor of Chemistry Education at the University of Hull, UK. She joined the chemistry department at the University of Hull in 1992, first as a teaching fellow, then as lecturer, senior lecturer, and then as Professor. She has published on the topics of critical thinking, context and problem-based learning and their role in developing conceptual understanding and cognitive skills and the development of problem solving skills. She has published learning resources which have been adopted in many institutions and has co-authored several textbooks in inorganic chemistry. She was Director of the national Higher Education Academy UK Physical Sciences Centre which supported teaching and learning across chemistry, physics and astronomy. She has been awarded the Royal Society of Chemistry's HE Teaching Award, Tertiary Education Award and Nyholm Prize and is a National Teaching Fellow and Senior Fellow of the Higher Education Academy.

Professor Mark Russell is the Director of Technology Enhanced Learning (TEL) and the Head of the Centre for Technology Enhanced Learning at King's College London, UK. Defined by his role and interests, Mark has significant responsibility for developing the TEL activity and aspiration at King's. In relation to TEL, such development includes the need to promote innovation, build capacity and stimulate research vibrancy. Prior to joining King's in 2012, Mark held various academic positions at the University of Hertfordshire. He has led University-wide curriculum enhancement (assessment) projects and particularly enjoys bringing others together to respond to institutional challenges and aspirations. Mark's disciplinary roots are in engineering and he has taught in the area of thermo-fluid science for around 15 years. Mark is a Professor of Learning and Assessment in Higher Education and appreciates opportunities to work across disciplinary boundaries.

PREFACE

The text is intended to serve as a core textbook for use in Higher Education Institutions (HEIs) that offer Higher Education Academy (HEA) and other accredited qualifications (for example, Postgraduate Certificates in Learning and teaching, Higher Education or Academic Practice) for staff who teach and support student learning. It sets out to meet a key need that we have identified during the course of our careers in professional and academic practice development across a range of HEIs. With growing calls for HEIs to identify, map and monitor world-class quality learning and teaching experiences, alongside evidence from research and theory which draws our attention to the diverse learning needs of students in HE, there has been a shift of emphasis. HEIs now encourage their staff to focus not only on the up-to-date *content* of their teaching, but also to identify more effective ways to engage students in *learning* this content, often alongside other key trans-ferrable skills. In addition, the changing fees landscape is positioning students into an ever more consumer-type stance and HEIs are now expected to be able to evidence the quality of their teaching and the format of their courses much more than ever before.

Our conversations with academic staff and educational developers across the HE sector, combined with our knowledge of a range of HEA accredited professional courses, reveal that this shift is increasingly manifesting itself in an expectation that academic staff will not only adopt a scholarly approach to updating the content of their teaching, but will also enhance their teaching and their students' learning through undertaking research and evaluation activities. This text aims to support academic staff to do this by exploring how such activities which, at first glance, may seem challenging, can in fact be undertaken from within familiar disciplinary contexts using research and evaluation processes and practices with which staff are conversant. In taking this approach we hope that staff will feel confident to engage more formally with the development of their teaching and, in turn, to impact actively on the experience of their students.

Throughout the text we use the term 'educational enquiry' to encompass a range of scholarly activities including research into, as well as the evaluation *of*, teaching and learning activities. This choice of words stems from our experience of working with academics that often have a well-developed understanding from their own subject backgrounds of what constitutes 'real' research, resulting in preconceptions that can be difficult to challenge. In using the term 'enquiry' we are seeking to engage academics in debates which will help them to reconsider such preconceptions, and to create a notional 'shared space' in which colleagues from different ends of the campus can meet to compare and discuss developments in the learning and teaching experiences they create.

The text is divided into two parts. The purpose of this approach is to provide a comfortable and accessible introduction to educational enquiry for staff from across the range of academic disciplines.

Part One introduces common approaches to, and methods for, undertaking enquiry into learning and teaching which stem largely from the social sciences. We have assumed that readers may be starting from a very different disciplinary perspective, and may need guiding through the language, logic and practice of educational enquiry. Our aim is to support academics from a range of disciplines to build the foundations from which an informed reading and understanding of existing educational literature can take place. Part One additionally offers readers an opportunity to consider where their particular disciplinary understandings of research approaches and methods sit in relation to those predominantly used in the field of education. We hope, in taking this approach, to engage academics in identifying and reflecting on the differences and similarities and the pros and cons of each.

In Part Two, seven discipline-focused chapters challenge the often unquestioned assumption that educational enquiry is the preserve of the social sciences and that those who wish to undertake such enquiry should adopt social science (often qualitative) approaches and methods. Each chapter begins from the premise that different disciplines can bring new and helpful methodological and conceptual resources to the process of educational enquiry and that they can, and should, play a central role in expanding our understanding of learning and teaching. This not only adds to the richness of educational enquiry but, more fundamentally, allows staff from different disciplines to undertake such enquiry without having to jump wholesale into a new and often alien disciplinary camp. This is not to say that a move towards social science methods is either substantively wrong or impossible; simply that the starting point on this journey may be closer to their disciplinary 'home' than many academics think. Once confidence in undertaking disciplinary educational enquiry is established, a move towards social science or hybrid disciplinary/social science approaches to enquiry may grow as staff members identify the most appropriate fit of particular approaches and methods to different aims and foci of enquiry.

Each of the chapter authors is an established academic within higher education with a keen interest in learning and teaching. Educational enquiry is a core strand of their activities in their respective disciplines, with dissemination an important part of the scholarly nature of their role. We hope that by reading their contributions, readers will be encouraged to identify aspects of their disciplinary modes of research that could usefully be adapted and adopted and will feel more confident in navigating a pathway towards more rigorous enquiry into their own learning and teaching practice. If so, we will have gone some way to achieving the main aim of this text.

We do not wish to be overly prescriptive about the order in which you read the chapters that follow. We are conscious that rather than reading from start to finish you may wish to start with the chapter closest to your disciplinary area, drawing on the more generic chapters at the front of the book at a later date. The book has been written in a way that supports both approaches and we hope that you find it accessible and useful.

Elizabeth Cleaver
Maxine Lintern
Mike McLinden

FOREWORD

Enquiry-based learning has long been recognised as an effective way to engage *students* in their learning, whereas engaging *staff/faculty* in educational enquiry is a more recent phenomenon. The latter was stimulated particularly by Boyer's (1990) popularisation of the concept of the 'scholarship of teaching', later more commonly called the 'scholarship of teaching *and* learning' (SoTL). Even more recently there is an emerging interest in staff *and* students collaborating in investigating teaching and learning in higher education, a trend which has variously been titled as 'students as partners' and 'students as change agents'.

Two of the drivers for the emergence of interest in educational enquiry in higher education are the professionalisation of teaching and the growing importance of accountability. In the UK the first has been stimulated by the development of the UK Professional Standards Framework for Teaching and Supporting Learning in Higher Education and the second by the marketisation of higher education and the actions of the Quality Assurance Agency. It is common practice in the UK that academics with less than three years' teaching experience should undertake a certificated course in teaching and learning in higher education. There is a related growth of interest in providing continuing professional development for all teaching staff. A further factor in the growth of interest in educational enquiry is the desire to provide greater recognition and reward for academic staff in their role as teachers, particularly for those on teaching-only or teaching-intensive contracts. Engaging academics in educational enquiry is, moreover, a way to foster the links between teaching and research and encourage lecturers to recognise that excellent teaching goes beyond student satisfaction scores and requires evidence of impact on learning.

However, though these factors may be important in influencing the priorities of senior managers in higher education institutions, to change the behaviour of individual staff I believe that you need first to motivate them. Appealing to lecturers that engaging in educational enquiry would be good for them and their students may win over a few dedicated individuals, but the key way to engage colleagues in their development as critical and reflective teachers is to stimulate their intellectual curiosity. After all, most staff came into higher education because they had an intense curiosity about their subject and a desire to share that with their colleagues and students. Asking questions about how students are learning in the lecture hall, seminar room and laboratory and what types of assignment lead to deep and retained learning is at the heart of intellectual curiosity and central to educational enquiry.

The simplest way to develop the intellectual curiosity of staff is to start where they are; which for most academics is their identity as disciplinary specialists. A discipline-based approach to developing educational enquiry recognises the 'academic tribes' to which most academics belong. Many staff will remain as discipline specialists in developing their educational enquiries; a few will go on to develop as higher education specialists. Both groups need to recognise the contribution of the other to avoid recreating wheels.

This book addresses these various issues in a novel way. It is divided into two parts. The first provides a helpful account of how to engage in educational enquiry, including an introduction to the educational literature and what counts as evidence; the ethics of enquiry; how data are collected and analysed; and how the findings are disseminated. In the second part, discipline specialists review the nature of enquiry into teaching and learning in seven different disciplinary areas. The text is brought alive by the frequent use of case studies and activities.

The authors are to be congratulated for producing a very readable narrative which should appeal to a wide readership, not only of staff taking postgraduate certificate courses in teaching and learning, but also to anyone interested in starting to explore the world of educational enquiry. Though all the authors come from the UK, the issues they raise are applicable world-wide. The potential tensions between discipline-based and generic approaches to educational enquiry are carefully nuanced. I can highly recommend this book. It is the one which I wish I had written!

Mick Healey BA PhD FRGS NTF PFHEA
Higher Educational Consultant and Researcher
Emeritus Professor University of Gloucestershire
Recipient of SEDA@20 Legacy Award for Disciplinary Development

PART ONE

UNDERSTANDING EDUCATIONAL ENQUIRY

CHAPTER 1

WHAT IS EDUCATIONAL ENQUIRY AND WHY IS IT IMPORTANT?

Elizabeth Cleaver, Maxine Lintern and Mike McLinden

Learning outcomes

By the end of this chapter it is anticipated that you will:

- Understand the broad context in which the growing emphasis on and expectations around educational enquiry are taking place;
- Recognise the skills, understanding and knowledge that you can bring to the educational enquiry process; and
- Understand the benefits of taking an enquiry-based approach to improving your own teaching practice and the learning of your students.

Introduction

This first chapter provides an overview of the broad context in which the current refocusing of government and institutional policies towards excellence in learning and teaching practice within higher education has taken place in the United Kingdom. In doing so it examines the growing expectation for academic staff to use their skills of research, scholarship and higher-order thinking to improve and enhance their teaching practice and their students' learning experiences. We hope that your reading of this chapter will help you to understand the context in which these expectations have arisen and the reasons why we consider that undertaking educational improvements and enhancements are important. Our main aim is to encourage you as researchers and lecturers in higher education to enhance your practice and the learning experience of your students by asking the right questions, carefully monitoring and evaluating any changes made to practice and making evidence-informed decisions for change. Such an approach should not be alien to you as it informs all research work in higher education or industry. Through this book we hope to show you how you can apply some of approaches to and methods of research with which you are familiar within your disciplinary areas, to your own learning and teaching practice.

We recognise that for many readers, this will not be the first time you use your skills of research, scholarship and higher-order thinking for the improvement of your learning and teaching: we are all responsible for ensuring that the latest developments in disciplinary knowledge are synthesised and integrated into higher education curricula. What may be new, however, is the focus on making sure the methods of and approaches to teaching this knowledge are also the most up to date and appropriate ones for your subject area. The challenge for us all is, in essence, no different from the challenge that we pose our students on a daily basis: namely that of moving from assumption, supposition and non-informed opinion, to a more evidence-based approach that includes information gathering, analysis, conclusion drawing and decision making.

Our experience suggests that for many teachers and researchers in higher education this is not always an easy journey to make. Research, scholarship and higher-order thinking can be conceived of and defined in very particular ways within each disciplinary area. Yet within formal development programmes in UK higher education (such as Postgraduate Certificates in Learning and Teaching in HE or Academic Practice) or continuing professional development opportunities, there is usually an unacknowledged expectation that academics will accept and adopt a 'social-scientific' approach to research and writing about their learning and teaching. Such an approach may require venturing into largely unknown territory: a new subject area framed by unfamiliar paradigms, language, research approaches and methods as well as a different understanding of what constitutes 'validity'. As Stierer notes, many academics can find entering the 'strange land' of higher education studies extremely challenging (2008: 35), while MacDonald-Ross argues that '[t]here is widespread dissatisfaction with educational research as being restricted to a relatively narrow range of techniques and values, and complaints come from all quarters' (2005: 17).

While we believe that the process of 'enhancement' is key to educational improvements (both curricular and experiential) in higher education, we question a frequently unquestioned approach to teaching and learning development: that academics from *all* disciplines should draw on writing approaches and research paradigms from within the social sciences. Practitioners from a range of professions (including teachers in the compulsory and further education sectors; nurses and other health professionals, as well as social and youth workers), are now expected, as part of their training and continuing professional development, to undertake critical reflection and practitioner research to inform their own and others' practice. This is seen to be fundamental to the continuing health of their respective professions and their own professional practice. However, many of these practitioners may not have engaged with research and scholarship since undertaking their first degrees or early training and so can require significant 'up-skilling' in order to adopt an evidence-based approach successfully. However, for many of you, as practising academics in higher education, the position is likely to be very different. You may, for example, have been engaging with research in your respective disciplines at a high level for a number of years. Some of you will be seasoned researchers with a clear understanding of the academic processes of peer-review, publication and sharing of results and data to inform the development of your discipline *and* the acknowledged approaches to research within that discipline. Such disciplinary research experiences provide a valid and useful starting point from which you can develop your own teaching and learning practice.

As educational developers we are aware that many researchers do not need to develop, or indeed have the time to develop new or additional research skills. We also understand that some academics may not recognise or identify with the approaches, methods and settings used for pedagogic research as these may be very far removed from their own current practices (an issue explored further in Chapter 2; see also Poole, 2013). To this end, we have opted where possible against using terminology that makes explicit reference to 'research' in this book, given that to do so could invite unnecessary comparison and confusion with the research undertaken within a disciplinary context. Similarly, we have also decided against using 'practitioner' research; a term that is already widely used in a number of professions (see for example, Foreman-Peck and Winch, 2010). In addition to the confusions that can arise amongst academics when the term 'research' is used to describe small-scale localised data collection and analysis in the work setting, we acknowledge that the term 'practitioner' does not necessarily resonate with our identities as 'academics' in higher education. Our experience suggests that speaking to academics about their academic 'practice' and identifying them as academic 'practitioners' can leave them confused. You may not see yourselves as a 'practitioner' and as such may even reject this label outright. This term may be more acceptable to those of you whose professional identity and role have an academic overlap, such as those who are clinically qualified and who must maintain registration as a 'practitioner' as well as an academic. However, we recognise that for many of you these two identities can be seen as quite separate and discrete aspects of your academic working life.

In the United States an alternative term that has been developed to describe the process of engaging in evidence-based improvement of learning and teaching (often from a disciplinary starting point) is the 'Scholarship of Teaching and Learning' (SoTL), a term that we will explore in greater depth later in this chapter. Briefly, this term encompasses research, scholarship and higher-order thinking activities which provide 'the mechanism through which the profession of teaching itself advances, through which teaching can be something other than a seat-of-the-pants operation, with each of us out there making it up as we go' (Hutchings and Shulman, 1999).

However, despite the usefulness of the debates and insights from this established area of work, there is one key sticking point with using the term *scholarship* in the United Kingdom (UK). In short, the UK Government's Research Excellence Framework (REF) audit of academic research and its impact, defines scholarship in a different way (at time of writing):

> as the creation, development and maintenance of the intellectual infrastructure of subjects and disciplines, in forms such as dictionaries, scholarly editions, catalogues and contributions to major research databases. (HEFCE, 2011: 71)

With this definition so prominent in academia within the UK at the time of writing, to use the term scholarship may simply serve to confuse and undermine the role that the Scholarship of Teaching and Learning can play in underpinning academic professional development and ensuring the continuing health of learning and teaching in the disciplines.

With this in mind we have adopted a different term for use within this text; a term which describes a process through which you can draw on your disciplinary skills and understandings of research, recognising that these may be employed at a different level, and with a different focus and outcome, but with the primary aim of improving your understanding and practice in learning and teaching. The term we use for this process is *educational enquiry*. In this chapter we consider why we believe educational enquiry has become an important element of the changing academic role in the twenty-first century, and explain why we feel the term 'enquiry' serves as a useful vehicle for encouraging academics to reflect on their learning and teaching in a scholarly and rigorous fashion with a view to enhancing practice. We begin by examining the wider context in which improving learning and teaching within higher education has been developed and consolidated.

The higher education context

As you will be aware, the broad context in which learning and teaching activities take place within higher education is changing at a rapid pace. Current drivers for change include the move towards broader access to education (termed the 'widening participation' agenda in the UK), drives towards increasing quality, flexibility and diversity, as well as a curriculum that has, as a central focus, student engagement, employability and transferable skills. These changes inevitably interact with a range of other shifts and advances including the growth of information and digital technologies, the growing recognition that learning takes place beyond the classroom, as well as an increasing recognition that learning is not a one-off but a life-long and life-wide experience.

As educators in higher education, we are required to think differently about the needs of a more diverse student group and how to meet these needs in terms of curriculum design, delivery and assessment. This shifting landscape has resulted in a greater emphasis on enhancing the quality of the learning experience, with students increasingly viewed as active participants, or indeed 'partners', in the learning process. Alongside this shift, the profile of teachers' roles in higher education has also changed, with what has been termed a 'scholarship of teaching' (Boyer, 1990) increasingly being given a higher profile. Teachers in higher education are therefore expected not just to know their subject area for the purpose of transmitting an established body of knowledge to their students, but rather to engage in broader debates about what makes for effective teaching of this knowledge and to consider their own role in facilitating effective student learning. Indeed, a consequence of such a shift in emphasis requires both teachers and learners to reframe their roles and identities within the wider learning process (Deignan, 2009).

Of significance in helping to facilitate this pedagogical shift has been the report of the Boyer Commission (1998) that called for a new 'model' of undergraduate education at research-intensive universities in the United States. The Boyer Commission's central thesis was that research should be the basis of all learning at university, from first year undergraduate to graduate, with opportunities provided for group work and other participatory activities. It further argued that the production of knowledge should not be an elite activity, but one participated in by all members of an institution. This influential report additionally proposed that undergraduates who enter such universities should engage in discovery activities as active participants, including opportunities to 'learn through inquiry'[1] rather than through simple knowledge transmission. In essence, Boyer advocated a more 'student-centred' approach to teaching, with students engaging in enquiry-based activities associated with research.

As noted by McLinden and Edwards (2011), over a decade later the notion of 'learning through inquiry' has been explicitly drawn upon by a wide range of universities across the globe to ensure that students have opportunities to engage in enquiry-led activities from an early stage in their learning experience. McKinney and Levy (2006) report that such a commitment reflects the widespread move in HE over recent years from a 'teacher-centred' conception of the learning process towards a more 'student-centred model'. Moreover, it engages with Boyer's earlier critique of the relationship between research and teaching in the United States system, as well as with the associated 'international reform movement' that aims to make student enquiry central to the student learning experience (1990).

Linking research and teaching through enquiry

Paralleling and informing such developments, moves have been made to develop and recognise the links and synergies between research and teaching. As noted by Jenkins and Healey (2005), discussion of the relationship between teaching and research often makes reference to the work of two notable nineteenth-century scholars: Cardinal Newman in England and von Humboldt in Germany.

Graham-Matheson (2010) notes that the work of Cardinal Newman is often cited as an important influence on defining the role of modern universities, given the emphasis he placed on describing a university as a place where the pursuit of knowledge and the education of the intellect were 'mutually supportive'. This view went on to provide a template for 'liberal education' in an expanding university sector for the next 100 years (Graham-Matheson, 2010). During a similar period the Humboltian university ethos was emerging. Robertson notes that von Humboldt conceived of a community of learners (teachers and their students) working together at the University of Berlin in the pursuit of knowledge. Thus, rather than the presentation of finished results to students in the form of knowledge, this approach advocated student involvement in the construction of knowledge

---

[1]In this text we recognise the interchangeable nature of the terms 'inquiry' (largely present in US literature) and 'enquiry' (largely present in UK literature). For the purposes of this book, and true to our own national origins, the authors of the chapters use the term enquiry. However, when referring to the work of others, or directly quoting, the term 'inquiry' may be substituted.

and ideas. Indeed, teaching was viewed as being embedded in research and undertaken through research – as such teaching and research were considered to be 'inseparable' (Robertson, 2007: 542).

This coming together of the two core strands of higher education activity is commonly referred to as the 'research–teaching' nexus; a term originally attributed to Neumann (1994) who makes reference to such a nexus in a study exploring its relevance to university students' learning experiences (Graham-Matheson, 2010). The concepts underpinning this nexus have been debated, developed and refined extensively (see for example Brew, 2006; Healey, 2005; Jenkins and Healey, 2005) and have been more recently examined in relation to particular disciplinary activities (see for example Spronken-Smith and Walker, 2010) and to ontological and epistemological perspectives (see for example Robertson, 2007).

However, your own experience may lead to the conclusion that in spite of these debates, the lines drawn between teaching and research activities within higher education appear more pronounced than ever. Many institutions are developing promotions criteria for academics which, rather than being based on excellence in all three areas of an academic contract (broadly captured as 'research and scholarship', 'teaching and learning' and 'administration and service'[2]), appear to be increasingly based on excellence in *either* research and scholarship *or* learning and teaching. Moreover, while academics have, in recent years, been increasingly employed on 'research-only' contracts at the beginning of their academic careers, the rise in teaching-focused contracts is a relatively new phenomenon.

While at first glance this could be seen as levelling what has become a quite uneven playing field in the last few decades, the reality can be starkly different. Many teaching-focused contracts have little or no 'research-time' allocated within them and if funding for, or publications from, research into learning and teaching are somehow achieved, these can be viewed as less important or worthy than disciplinary research funding and outputs. Furthermore, while researchers can make the transition to a full academic contract, often without any experience of teaching or evidence that they can teach, the equivalent journey from teaching to research may be less well tolerated or supported. An underlying factor which may help to explain these observations is the series of UK policy changes, driven by market economy imperatives and associated accountability demands that have been

---

[2]Service is a term which is used to describe academic activities that take place, within institutions and beyond, some of which support the deliberative committee structures of higher education decision making and the peer-reviewed quality assurance processes in research and teaching. These may include, for example, acting as a reviewer for journals and books, sitting on institutional quality assurance committees, hosting or presenting at international conferences and taking on external examining roles across the sector (see MacFarlane, 2007).

recognised to have forged a potential divide between research and teaching (Robertson, 2007).

This may seem a somewhat perverse outcome given the significant amount of public finance that has been invested in connecting research and teaching and learning in the last decade in the UK. For example, £40 million of Government funding was released by the Higher Education Funding Council for England's (HEFCE) Teaching Quality Enhancement Fund (TQEF) in 2006 to provide support for the development of teaching informed and enriched by research and research-informed teaching environments. What such funding did ensure, however, was that despite the 'unstable terrain of the research–teaching nexus' (Robertson, 2007: 543), a number of attempts to emphasise the varying relationships between teaching and research, which might have otherwise remained internal academic conversations within the educational development community, were debated, applied and critiqued more broadly.

A notable example is a typology developed by Griffiths (2004) to help understand what is meant by 'linking teaching and research'. As reported by Jenkins and Healey (2005), this typology describes four main categories that illustrate different relationships between teaching and research:

- Teaching can be *research-led*. In this relationship, the curriculum is structured around subject content with content to be directly based on the disciplinary interest of teaching staff. The emphasis tends to be on understanding research findings rather than research processes. A common example would be informing students about your own research findings or the work of other academics in the field.
- Teaching can be *research-oriented*. In this relationship, the curriculum is structured to place as much emphasis on understanding the processes by which knowledge is produced, as on learning how knowledge has been achieved in a particular discipline. Attention is given to the teaching of enquiry skills and on developing a 'research ethos'. This can be viewed as students learning how to 'do' research, in principle if not actually in practice.
- Teaching can be *research-based*. In this relationship, the curriculum is mainly designed around activities that are enquiry-led in nature with the potential for interactions between research and teaching emphasised. In this category, students may be expected to use some research skills to find out things for themselves, alone or in groups.
- Teaching can be *research-informed*. In this relationship teaching draws on systematic enquiry into the teaching and learning process itself. Thus research on *how* to teach, conducted by yourself or others, is used to inform the decision on what method or approach is employed to achieve the best outcomes for students' learning.

Healey (2005) has drawn on these first three categories and replaced the broader notion of 'research-informed teaching' with that of *research-tutored*, which emphasises learning that is focused on students writing and discussing essays and papers. The type of nexus that results from each of these relationships is captured along two axes, one of which shows a continuum from an emphasis on 'research content' to an emphasis on 'research processes and problems', and the other from approaches that are considered to be 'student-focused' to those that are 'teacher-focused' (see Figure 1.1). As noted by Jenkins and Healey (2005), many learning and teaching activities involve a mixture of these four approaches, the particular blend very much dependent on the context in which teaching takes place.

We have introduced this typology to help to explore further why we feel the term *educational enquiry* is useful in helping you to understand how to approach the enhancement of your own learning and teaching through its connections with research. At the heart of the relationship in the top right-hand quadrant in Figure 1.1 (research and teaching which is 'research-based') is the concept of learning that is led through *enquiry*. Rowland reminds us that whilst universities are in the business of teaching *and* research, and while each may be seen as a form of enquiry, academics' 'experience of teaching is normally somewhat different from their experience of research' (2006: 104). Further support for this view comes from Barnett (2005) who notes that the conclusion of many writers (see Elton, 2005; Brew, 2001) is that teaching and research are more likely to be closely linked when both teaching and learning are 'enquiry-led' and 'enquiry-based'. Indeed, citing the work of Brew and Boud (1995), Barnett argues that the common feature of both research and teaching 'is that they

STUDENTS AS PARTICIPANTS

	Research-tutored Curriculum emphasises learning focused on students' writing and discussing essays and papers	**Research-based** Curriculum emphasises students undertaking inquiry-based learning	
EMPHASIS ON RESEARCH CONTENT	**Research-led** Curriculum is structured around teaching current subject content	**Research-oriented** Curriculum emphasises teaching processes of knowledge construction in the subject	**EMPHASIS ON RESEARCH PROCESS AND PROBLEMS**

TEACHER-FOCUSED
AUDIENCE AS STUDENTS

Figure 1.1　Curriculum design and the research–teaching nexus (adapted from Jenkins and Healey, 2005)

are both acts of learning … in as much as learning can be a form of enquiry' (2005: 100).

With this in mind, we find it useful to conceptualise enquiry as meaning 'seeking' (Rowland, 2006) as this resonates well with the process of research with which many of us are familiar (that is, seeking out information through a process of structured or disciplined enquiry in order to address a particular research hypothesis, question or issue). The association between 'seeking' and teaching, however, may not prove quite so apparent to many of you; particularly if the commonly held view of teaching in your institution or discipline appears to be based on the transmission of incontestable information and fact. If this is the case, then Rowland's view that, 'the most important task of the teacher is to develop an atmosphere or an attitude in which students *seek*, to build and understand knowledge' (2006: 109, our emphasis), may prove difficult to realise.

One way in which this can be approached is through enquiry-based teaching approaches. Such approaches, in line with Jenkins and Healey's (2005) notion of *research-based teaching,* are designed to foster deep engagement with complex problems and to encourage students 'to create and conduct their own enquiries for learning' (Jackson, 2003: 1, see also Hutchings, 2007). This approach has recently been acknowledged by a number of 'research intensive' UK universities as an appropriate way of conceptualising teaching and learning within their particular institutional settings.

Within this rapidly changing landscape, we argue that teaching needs to be reconceptualised within the academic's role; a reconceptualisation that is broadly captured in the literature which explores and develops the *scholarship of teaching and learning.*

Towards a scholarship of teaching and learning

The second area of debate and development which has contributed towards our use of the term 'educational enquiry' is a growing literature and set of activities which together are conceptualised as the Scholarship of Teaching and Learning (SoTL).

Earnest Boyer's seminal report published in 1990, *Scholarship Reconsidered: Priorities of the Professoriate,* documents how (similar to shifts in the UK) the rewards for academics (faculty) in the United States narrowed to focus on research just at the time that the American sector began to widen participation and expand its intake. These two requirements – the requirement for high-level research and outputs and the requirement for different teaching and support methods and approaches to support the changing student body – led academics to feel 'caught in the crossfire of … competing goals' (1990: xi). Boyer called for a reconceptualisation of what it means to undertake academic work to reflect better the demands of the changing higher education sector. He argued for a move away from the pitching of teaching against research in academic workloads towards a recognition of four 'scholarships' which he claimed would bring legitimacy to the full range of academic duties:

- *The scholarship of discovery*, which reflects the investigative aspect of academic work; that is 'the commitment to knowledge for its own sake, to freedom of inquiry and to following, in a disciplined fashion, an investigation wherever it may lead' (1990: 16);
- *The scholarship of integration*, which recognises the importance of synthesis and the value of work that gives 'meaning to isolated facts, putting them in perspective … making connections across the disciplines, placing the specialties in larger context, illuminating data in a revealing way' (1990: 18);
- *The scholarship of application*, which views 'scholarly service' as key to the academic's role, ensuring the application and contribution of academic insight can help to solve problems and facilitate change (1990: 23); and
- *The scholarship of teaching*, which views teaching not as a routine function but as a process in which '[p]edagogical procedures must be carefully planned, continuously examined, and relate directly to the subject taught … good teaching means that faculty, as scholars, are also learners' (1990: 24–25).

In the UK, similar concerns which parallel and reflect those voiced by Boyer were contained in the Government White Paper, 'The Future of Higher Education' which stated that '[t]eaching has for too long been the poor relation in higher education' (Department for Education and Skills, 2003: 15). It continued, both in the spirit of Boyer and reflecting ideas presented in the earlier Dearing Report (National Committee of Enquiry into Higher Education, 1997), that it is not necessary for every academic to be engaged in cutting edge research but that 'it is clear that good scholarship, in the sense of remaining aware of the latest research and thinking within a subject, is essential for good teaching' (Department for Education and Skills, 2003: 54). This suggests that it is not just the level or type of the teaching that academics in higher education undertake that differentiates them from other educators, but the fact that as a group they can apply their skills of higher-order thinking to their own teaching design and practice: taking a scholarly approach to their teaching and learning.

While fundamental change towards these goals has been slow in the UK, and you may not recognise them as happening in your own immediate departments and faculties, it cannot be denied that a reordering of priorities of staff in the higher education system is now underway. As an example, many universities are now 'rewarding' teaching through their promotions process and the first tranche of 'teaching-focused' professors are beginning to appear in the UK higher education sector. Further, institutions are increasingly expecting staff to undertake some form of training in teaching, often as a probationary requirement, which aligns to the sector-owned UK

Professional Standards for Teaching and Supporting Learning in Higher Education (HEA, 2011). Moreover, the Higher Education Statistics Agency (HESA), which requires all UK higher education institutions to return statistical data in a range of areas on an annual basis has, in 2013 for the first time, requested information about academic staff teaching qualifications and professional affiliations.

However, a growing movement in the United States and beyond has called for more than simply a 'scholarly' approach to teaching, and has actively reconceptualised the academic role as involving the Scholarship of Teaching and Learning (SoTL). This movement, broadly recognised as being introduced by Hutchings and Shulman (1999), has grown in scope and influence over the last decade and is based around the argument that equipped with the skills of higher-order thinking, research and scholarship, academics can move beyond a synthesis of the latest thinking and practices within their subject area, to actively enter into and lead debates about appropriate modes of teaching and good practice in facilitating student learning. Key to this movement is an emphasis on making any work we do 'community property' (Shulman, 1993) so that colleagues can use and build on one another's work to avoid reinventing the pedagogic wheel.

While there remains no one definition of the Scholarship of Teaching and Learning, and the methods and approaches that it encompasses remain the focus of continuing debate, one clear exposition, drawing on Boyer's *Scholarship Reconsidered* (1990) provides a useful staging post for this discussion. Healey (2003) argues that the Scholarship of Teaching and Learning should comprise Boyer's first three types of scholarship: the scholarships of discovery, integration and application. This conceptualisation helps us to move forward in our quest for an approach to the enhancement of teaching which draws upon academics' existing skills-sets: the skills of higher-order thinking, scholarship and research. Key texts in this field that may be of interest to those reading this volume are listed at the end of this chapter (see McKinney, 2007; McKinney, 2013 and Huber and Morreale, 2002).

Despite the usefulness of these debates and insights there is one key sticking point: the meaning of the term *scholarship* in the UK. As stated earlier in this chapter, the UK Government's appropriation of the term scholarship to describe a particular form of academic output for the Research Excellence Framework (REF) creates a climate in which this term cannot be fruitfully used. The contested nature of the term 'scholarship' is clearly exemplified by a document entitled 'Definitions of Scholarship' produced by the University of Leeds (2013) for the purposes of academic promotions. With the REF definition so prominent in the collective minds of universities and their staff members, we argue that to use this terminology would act to undermine the very effective role that the Scholarship of Teaching and Learning could play in the UK, particularly in research-intensive universities. In short, it may be deemed a worthy activity, but only insofar as academics have time to undertake it when they have completed their other 'core' research activities and teaching and administrative duties. With this in mind, we turn to a consideration of alternative terminology which has the potential to engage academic staff in research into their learning and teaching.

Exploring the challenges of educational enquiry

In this final section we draw together key themes from this chapter and explore the nature of educational enquiry in the context of this text. We have noted the link between the terms 'enquiry' and 'seeking' in relation to student learning and considered the role of the teacher in developing an atmosphere in which students can seek information and create understanding through adopting an enquiry-based approach to learning. The discussion of the Scholarship of Teaching and Learning highlights the importance of teachers in higher education adopting a similar approach in relation to their own practice. This, in turn, gives rise to the notion of 'educational enquiry' which, for the purposes of this text, we view as being a suitable vehicle by which teachers in UK higher education can seek to gather, analyse and produce information, through a process of structured or disciplined enquiry, to address a particular research hypothesis, question or issue. They can then draw on these findings to reflect on their learning and teaching with a view to informing and enhancing their practice and, where relevant, to sharing these results with others through the normal channels of academic dissemination (conferences, books and journal articles) and perhaps other new avenues for sharing. Through knowing how to engage in the process of educational enquiry, teachers are potentially equipped to provide evidence for, and to enter into and lead debates about, appropriate modes of teaching and good practice in facilitating student learning within their departments, faculties and disciplines.

Any academic who wishes to undertake such a process of structured enquiry into their learning and teaching practice will need a set of skills and knowledge to begin this process. In most higher education institutions in the UK, these are now often developed as part of often compulsory programmes of study in higher education teaching (known variously in the UK as Postgraduate Certificates in Learning and Teaching, Higher Education or Academic Practice). Yet, as stated earlier in this chapter, such programmes (and other continuing professional development initiatives) often expect that academics will study, assimilate and adopt a 'social-scientific' approach when they undertake educational enquiry. For those of you from almost any subject area other than education itself, and some linked areas of the social sciences, it is highly probable that this will confront you with unfamiliar paradigms, language, research approaches and methods and understandings of 'validity'. Prosser et al. (2006) in their study of such programmes, further confirm that the needs and approaches of different disciplines are not writ large. And as registration on such programmes may not be optional and can often accompany the early career expectations of establishing a new research team, getting to grips with departmental administration roles as well as the details of new taught programmes, together it can all amount to an immense challenge.

To put early career academics at ease, one of the key messages that educational developers regularly impart is that programme participants are not expected to become 'experts' in education; simply to recognise and understand the range of paradigms, approaches and methods used in education is enough. Yet this often goes against the grain of everything that academics have learnt so far in their careers where every qualification from their degree onwards has led further down the pathway of developing their expertise. To suddenly take a qualification in an area in which they are not expected to become 'expert' may leave them feeling uneasy. Indeed it could be argued that to suggest that such a qualification can be gained without an element of expertise, somewhat undermines the value and validity of the qualification and may further compound already negative views of social science disciplines.

If perceived as a venture into the unknown, particularly if the unknown is unvalued, this can prove unsatisfying for all involved. As Savin-Baden (2008) argues, moving between disciplines may cause a sense of disjunction and a threat to an individual's identity. Stierer highlights this disjuncture further, arguing that for many lecturers, entering the field of higher education studies can feel like becoming 'a stranger in a strange land' (2008: 35). Indeed he argues that for academics, entry onto such programmes may be even more challenging than for other university students as few academic programmes admit students with little or no knowledge of the academic subject area. To this we would add that few academic programmes admit students who may not wish to study and even when expected to, are often not granted adequate time to study as part of their broader workload. This disjuncture has been further explored by one of our chapter authors, Rebecca O'Loughlin, who notes that academics within her own discipline can experience difficulties in engaging with educational research 'because of the[ir] differing research paradigms: empirical (educational research) and theoretical/discursive (theology and religious studies)' (2008: 69). O'Loughlin argues that this makes engaging with existing literature on learning and teaching difficult for those from a humanities background as educational researchers tend to adopt social science research models and referencing conventions[3] that can be difficult to navigate. These arguments have recently been revisited by Chick (2013), Grauerholz and Main (2013) and Poole (2013) in a recent edited volume *The Scholarship of Teaching and Learning in and across the Disciplines* (McKinney, 2013).

---

[3]Using social science referencing conventions is something we are very conscious that we are doing in this text! For further information on the Harvard referencing system that we are using please refer to Chapter 3.

From our own experience, the various circumstances described above can leave early career lecturers struggling to make connections between the requirements of a new and possibly alien field of study and any potential beneficial transfer to and impact on their teaching and students' learning.

Starting from your discipline

How then can we best help discipline-based academics to engage with educational enquiry which is meaningful and helpful, and through which they can advance their teaching and learning practice using familiar evidence-based approaches to inform changes and improvements?

Our starting point for this book is your own starting point: your discipline. Trowler describes the 'power of disciplines to condition the behaviour of academics, their practices, values and attitudes' (2009: 181). We recognise that like most academics you will be steeped in your discipline; the discipline is where you are likely to have undergone most if not all of your formative education (often from school age). It is within this disciplinary context that you will define *what* you research and teach, as well as *how* you research and teach. In relation to teaching, such disciplinary approaches have been termed 'signature pedagogies'; a term first coined by Lee Shulman (2005) which has been further explored and extended in two recent volumes focusing on signature pedagogies across a range of disciplinary contexts (see Chick et al. 2012; Gurung et al. 2009). This parallels and reflects a growing interest in, and awareness of, the ways in which academic disciplines teach and develop ways of thinking (Donald, 2002; King et al., 2012; Pace and Middendorf, 2004) and writing (Elton, 2009). As such, there has been a recognition of the need to approach not just the study of learning and teaching, but the development of learning and teaching, from within its disciplinary context (Huber, 2006; Huber and Morreale, 2002; Kreber, 2009; McKinney, 2013; Potter, 2008). Disciplinary starting points not only appeal at the personal level; they additionally chime with the needs of disciplinary groupings, further evidenced in the UK through the Higher Education Academy continuing to employ disciplinary learning and teaching experts and to host discipline-focused resources (HEA, 2013a).

We argue that given academics' varied disciplinary starting points, identities and cultures, it may not be enough to claim as Shulman has, that education is not a discipline but a broad interdisciplinary field of study in which 'the perspectives and procedures of many disciplines can be brought to bear' (2004: 279, cited in Potter, 2008). The reality is that for many looking into 'education' from the outside, the apparent dominance of social science approaches and methods will suggest that it is not as interdisciplinary as might be hoped. McCarthy's recognition that 'all academics have a research discipline in which they are embedded [which is why SoTL must reach] ... *beyond the boundaries of educational research*' (2008: 14; our emphasis) points us in the right direction. As Huber states (citing Grauerholz and Main, 2013) it is important to 'free the scholarship of teaching and learning from inappropriate methodological expectations' (2013: xii).

In encouraging you to engage in disciplinary approaches to educational enquiry we aim to do just this: to look beyond the boundaries of the current dominant methods in educational research. We hope, in doing so, to help and encourage you to utilise your disciplinary research expertise to improve not just the content of your teaching, but also its approach, design and delivery.

Concluding thoughts

We hope this introductory chapter has inspired you to continue reading the rest of this book and, in particular, to reflect on and develop ways to use your current disciplinary research expertise for the benefit of your own and colleagues' learning and teaching practice. However, it is important to recognise that this cannot be done in complete isolation from other types of educational enquiry. To do this effectively, an understanding of where disciplinary enquiry sits in relation to the approaches and methods which dominate educational enquiry is of key importance. We have therefore chosen to begin this book with an accessible introduction to the social science approaches that currently influence educational enquiry. Such approaches and methods form the backbone of a significant proportion of existing enquiry into learning and teaching and developing an understanding of them (even if you do not 'practise' them) is important for two reasons. First, it means you will be able to engage with, and understand the language and logic of social sciences methods and read existing literature in an informed way. Secondly, it offers you an opportunity to reflect on where your particular disciplinary understanding of research approaches and methods sits in relation to these dominant approaches. With this in mind, Chapters 2 to 6 introduce social scientific approaches to, and methods for, undertaking enquiry into learning and teaching.

Suggested further reading

Huber, M.T. and Morreale, S. (eds) (2002) *Disciplinary Styles in the Scholarship of Teaching and Learning: Exploring Common Ground*. Washington, DC: American Association for HE and the Carnegie Foundation.

McKinney, K. (2007) *Enhancing Learning through the Scholarship of Teaching and Learning: the Challenges and Joys of Juggling*. San Francisco, CA: Jossey Bass.

McKinney, K. (ed.) (2013) *The Scholarship of Teaching and Learning in and Across the Disciplines*. Bloomington, IN: Indiana University Press.

CHAPTER 2

WHAT DO I NEED TO KNOW BEFORE I READ EDUCATIONAL LITERATURE?

Mike McLinden, Elizabeth Cleaver and Maxine Lintern

Learning outcomes

By the end of this chapter it is anticipated that you will be able to:

- Identify the different approaches to, or models of research and enquiry (paradigms) that you are likely to encounter in the literature on learning and teaching in higher education;
- Identify where your own disciplinary research approaches sit in relation to these research paradigms; and
- Explore the opportunities, as well as the limitations, that adapting your own disciplinary methods to the study of learning and teaching can afford.

Introduction

As noted in Chapter 1, a number of academics that we have worked with in our respective institutions have found the terminology, approach and methods of educational research very different to those which they use in their own disciplines. This often makes them feel at the very least disengaged from, or at worst hostile to, educational research. It is possible, if you are reading this book, that you will class yourself as one of this group. For those of you who come from disciplines where educational research does not underpin your work, it can be easy to view research and theory about higher education pedagogy as the preserve of those who work in education, in the same way as, for example, chemical engineering or law academic publications are written for academic audiences in their respective disciplines. Our starting point for this chapter however, is that just as aspects of chemical engineering papers can be useful to those outside of academia – in industry perhaps – and law papers can be used by those in wider legal practice, so too publications about higher education and academic practice may be useful to anyone involved in supporting students learning in higher education, from a range of disciplines.

In order to begin navigating the educational literature which can appear to a newcomer, like all academic fields, to be complex and jargon laden, it is useful to explore some of the philosophical underpinnings that serve as the bedrock of all research. Our experience suggests that an understanding of these will help you to make informed judgements about the utility, validity and reliability of the research found in the literature on higher education teaching and learning. This exploration will help you to understand *why* the educational literature tends to draw on particular research approaches and methods and *how* it goes about it. It should also help you to consider how you can embed your own educational enquiry within this wider literature and evidence base and to understand the potential opportunities as well as limitations that your own disciplinary methods can offer as a vehicle for educational enquiry.

Navigation of this field requires you to become familiar with a number of important terms. We are aware that the language of another discipline may seem as alien and counterintuitive to you as an unfamiliar foreign language. This is something your own discipline will also do: we all develop terminological shortcuts to help to explain concepts, theories, ideas and processes. As Wenger (1998) points out, this terminology and its role in engaging others in understanding meaning and process, forms the bedrock of *communities of practice* which, for the purpose of this chapter, could be subject discipline communities. However, in spite of this recognition, new educational terminology may still remain what Perkins (1999, 2006) terms 'troublesome knowledge'. The term 'troublesome knowledge' describes, amongst other things, terminology that is new or is used in a new way, that can seem conceptually difficult or alien and relies on other underpinning knowledge and assumptions to become meaningful. We would encourage you to recognise the importance of such terminology in the field of educational studies. It is not there to trip you up, or indeed to obfuscate, but to help the discipline to make sense of the world around it. This is why the literature that you read on learning and teaching may appear so jargon laden and why we need to find a pathway through this to gain an understanding of the literature. As a way of helping you with this, as we go through the text we will endeavour to ensure that any terminology that may be unfamiliar to you is clearly defined.

What do I need to know?

Unless you are thinking of moving on to specialise in educational research and to gain promotion and standing based on your research in this field (which we recognise will not be the case for most people reading this book), then it is suggested that a broad overview, rather than a comprehensive understanding of the methodological approaches, data collection and analysis methods used in educational research should be your starting point. In this chapter we provide a basic introduction to the terminology, trends, values, understandings and expectations that underpin educational research to inform your reading of the literature. This should enable you to comfortably dip your toe in the water, without expecting you to dive right in!

Such an approach may seem alien to those of you who are researchers in another field where in-depth expertise has been key to your career and the status of your work. We would reiterate therefore that this text aims to meet the needs of practitioner researchers in this field who intend to draw on their existing expertise and use their established skills of research to improve their own and their colleagues' teaching and learning practice. For those of you who wish to move beyond this professional development approach and to undertake educational enquiry with a reach beyond your immediate practice, there are many texts on the market that provide comprehensive overviews of, and guidance on, educational research approaches and methods (see for example the list of recommended texts at the end of this chapter). However, for those of you who just wish to broaden your understanding and engage with the literature, or are starting to think about *how* to research within the teaching of your own subject, a good place to start is with what you already know.

Before reading further you may find it helpful to pause for a moment and reflect on your own understanding of the term 'research' in the context of your own discipline. A useful way of doing this is to think about key points you might include when completing the following three sentences (adapted from Opie, 2004):

1. My understanding of the term research is …
2. Research should be undertaken by …
3. I believe research is something that requires …

As you will probably be aware, there is no single right or wrong answer to each of these sentences; indeed you may well have thought of a number of different key points for each one. However, as we consider below, your answers to each may well reflect your own (and your discipline's) view of how knowledge is created and the ways in which it is communicated to others.

As noted in Chapter 1 we propose that research has parallels with the term 'enquiry' – a view supported by Robson who uses the terms interchangeably, noting that the word *research* 'tends to put some people off' as it can be seen as 'some esoteric enterprise necessarily done by outside experts' (2002: xv). We have made reference to enquiry as being a suitable vehicle by which teachers in higher education can seek out knowledge, through a structured process, to address a particular research hypothesis, question or issue. They can then draw on these findings to reflect on their learning and teaching with a view to informing and enhancing their practice and, where appropriate, to sharing these results with others. You will note that these steps associated with educational enquiry are in actuality very similar to the research processes and practices that you engage in within the discipline.

However, while there may be broad agreement as to what we mean by the term 'research', if you were to compare your key points with a colleague from another discipline you would probably find some important differences; different disciplines have different ways of viewing what constitutes knowledge and how to create or move this knowledge forward. A brief overview of these differences should help you to engage with the types of research that you are likely to encounter in the educational literature.

We start by introducing an important term in educational research – namely *epistemology*. Whilst this may not be a term you are familiar with, it is vital to your growing understanding of educational research as it relates to how we all, from within our disciplinary contexts define, understand and create knowledge. As noted by Cohen et al., epistemology can be viewed as one set of assumptions made about the world and is concerned with 'the very bases of knowledge – its nature and forms, how it can be acquired, and how communicated to other human beings' (2011: 6). With reference to the work of Burrell and Morgan (1979), Cohen et al. go on to explore two views of the nature of knowledge in the context of educational research – knowledge that can be described as being 'hard, objective and tangible' compared with knowledge viewed as being 'personal, subjective and unique'. They further note that how one aligns oneself in this debate affects how one will go about uncovering and building knowledge:

> The view that knowledge is hard, objective and tangible will demand of researchers an observer role, together with an allegiance to the methods of natural science; to see knowledge as personal, subjective and unique, however, imposes on researchers an involvement with their subjects and a rejection of the ways of the natural scientist. (2011: 6)

However, we wish to stress at this point that you do not have to always 'reject' all that you hold dear to engage in a different approach to research or enquiry!

Ultimately your epistemological beliefs are likely to be reflected in your whole approach to the research process, from formulating the research problem, to choosing a methodology, and collecting, analysing and disseminating data. This is captured succinctly by Robson who describes his own epistemological journey as he changed his research interests:

> As an experimental psychologist I started with the virtually unquestioned assumption that rigorous and worthwhile enquiry entailed a laboratory, and the statistical analysis of quantitative data obtained from carefully controlled experiments. More recently I have developed doubts – in part explained by working in a department alongside social psychologists and ... [a]lso, my developing interests in more 'applied' fields ... [This] precipitated a fundamental reconsideration of the style and approach to enquiry which is appropriate if one wants to say something sensible about such complex, messy, poorly controlled 'field' settings. (2002: xv–xvi)

This description demonstrates the shift in the author's epistemological assumptions in line with his research focus from one end of Cohen et al.s' 'hard, objective and tangible' and 'personal, subjective and unique' continuum to the other. It also leads us towards a further term that it is useful to explore briefly here, which may also be unfamiliar to you: *ontology*. Similar to epistemology, this term also helps us to identify and differentiate between different sets of understandings and viewpoints that underpin our approaches to research. It refers to our assumptions, or theories about, the nature of what exists: our perspectives on and understandings of the nature of 'reality'. The different epistemological starting points outlined above begin to indicate their own ontological underpinnings: one alludes to reality being tangible and observable while the other infers that reality is personally and situationally defined and therefore unique.

It is important to state, however, that we do not assume that every researcher undertaking educational enquiry must always embrace alternative understandings of knowledge and reality to those that they are used to in their discipline. We introduce this discussion with the aim of helping you to understand the advantages and limitations of your disciplinary starting points and any related choices that you make within the educational enquiry process. It is also necessary to recognise that there is no reason why your research, or the literature that you read, cannot embrace both approaches.

Paradigms in educational enquiry (and beyond)

So far we have introduced the idea that our approaches to research and the disciplinary conventions and cultures that we work within, are underpinned by our philosophical (epistemological and ontological) assumptions about knowledge and reality. Our understanding of how these different philosophical starting points came to be recognised and categorised, is often associated with the work of Thomas Kuhn (1962/1996). As Hammersley states, Kuhn's work, alongside other developments in the second half of the twentieth century, resulted in the growing adoption of the idea that there are competing research *paradigms*; that is, a competing set of 'philosophical assumptions about the phenomena to be studied, about how they can be understood, and even about the proper purpose and product of research' (2012: 2).

While we acknowledge that there are a number of competing and often self-identifying research paradigms that can be associated with educational enquiry (see Hammersley, 2012), for the purposes of this text we focus on two key paradigms that we feel you are most likely to encounter within the field of educational enquiry: *positivism* and *interpretivism*. Each one of these paradigms embodies different understandings of, and assumptions about, the nature of research and associated modes of enquiry, the nature and creation of knowledge and the basis of truth. Elements of one, the other or both paradigms may resonate with your own disciplinary understandings and experiences of research. Below, we explore these paradigms in further detail with the aim of further demystifying and clarifying some more of the difficult or different terminology that you may encounter in the educational literature.

Positivism

Although there is no one absolute definition, positivism broadly encompassed the view that there is one version of the truth, that truth is 'out there' to be discovered and by planning and conducting appropriately robust experiments we will get ever closer to understanding that truth. Truth here might be defined as authentic knowledge, empirical evidence, scientifically verifiable facts or logical information.

Robson notes that whilst positivism can be described in different ways, in a 'standard view', science (including social science) has 'explanation as a central aim'. He continues that such explanation is considered in a very restricted manner: 'namely, if you can relate an event, observation or other phenomenon to a general law (sometimes called a "covering" law), then you have explained it' (2002: 20).

This understanding is most commonly found in the life and physical sciences where researchers strive better to understand the physical and biological world, what is in it, how it works and what the interactions within it and influences on it are. The approach uses logic, cause and effect, isolation of factors and the proposing of testable hypotheses to help generate an understanding of the world via a series of interlinked theories. These 'truths' can often be counterintuitive to everyday experience, but the theories created are used to power many of our technological advancements. The explosion of biological understanding in the latter half of the twentieth century, following the discovery of the structure of DNA, is a classic example. DNA has always been there doing its job, but once we knew what it looked like and started to understand how it works, the advancements in all areas of cell biology and medical science have been exponential. However, we know our understanding of DNA and its role in living organisms is as yet incomplete as the more we understand, the more questions appear.

Positivists also recognise that using an incomplete model can be 'good enough' for the job in hand; Newton's Laws of Motion are sufficient to facilitate man's landing on the moon but we need Einstein's theories of relativity to keep global positioning satellites in place and our satnavs and mobile phones working. New ideas in quantum physics including the 'hunt' for the Higgs boson particle seem strange (and perhaps counterintuitive) to many, but will help us address fundamental questions such as the origins and purpose of 'mass' and 'gravity'. The application of these empirical theories in industries and disciplines such as engineering and computing provide us with many of our everyday comforts and form the basis of the contemporary world.

In *positivism*, observation, data and the occasional hunch are used to construct a hypothesis about how something works. An experiment is then devised to test that hypothesis and prove it wrong. Only once the evidence is overwhelming that the hypothesis cannot be disproved does it then become a theory. A 'good' theory can be used to make predictions about the outcomes of certain sets of circumstances. However, this does not mean that future research will not disprove the theory or change our understanding of it.

A medical 'randomised control trial' (RCT) is a good example of this process in action. In RCTs, a researcher may hypothesise that a chemical they have extracted from a plant which historically has been used to treat a disease has some functional properties and could be developed into a new drug. As such, they may take two groups of samples (cells in a dish, animal models or human test subjects depending on how far the trial has progressed) and test one set with the new drug and the other with nothing or perhaps a placebo drug. They would then measure, objectively, the effect of that drug compared to no drug, with the assumption that no other factors have been changed. If they can show a bulk of robust evidence that the drug has a positive impact on that disease then they have a theory of effect and can move towards making it available for medical treatment.

The key factor at play here is *objectivity*: the researcher does not influence the outcome. Often real drug trials are conducted 'blind' where neither the researcher nor the patient are aware which is the real drug in order to reduce any form of bias. Whether bias or influence can ever really be fully avoided remains a key debate, but the intention is always to design bias out of the experimental plan.

Most academics hailing from a science, engineering or mathematics background are likely to have only been exposed to this kind of approach to research. In fact, in our experience some may not even be aware of there being any other kind of (valid) research approach. As such, educational research that does not embrace this view and follow similar procedures can appear trivial and based on a subjective viewpoint rather than being viewed as objective 'research'.

While we argue that educational enquiry cannot simply or exclusively take a positivist stance (and explore later how this would limit the findings and results of enquiry), we acknowledge that academics in such disciplines may find it less straightforward to engage with, understand or appreciate research using a different paradigm. As such, focusing on literature describing projects that take a broadly positivistic approach may be an easier and more comfortable starting point, as the approach and design of the research will seem more familiar. Case Study 2.1 illustrates an example of this approach in action.

 Case Study 2.1   Effect of A level maths knowledge on university learning

A maths lecturer was concerned that many of his first years seemed to be struggling with his module on mechanics. He hypothesised that it might be to do with which A level syllabus they had studied and that the amount of experience they had had with mechanics at school may impact on their ability to engage with it at a higher level. He collated the data on test performance at the end of the module and tried to correlate it with whether mechanics had been part of each students' A level work or not. He found a correlation, but it was not what he expected. He found that those who had done mechanics at A level had, on average, done worse in the module than their peers who had not. This seemed counter-intuitive. Further enquiry into the way students attempted the questions in the test, through implementing carefully designed research instruments in the form of a questionnaire and follow-up semi-structured interview schedules, shed some light on what was happening. He discovered that those with A level experience did well on the first few 'easy' questions that required not much more than A level knowledge of the equations. Effectively the students could recall equations they had previously learned and apply them. However, as the test went on the questions became more difficult and a deeper knowledge was required. The students needed to be able to derive the correct equation from first principles to answer the questions. Those that had only had mechanics instruction in the module were able to do this. However, those that already 'knew' mechanics from their A level experience were falling back on their default knowledge and seemingly had not engaged with the 'new knowledge' of the underpinning principles and therefore could not address the test questions. Once this difference in approach by the two sets of students was understood, the lecturer could address it in the way the module was taught resulting in better success for all students.

This case study serves to illustrate an important point made by Robson in relation to research that involves people. He notes that researchers who adopt a positivist approach are looking for

> the existence of a constant relationship between events, or in the language of experimentation, between two variables. This can be relatively straightforward when dealing with the natural world, although calling for considerable ingenuity and the ability to control the conditions of the experiment – which is why laboratories exist. However, when people are the focus of the study, particularly when it is taking place in a social real world context, 'constant conjunction' in a strict sense is so rare as to be virtually non-existent. (2002: 21)

For the maths lecturer in the case study, adopting a 'positivist' approach clearly provided him with an indication of the source of the problem. However, to obtain a full answer to the question 'why are certain students performing better than others?', he required a different approach that would have required him to ask students in a systematic manner about why they were approaching questions in a certain observed way. This approach would fall into the alternative paradigm that we introduce in this chapter: namely interpretivism (sometimes referred to as 'antipositivism' or 'naturalism').

Interpretivism

Interpretivism underpins a number of research approaches, but fundamental to all is the wish to understand *social* phenomena within their particular context. As such, the researcher does not attempt to research phenomena in objective ways, abstract from their broader context, but recognises that any account of phenomena necessarily needs to take their setting into account. This view is captured succinctly by Cohen et al. who note:

> In rejecting the viewpoint of the detached, objective observer – a mandatory feature of traditional research – anti-positivists and post-positivists would argue that individuals' behaviour can only be understood by the researcher sharing their frame of reference: understanding of individuals' interpretations of the world around them has to come from the inside, not the outside. Social science is thus seen as a subjective rather than an objective undertaking, as a means of dealing with the direct experience of people in specific contexts.
> (2011: 15)

In contrast to the positivist approaches outlined above, the interpretivist paradigm is based around contextual illumination and understanding. As such, reliability and replication (breadth of understanding and applicability) are not central to this approach; rather the extrapolation of understandings and interpretations to similar (but not identical) situations is underpinned by the recognition that no social situation is the same and that depth of situational understanding, rather than breadth of understanding and wider applicability, is key. Quoting Bassey (1981), Opie (2004) notes that the study of particular or singular situations or events in educational contexts can often be seen as more useful (when usefulness is defined and judged by teachers) than approaches which aim to produce generalisable results. As such, he concludes, the *relatability* of educational enquiry (its relevance or similarity to other settings) is more important than its generalisability. In this vein, you may indeed find that you are drawn to educational enquiry undertaken from within your discipline, irrespective of its approach or methods, due to its relevance to your own setting and resonance with your own experiences.

The knowledge created by employing this approach is not seen as a universal truth but as an interpretation based on the people involved, the situation and observable or perceived practices, processes, interpretations and outcomes. Important to this process is the recognition that perceptions (however subjective and unobservable) can result in outcomes that have very real consequences. Thomas and Thomas, writing at the early part of the twentieth century in America, provide insight into this process that remains, nearly one hundred years later, clear, succinct and relevant: 'If men [*sic*] define situations as real, then they are real in their consequences' (1928: 572, cited in Gross, 2007: 194). This insight has become known as 'the Thomas Theorem' and underpins Robert K. Merton's concept of the *self-fulfilling prophecy*: 'a *false* definition of the situation evoking a new behaviour which makes the originally false conception come *true*' (Merton, 1948: 195; original emphasis).

An example of this process in action might be that a teacher in a classroom decides to set a mid-semester test to identify how students are doing in relation to a module's learning outcomes in order that future sessions can be tailored to students' learning needs. The test does not contribute to the final module mark and this is clearly conveyed to the students to ensure that students do their best, but are not overly worried about their results.

The students, in contrast, perceive this test to be a minor diversion which will waste their time when they need to study for their final exam. As a result very few turn up to the test and the results are not a reliable measure of whole class need.

In recognition that there may be many 'realities' out there to study and that one approach or method may not capture all of these, interpretive studies often use a variety of methods to ensure that a range of perspectives and interpretations are taken into account. These approaches are viewed as being framed by, and adding to, existing theoretical debates in a given area thus providing answers to research questions that may help others to understand similar (if not identical) situations.

Methods such as interviews and observations are common, which allow for a range of interpretations to be gathered and *triangulated* to ensure that any theoretical developments that result from the study are multi-dimensional and have taken a range of views and observations into account. This process is illustrated in Case Study 2.2.

Case Study 2.2   Exploring students' understanding of feedback

A lecturer notices that while student satisfaction survey results are very positive in terms of the promptness and quantity of feedback on assessed work, students appear to be significantly less satisfied with the effectiveness of the feedback they receive. The questionnaire used for the survey does not provide any insight as to why this is the case. She and her colleagues have spent a long period of time discussing the appropriate content and length of feedback and are struggling to come up with hypotheses. She decides that the only way to find out why feedback is deemed by students to be ineffective is to talk to the students themselves. While asking students directly what they view as effective feedback, and why, may provide one possible route to understanding this phenomenon, the lecturer is aware that this may simply highlight students' perceptions of what they think would constitute effective feedback rather than uncovering what is and is not working in current practice.

To address this, a three-pronged approach to gathering data is used. First, students are asked to explain their views on the role and purpose of feedback. Secondly, focus groups of students are asked to discuss what constitutes constructive and effective feedback. Finally, individual students are invited to sit down with a researcher using the 'think aloud'

(Continued)

> *(Continued)*
>
> or cognitive interviewing technique, in which they read through feedback to a piece of work and tell the researcher how they are interpreting it in real time. In combination, these three approaches to data collection provide the lecturer with a clear understanding of students' views of, and approaches to, using feedback from which evidence-based changes to the department's feedback policy and practice can be made.

It is also worth noting the recognition, from within this paradigm, that research is only able to be communicated using the frameworks available at the time (the norms of linguistic and explanatory communication). To this end, Cousin (2009) makes the important point that our research (data collection, analysis and dissemination) can only 're-present' our observations and analysis within certain limits. At a very simple level, our experience of *riding* a horse will always be different from our re-telling of this experience (our narrative).

The paradigms in brief

As we have discussed, each of the two paradigms introduced in this chapter has different philosophical underpinnings which are useful to understand as they provide the basis for the particular research methods that you may come across in educational literature. Figure 2.1 (drawing on the work of Burton et al., 2008: 61–62) brings together the discussion so far to illustrate these differences in relation to the following questions:

- How is knowledge defined and created?
- What role do theory, research questions and hypotheses play in the research process?
- What is the role and status of the 'researcher' and 'researched'?
- What actually exists or can be said to exist (what is real; what is reality)?
- What constitutes validity, reliability and credibility in research?

What does this mean in practice?

Every disciplinary area, reflecting the paradigms that they align to, will have its own preferred and expected research methods to study a given phenomenon or research problem. Indeed, many academic disciplines will ensure that their students learn about and apply such disciplinary methods as part of their undergraduate degree programmes. As you will have gathered from the discussion and case studies above, positivism emphasises research methods that focus on relatively objective approaches to gathering data (for example, surveys and experiments) and tends to draw on deductive means of analysis (statistical analysis and other systematic coding of data using predefined, controlled and objectively applied coding frames).

Positivism	Interpretivism
How is knowledge defined and created? (Epistemology)	
Knowledge is truth as defined by testable hypotheses. It is not created, only discovered or identified. The objective researcher is key to this process and occupies an 'expert' position in relation to the subject of the research	The construction of knowledge is a social process involving all who are involved in the research process. Knowledge is constructed from multiple perspectives and subjective biases are expected, recognised and identified.
What role do theory, research questions or hypotheses play in the research process?	
Theories are models of reality that have been constructed out of a series of tested hypotheses. They are testable and can be used to make predictions and form the basis through which research design is predetermined (*deduction*). They are 'true' as long as the consensus of research supports them and will be disproved should a 'better' theory or model comes along.	Theories are ever-developing 'understandings' of the world around us. They form an overarching explanatory framework for the social world and research questions are contextualised by these frameworks. Theories are not disproved; rather they emerge and develop from a dialogue between research and theory (*induction*).
What is the role and status of the researcher and researched? (Positionality)	
The researcher is an objective observer that ideally has no influence over the researched. They design the experiment, control all of the variables bar the one of interest and eliminate confounding factors so as to ensure only the object of interest can influence the outcomes. That way the results and outcomes can be directly attributed to the variable factor and its role in the system can be described.	The researcher recognises the multiple perspectives that come to play on any given social situation and recognises how they (and their respondents) form an artificially created research setting and may all be affected by this. Issues related to status and power (for example, gender, role, ownerships, space, culture) are all deemed to be important in this process. Research subjects are given equal status in co-constructing understanding, knowledge and outcomes.
What actually exists or can be said to exist; what is reality? (Ontology)	
Reality is objective, rational and exists independent of observation or from the perspective of the observer. It is 'out there' waiting to be discovered and observed.	Reality is socially and culturally constructed; it has many dimensions and its particular form will depend on the frame of reference within which it is being observed.
What constitutes validity, reliability and credibility?	

(Continued)

Figure 2.1   (Continued)

A valid theory must have no other plausible, simpler explanation and the chain of cause and effect should have no gaps or assumptions but be made of clear, logical, testable steps. Validity also refers to the means of measurement, whether they are accurate and whether they are intended to measure. A reliable theory must always give the same result under the same conditions. The replicability of results or observations is key, and central to this process is the method of data collection and the objectivity of the researcher.	Validity involves the recognition that there is confidence in the accuracy of the data (due to the methods of gathering and analysing data). Reliability comes not from a predictability of result through replication, but from a recognition and awareness of the multiple sources and ways of creating knowledge in any given situation. Although reliability and validity are treated separately in positivism, these terms are not viewed separately in interpretivism. Instead, terminology that encompasses both, such as credibility, transferability and trustworthiness are often used.
How can we communicate our findings?	
Research dissemination and communication techniques are rigorous and objective and present, using techniques which have been developed to ensure objectivity and a reliable representation of reality.	Research dissemination and communication techniques rely on the conventions and linguistic and explanatory frameworks available. As such we are unlikely to represent 'reality' as it happened, but only our lingustic or written interpretation of it, often within particular predefined parameters.

Figure 2.1   An overview of key differences between the two paradigms

Conversely, interpretivism emphasises research methods that tend to focus on relatively subjective approaches (for example, interviews and observations) and tends to draw on inductive means of analysis, allowing *codes* (analytical themes and categories) to emerge from the data with no predefined analysis framework in place.

However, it should be noted that the overall research approach taken does not prescribe or negate a particular procedure or method being used. As our case studies in this chapter have illustrated, research studies in the field of education can, and often need to, adopt what is termed a *mixed-method approach*. This ensures that a range of different data on a given issue, phenomenon or practice are collected and analysed. It is now increasingly viewed, within social and educational research, as a 'third paradigm ... a platform of ideas and practices that are credible and distinctive and that mark the approach out as a viable alternative to [positivist and interpretivist] paradigms' (Denscombe, 2008b: 270).

Concluding thoughts

The main focus of this chapter has been to help you to think about the differences and similarities between positivist and interpretivist approaches to research. Ultimately which of these approaches is most appropriate for your own educational enquiry project will be largely determined by the research question under scrutiny and the issue to be addressed. The approach needs to be carefully thought out and tailored to the task in hand: different questions or problems require you to take different approaches to find a solution.

What is important to recognise is that there is not one 'best' way to undertake educational enquiry. Reflecting on where you sit in relation to the two prevailing paradigms, as a result of your subject background, will enable you to identify what you do not know about different approaches to research. It will hopefully also help you to recognise that just because a particular approach is not familiar to you, does not mean that it is not a valid way of undertaking educational enquiry.

This notwithstanding, we highly recommend that your first steps into educational enquiry are taken within a familiar paradigm as this is likely to help you to engage most comfortably with this new field. Whether this means you primarily read educational literature from your subject area, focus on reports that use methods that you understand or use a method that is familiar to you from your own disciplinary research, does not really matter. Most important is the fact that your teaching developments become increasingly evidence-based. As you gain experience and confidence in this area of work and start to ask yourself questions about your own teaching practice, you will begin to see how a range of different data- and evidence-gathering techniques could be relevant to you and your work. There is no right or wrong way forward here. We argue only for an understanding of all of the options so that you can choose the right tool for the job, adapt the job to the tools in hand or partner up with someone (perhaps from a different discipline) who can bring different skills, understandings and approaches to a project to support the development of a mixed-methods approach.

Suggested further reading

Cohen, L., Manion, L. and Morrison, K. (2011) *Research Methods in Education* (7th edition). Abingdon: Routledge.
Denscombe, M. (2010) *The Good Research Guide: For Small-scale Social Research Projects* (4th edition). Maidenhead: Open University Press.
Robson, C. (2011) *Real World Research* (3rd edition). Chichester: Wiley.

CHAPTER 3

HOW IS EDUCATIONAL LITERATURE EVIDENCED AND REVIEWED?

Mike McLinden, Elizabeth Cleaver and Maxine Lintern

Learning outcomes

By the end of this chapter it is anticipated that you will:

- Have an understanding as to why drawing on an evidence base is an important foundation for any educational enquiry project;
- Recognise the key criteria that can be drawn upon when assessing the quality of sources; and
- Understand how reviews of educational literature can form part of your own professional development activities.

Introduction

As an academic working in higher education, you will be very familiar with the concept and process of reviewing an evidence base within your own discipline. You are likely to have undertaken at least one review of literature as part of a research study (either at undergraduate or postgraduate level) at some point in your academic career. You may not, however, be as familiar with reviews undertaken as part of educational research and in particular, those which are focused on educational enquiry within the context of higher education. Thus, while you will have developed an extensive knowledge base in your area, it is probable that educational enquiry papers, articles and books will not feature in the databases, journals or other forms of dissemination used within your discipline.

The main purpose of this chapter is therefore to help you to understand and evaluate the usefulness of existing literature reviews, or to undertake such a review yourself, in a potentially unfamiliar landscape which draws on traditions that may differ from those with which you are familiar. Indeed, some of the literature that you explore as part of an educational enquiry project may not be recognised as 'valid' literature within your own field.

With this in mind, we start the chapter with a brief consideration of the broad purpose of a literature review in the context of educational enquiry. Within this discussion, we revisit the notion of 'scholarship' introduced in Chapter 1, arguing that drawing on an evidence base is an important foundation for any educational enquiry projects that you embark upon. Just as any academic paper in your discipline will make reference to work that has gone before – either to critique this, support it or build upon it – so too your educational enquiry will need to make reference to literature in this way. This is arguably of even greater importance in the field of education where policy evidence (both local institutional and broader national) as well as research evidence can be key in framing practice; particularly if we recognise that our classroom practice is not separable from the broader policy and socio-economic context in which it sits. Brew provides support for this approach, arguing that within any field of study,

> making a contribution to knowledge involves relating work to an on-going story of the development of ideas in the field. This means that academics coming to the scholarship of teaching and learning, need to have an understanding of how ideas in the field of higher education have developed. (2011: 1)

The chapter also includes a consideration of the different types of review that you may encounter within education studies and offers some practical guidance to help get you started on your own literature review.

Why review the literature?

In Chapter 1 we briefly considered the notion of the 'scholarship of teaching' in relation to educational enquiry within higher education. As Brew (2011) argues, the purpose of such scholarship is to 'infuse' teaching with scholarly qualities in order to enhance learning. In line with this, we argued that to infuse educational enquiry with scholarly qualities, you should build any enquiry on secure evidence-based foundations. If you have been teaching for a number of years, you will probably agree with the view eloquently expressed by Hutchings and Shulman that teaching does not automatically 'renew' itself. Indeed, they argue that it is possible to teach for years without the *development* of that teaching, and refer to the scholarly aspect of teaching and learning as involving 'going meta' (1999: 13). This approach encourages the framing of questions that can be used systematically to investigate teaching and students' learning. Part of this systematic investigation, when 'going meta', is knowing how to locate relevant evidence upon which to build your own study, or to show how others have addressed a similar focus of enquiry. This is supported by Trigwell et al. who argue that the aim of scholarly teaching is to 'make transparent how we have made learning possible', arguing that 'teachers must be informed of the theoretical perspectives and literature of teaching and learning in their discipline, and be able to collect and present rigorous evidence of effectiveness' (2000: 156).

A useful way of thinking about the importance of a review is therefore to consider how a study or project within your own discipline that you have recently undertaken, or are planning, would look without reference to relevant literature. As Hart (1998) argues, a review is important because 'without it you will not acquire an understanding of your topic, of what has already been done on it, how it has been researched, and what the key issues are'. In essence, then, the main purpose of a review of literature can be seen to be 'to analyse ideas, find relationships between different ideas and understand the nature and use of argument in research' (Hart, 1998: 1–2). This highlights that a review of an evidence base should not be just a bibliography of relevant sources but will require an appropriate breadth and depth as well as rigour and consistency 'to justify the particular approach to the topic, the selection of methods, and demonstration that this research contributes something new' (1998: 1–2).

The nature of evidence

As argued above, the literature sources that you use to develop your own educational enquiry project may be different to those you are used to using within your discipline. In sifting through this potentially new literature base you will need to make decisions as to the relevance and quality of any given source. This need for 'information literacy' is captured by Thomas who notes something that you will doubtless tell your own students on a regular basis: that some sources have more credibility than others and as such it is important 'not to be taken in by something – or to present it to others – just because it is in print' (2009: 31). However, as noted above, an idea or view presented in text that is relevant for an educational enquiry project may not be evidence-based (a policy, for example), but may help you to set the scene or to formulate a research question or focus. As such it can be appropriate to include reference to it in any review you do or for others to have done similarly themselves.

It is probably useful at this point to consider further the types of evidence that you are likely to come across in the educational evidence base. You will be very familiar with the distinction between 'primary' and 'secondary' sources of information in relation to your own discipline. As Thomas notes, the main difference between these sources is 'in the directness of the data or evidence being presented' (2009: 31). Primary sources usually include materials that have not been further examined or analysed and in the context of educational enquiry may include data such as government or institutional statistics (for example, the number of students studying a particular subject area), published research reports, articles in research journals and so on. However within education they may also include types of evidence that are less familiar to you, including 'grey literature',[1] theoretical texts, opinion pieces and newspaper reports. Secondary sources, as the name suggests, will incorporate an analysis or some reworking of primary sources. Commonly used secondary sources you may draw upon within the field of education include texts that synthesise research published in other sources (such as this book) as well as review articles that seek to synthesise key themes from the educational literature.

Given the wide range of sources available and depending on how they are utilised within a review, it may be useful to compare different 'published' outputs. Outputs from even relatively small-scale studies can vary in their approaches to data collection, analysis and dissemination. Each of these factors may lead to some being more credible than others when placed within the context of your own review. With this in mind, an important aspect of adopting a scholarly approach to your learning and teaching is being able to rate the sources you draw on and to articulate their strengths and limitations in the context of your particular project.

---

[1]The Fourth International Conference on Grey Literature (1999) defined grey literature as '[t]hat which is produced on all levels of government, academics, business and industry in print and electronic formats, but which is not controlled by commercial publishers' (cited in New York Academy of Medicine Library, 2013). This body of literature is likely to grow exponentially with the open education movement and moves by many to publish under Creative Commons licencing agreements.

Activity 3.1   Problem-based learning for civil engineers

For this activity, consider the following sources in which the outputs of a small-scale educational enquiry study were published. Each source presents the outcomes of a study that describes how Problem-based Learning (PBL) was used to teach Year 1 students about structural forces within one module of an undergraduate degree in civil engineering.

A. Chapter describing the research study in an edited text on learning and teaching approaches such as this one (commissioned and reviewed by the editors of the text).
B. Article in a special edition of a discipline-focused professional journal (commissioned and edited by editor of the journal).
C. Research article presented in a peer-reviewed journal on learning and teaching in higher education (peer reviewed anonymously by three reviewers).
D. Unpublished study describing the research process – submitted by the module tutor as part of a master's dissertation and available in the university library.
E. Paper presented at a national academic conference on learning and teaching approaches in the physical sciences (peer-reviewed anonymously by an academic selection committee).
F. Summary of findings presented on the institutional website as part of 'new innovations in teaching practice' theme.

Consider first how you might determine the relative 'quality' of each of these sources if you were to draw on them for a review of literature (for example, as part of a review of literature on how PBL has been used within different disciplines in higher education). Next, consider how you might place each on a virtual continuum with sources of relatively 'high' quality on the one end and those of relatively 'low' quality at the other. You can then compare your analysis with our own.

Comment on Activity 3.1

You will be aware from your own discipline, that whilst peer-reviewed journals are usually considered to be the 'gold' standard' for determining the quality of evidence (Thomas, 2009), not all journals (or indeed conference presentations) will have the same rigour attached to them. In short then, further detective work would be required to find out about the quality of the respective sources as part of a review of literature seeking to analyse the evidence from this study. The relative quality of the sources will depend on a number of factors but based on this summary we would place source F (summary located on an institutional website) at the relatively 'low quality' end of the continuum with source C (article in a peer-reviewed journal) at the relatively 'high quality' end. A decision about the relative quality of the other sources is clearly open to debate – but generally we would place those outputs that had been subject to anonymous external peer review (for example, a paper presented at an academic conference with a peer-review selection committee) as being of a relatively higher quality than the other sources. You may wish to undertake a similar activity with colleagues in your place of work to compare their views with your own. We are sure it will be the focus of a stimulating discussion.

You will be familiar with published reviews of literature on particular themes within your own discipline. Increasingly such review articles feature in the educational literature and can provide a good starting point for your own review of published work. Review articles in education can be broadly divided into those that adopt a *systematic* approach to searching the literature and those which adopt a more *narrative* or *thematic* approach.

Thomas describes the systematic approach as using 'particular methods to search for research on a topic in a wide range of peer review sources', where only studies of a 'predetermined type and/or quality are included in the ultimate review' (2009: 34). Such reviews have at their very heart positivist understandings of rigour and validity (as discussed in Chapter 2) and often focus on studies with a larger sample size which are conducted in particular ways. The type of review illustrated in Case Study 3.1 is an example of a study that seeks to bring together 'high-quality evidence and then synthesises and summarises it for the reader' (2009: 35). There are a now a number of collaborative organisations that produce such resources. Some of the most well-known and well-regarded systematic reviews are the Cochrane Reviews which review 'primary research in human health care and health policy, and are internationally recognised as the highest standard in evidence-based health care' (Cochrane Collaboration, 2013). Other collaborative ventures include the Campbell Collaboration (social sciences) and the EPPI-Centre (education, social science and public policy). If you wish to explore the range of methods covered by the systematic review approach further, a good overview and critique is provided by Gough et al. (2012). Given the emerging nature of the area, such reviews are relatively rare in the broad context of educational enquiry within higher education. Those that have been undertaken, however, can provide a useful and robust resource that lay strong foundations for future pedagogical activities (as an example, a pilot systematic review of the effectiveness of problem-based learning within higher education is presented in Case Study 3.1).

It is worth noting also that to undertake a systematic review well takes time and other resources, which may not be at your disposal. Moreover, it is important to recognise that the approach, and its claim to be the highest standard of literature review, rests on certain epistemological assumptions. These may, in all actuality, not resonate with the particular nature of your educational enquiry problem or research questions. As such, you may find that the narrative approach to literature reviewing is more appropriate. This approach may not only be more practical in terms of its resource costs, but also has the potential to offer scope for the incorporation of a wider range of educational literature. As reported by Cronin et al. in this type of review, the body of literature is

> made up of the relevant studies and knowledge that address the subject area. It is typically selective in the material it uses ... This type of review is useful in gathering together a volume of literature in a specific subject area and summarizing and synthesizing it. Its primary purpose is to provide the reader with a comprehensive background for understanding current knowledge and highlighting the significance of new research. (2008: 38)

While such an approach is less specific about the types of literature that are included, and sometimes about the ways in which they have been selected, it can and does play an important role. In addition to empirical studies and reports, it can include a range of other resources including 'grey literature', expositions of theory, opinion pieces, newspaper reports and policy documents. This more comprehensive stance recognises that the concepts, ideas and understandings that emerge from a broad range of literature can provide insights which may prove important for an empirical study. Even if theoretical or opinion-based, such ideas may help you to formulate research questions that can be explored empirically through data collection. If other educational enquiry projects adopt this approach to reviewing the literature, however small your own educational enquiry project is, you may be cited and thus involved in advancing knowledge and providing evidence to support or question further educational developments.

Below we illustrate these two approaches through the use of two case studies; Case Study 3.1 focuses on the evidence base for problem-based learning (PBL) and Case Study 3.2 on evidence for best practice in the use of case-based teaching. While you may be familiar with one or both of these approaches, and may have used them in practice, you may not be as familiar with the evidence base upon which each approach has been built. In introducing these case studies we also hope that they can illustrate how drawing on an existing evidence base may be helpful in thinking through new approaches to your learning and teaching, whether you are thinking of undertaking educational enquiry or not.

Case Study 3.1   Example of a systematic review (Newman, 2003)

This case study explores a commissioned study which sought to review the 'effectiveness' of problem-based learning (PBL) within HE through a pilot systematic review. The focus was on health professional education at both pre- and post-registration levels. The study acknowledges that whilst there are many sources of published work on PBL in the field of education, the quality of these is wide ranging; existing overviews of the field do not provide high-quality evidence with which to offer 'robust' answers to questions about the 'effectiveness of PBL'.

To this end, this study reports on the development and piloting of a systematic review and meta-analysis on the effectiveness of PBL by an international group of teachers and researchers convened under the auspices of the Campbell Collaboration. The pilot systematic review established that the limited high-quality evidence available from existing reviews does not provide robust evidence about the effectiveness of different kinds of PBL in different contexts with different student groups. It concludes that there is scope for a systematic review of PBL that is specific in terms of the 'intervention' that is being evaluated, comprehensive in terms of strategy employed to identify potential evidence and methodologically rigorous in terms of the criteria used to evaluate the quality of evidence. The pilot review demonstrates the potential value of a systematic review and meta-analysis in summarising and synthesising existing research to begin to provide robust answers to questions of effectiveness and to identify issues for further primary research.

Case Study 3.2   Example of a narrative review (Kim et al., 2006)

This article, using the narrative review approach, aims to identify strategies to help teachers to construct 'cases' to aid teaching in a variety of learning settings. The evidence is gathered from studies from a range of disciplines reporting the development and use of case-based teaching.

(Continued)

(Continued)

The paper describes how the research team selected keywords for searching, reviewed the literature (moving from an initial search total of 974 to 100 pieces of literature) based on a broad set of inclusion criteria: 'journal articles, books and book chapters written in English that reported original data, descriptions or theoretical frameworks covering the structure, process and outcomes related to developing teaching cases' (Kim et al., 2006: 869). Studies which considered the benefits of case discussions, but did not point towards ways to develop cases for teaching, were excluded. The article charts how the authors were able to catalogue a series of emergent themes which point towards the development of *relevant, realistic, engaging, challenging* and *instructional* teaching cases.

The review concludes by arguing that many academic disciplines, whilst using case-based teaching as a core teaching method, appear to lack a coherent, evidence-based approach to teaching-case design, use and evaluation. The framework developed from existing literature is presented as a 'menu of case development options that educators can pilot and evaluate in their local settings' (2006: 873).

Undertaking your own review of educational literature

In this section we introduce a staged approach to help you to get started in your own review of educational literature. Cronin et al. (2008) outline five steps in undertaking a narrative review of literature, many of which are likely to be familiar to you but may, in fact, be subtly different from the approach that you would normally take within your own disciplinary area:

1. Selecting your topic for review
2. Beginning your search of the literature
3. Gathering, reading and analysing the literature
4. Writing your review
5. How to cite references

For the purpose of this chapter, and in order to highlight potential differences between your own and educational practices in this area, we focus particularly on Steps 1 and 2, illustrating these with appropriate reference to a worked example related to educational enquiry. We then briefly consider referencing conventions within the field of educational enquiry.

Step 1: Selecting your topic for review

Cronin et al. note that topics for review that are 'too broad will result in reviews that are either too long or too superficial. As a rule of thumb, it is better to start with a narrow and focused topic and if necessary broaden the scope of the review as you progress' (2008: 39).

As a worked example, imagine that you are planning to revise your teaching with a view to introducing 'small group' enquiry-based learning approaches (structured around authentic scenarios or cases) into a module for undergraduate science students that is currently based around 'large group' lectures. The broad topic area of interest may be whether this type of collaborative learning approach is more effective than the traditional large group lecture format. Whilst this is an interesting area for review, it is unlikely (unless you have a long time period and/or have secured external funding for the review) that you would have the resources to do it justice. Consider for example how many different types of 'collaborative' learning approaches there are which are structured around enquiry-based learning, the number of countries, institutions and disciplines within which this could take place and the many discussions about what might constitute a large group or a small group. In some disciplines or institutions, 'large' may equate to 50 students while in others it may mean 400 students; likewise, 'small' may mean one-to-one tuition or a group of 20 students depending on institutional and disciplinary context.

To develop a more focused topic area it would therefore be helpful to consider the following questions:

- What particular aspect of this topic is of relevance to you? Consider for example, the particular context of your own disciplinary setting, the type of teaching that you currently undertake and the type of institution you are based in.
- What approach are you thinking of taking to the research? What are your epistemological starting points and why is this the case?
- What kind of data will be most useful for helping you to address your research questions? Consider whether existing data held in university records (for example, module grades and student progression data) or new data (for example, student voice) will help you to evaluate its effectiveness.
- What timescale and sample size will the project cover? Is this a one-off 'snapshot' evaluation of change within a given cohort or will you also study other groups of students experiencing similar change over time?

These questions should help you to define a clearer focus for your project and, as we will see in Step 2, help also to define the keywords that you will use in your literature search.

Step 2: Beginning your search of the literature

As an academic located within a particular disciplinary area, you may not be familiar with key journals and the databases in which the latest evidence from higher educational research can be found. Such evidence is published in a wide range of journals and texts, some of which are more 'practitioner' based than others. We provide a summary of a selection of generic journals that have a focus on learning and teaching in HE in Figure 3.1, with a number of the later chapters in this text making reference to more discipline focused journals.

When planning to access this literature base, you will be aware of the changing nature of academic libraries which increasingly serve as a portal, providing access to a vast wealth of electronic information, rather than serving as a repository of information in more traditional hard copy format. As such, a keyword search using your own academic library is usually a good starting point for any review. You will be familiar with the skills required to undertake a review of literature in relation to your own discipline but it is worth reminding you of some basic techniques, and the importance of an accurate keyword search when accessing electronic databases.

Electronic databases

As Cronin et al. note, there are 'numerous electronic databases, many of which deal with specific fields of information. It is important, therefore, to identify which databases are relevant to the topic' (2008: 40). A number of institutions now offer or are moving towards a 'single sign-on' environment in the form of one 'gateway' to all of the electronic resources that they subscribe to, including for example, the full text of journals, searchable databases or any other type of electronic resources that they have access to.

As a starting point you may wish to check the arrangements in your own institution and find out which of the journals listed in Figure 3.1 your library subscribes to, and whether these are held in electronic format. If your institution does not subscribe to a particular journal you can consider using a comprehensive research database called Zetoc through your university library. This database provides subscribers with access to over 28,000 journals, and over 50 million article citations and conference papers through the British Library's electronic table of contents. You may wish to start your search with databases or search services that are of relevance to educational and broader social sciences literature. A number of commonly used search services are listed in Figure 3.2.

Use of keywords and descriptors

As indicated above, given the wealth of information now available in electronic format, it is important to think carefully about the keywords and related descriptors you will be drawing on for your search. As noted by

Cronin et al. (2008) the keywords used to identify terms may differ in spelling and/or meaning. As such it is a good practice to consider using alternative keywords that have a similar meaning and which could provide you with additional information. A common example in relation to the focus of this text is use of the terms 'enquiry' and 'inquiry'. As discussed in Chapter 1, these two terms are synonymous but are spelt differently according to UK English and American English conventions. A search in the ERIC (Education Resources Information Centre) database in Spring 2013 for the term 'enquiry based learning' produced 152 sources. This compares with 3550 when the term 'inquiry based learning' was typed in. Use of both terms as part of an extensive keyword search would probably therefore be advisable (with some consideration in the review itself of the use of terminology in the selected sources).

A useful facility incorporated into some databases allows you to search using particular subject headings. As an example, the ERIC database has a thesaurus of headings labelled as 'descriptors'. Effectively the database assigns terms to its records to organise them by subject and so make them easier to retrieve through an online search. Searching by descriptor, then, requires searching relevant terms from within this 'controlled' vocabulary. Although you can also search the ERIC records using keywords, it is stated on the website that more precise search results will be obtained if the Thesaurus subject terms are used, as searching by keywords will match the exact word found in a record, regardless of whether they are used in the same context as your own topic. As such, searching through the use of descriptors enables you to locate records by the subject area, and is not dependent on the terminology/keywords that the author of the published source may have used. A useful facility is to type in your keywords and view the related descriptors. These then provide the direction for a future search. Guidance on how you might search the ERIC database using the listed descriptors is presented on the ERIC website.

Continuing our worked example, if we type in the keywords 'enquiry based learning' into the Thesaurus no matches are revealed. Typing in the keywords 'inquiry based learning' reveals one descriptor, appropriately enough entitled 'inquiry based learning'. This descriptor is related to two other descriptors, namely 'active learning' and 'inquiry'. It is now possible to start a search using these descriptors and then adding additional keywords to refine our search. We can start by including the keyword 'higher education' to give:

((**Thesaurus Descriptors**: 'active learning' AND **Thesaurus Descriptors**: 'inquiry') and (**Keywords**: higher and **Keywords**: education))

This search undertaken in Spring 2013 reveals approximately 210 results, with a number having direct relevance to the topic we are interested in (that is they are concerned with student perspectives of engaging in a particular active learning approach).

As this particular project is about science students studying for a first degree, you could now start to refine your keyword search to include 'undergraduate' and/or 'science'. This now reduces the list of results to nine, which is a more manageable number to read through initially and from which to broaden the scope of your search. As an example, we might want to consider whether similar work has been undertaken in other discipline areas and may undertake the same search but replace 'science' with 'humanities' or with a more specific disciplinary name such as 'chemistry'. The use of the term 'undergraduate' may also have reduced the search results to those undertaken in the UK and you may wish to consider using a term such as 'bachelors' (used in the United States to signify an equivalent type of first degree).

As you would expect, there are many 'unknowns' associated with this process; the outcomes can depend simply on how much a particular topic area has been researched and reported on in the past which, in turn, can affect just how far you need to extend your search beyond initial narrow parameters. As you probably found when building your searching skills within your disciplinary area, your understanding of the way literature is coded within databases grows with experience and searching becomes less time-consuming and difficult with time. Ultimately keywords are generated by the author of a document who, in turn, selects these according to particular contextual (perhaps disciplinary) conventions. As such, it may take a little time to 'break the code' of literature searching in a new area.

Remember, however, that you are not alone. The subject-librarian in your institution who covers education and/or the social sciences may be able to help you with this process and provide ideas for keywords to start off your search. Moreover, colleagues from education, the social sciences or your institutional educational development team, may also be able to help you to think about your search parameters.

Steps 3 and 4: Making sense of it all

We have already covered many of the points salient to Cronin et al.s' (2008) two next steps – Step 3 'Gathering, reading and analysing the literature' and Step 4 'Writing your review' – in Chapters 1 and 2 of this text. Key to your understanding of the literature, and your ability to bring it all together into a coherent narrative and starting point from which your own project can begin, is your understanding of, and ability to tease out, the different epistemological underpinnings and associated methods presented in each piece of literature. This understanding, and your own decisions about approach and methods that stem from it, will help you to select the most relevant literature for your own study. However, as noted above, it is also appropriate to consider other types of literature that do not prove an 'exact' match to your own study either in terms of their focus or their approach. Their insights, whilst not directly replicable or transferable to your own study, may prove useful in formulating your ideas. This may, for some of you require experimenting with the adoption of a more 'interpretivist' mind-set which recognises that knowledge can be constructed from multiple perspectives, just as long as subjective differences or biases are expected, recognised and identified.

As identified by Thomas (2009), one of the potential risks of this approach, which you may not have encountered in your own disciplinary experience of collating and writing about literature, is ending up with an overwhelming range of literature to consider. For a small educational enquiry project this is neither desirable nor practicable. If you take the approach that multiple perspectives are useful, you will need to ask yourself at regular intervals: *what is the value of including this piece of work in my review?* This is a decision that cannot be prescribed for, or guided, to any great extent by a text such as this. Only you, on encountering the range of literature available in a given area will be able to judge just how far your literature review needs to stray from the direct focus of your study.

In preparing to write your review, it may be useful to familiarise yourselves with the ways in which literature is presented as a narrative. The difference between medical science and social sciences approaches to this was experienced by one of the editors at first hand recently, when a medical sciences colleague expressed surprise at some of the conventions used in constructing a social sciences introductory narrative to a research paper. Reading through some narrative literature reviews may help you to think though some of the different ways in which the literature that frames your project can be presented.

However, in the spirit of this text (and in particular its latter chapters) we do not advocate the absolute need to mirror or mimic others' approaches. It is, however, worth considering how your own approach differs from these approaches and whether any dominant techniques or common turns of phrase could enhance your own review.

Ultimately, it is worth remembering that the review is an important aspect of starting your project, raising questions and pointing forwards to areas to be explored and ways of exploring them. As such it is useful to reflect on a set of key questions to ensure that you have built a sound enough set of foundations from which to undertake the new project:

- What range of ideas, theories and understandings have already been developed or used in relation to a given issue?
- Are some ideas, theories and understandings more common than others? Why does this appear to be the case?

- Are there any key areas of disagreement?
- Are there any limitations to the approaches and methods used in the studies you are citing?
- Are there any obvious gaps in the research base that help you to frame the direction of your own study?
- How do your own study and its research questions relate to the body of literature that you have reviewed?

Step 5: How to cite references

If you are not familiar with the Harvard reference system it is worth taking a moment to become conversant with its key conventions. This is the most commonly used system in the social sciences and therefore is employed in much of the generic literature on learning and teaching in higher education. Many universities in the United Kingdom have now adopted the Harvard referencing system as their recognised referencing approach for undergraduate work. However, in some disciplinary areas, where many journals and publishers still use the convention of footnotes, the Harvard system with regular insertions within the text of 'author, date' in rounded brackets, can seem cluttered and distracting. This is particularly so when a large number of citations are included within a short space of time within a literature review. Rather than spend a long time discussing the pros and cons and conventions of the Harvard system here, we simply wish to highlight that this is a commonly adopted approach within educational literature and when reading educational publications (including this one) and potentially publishing your own educational enquiry project, you may be required to use it. Excellent and comprehensive overviews of the Harvard Referencing System have been produced by university libraries across the globe and a quick internet search will produce some reputable guidelines for you to follow. Moreover, if you are used to using an institutionally supported referencing tool such as Reference Manager or Endnote, you will be able to choose the Harvard citation option from within these packages.

At the time of writing, a number of free tools and 'apps' have also become available on the internet (for example Harvard Generator and Mendeley) which may also be helpful in generating a correctly cited reference list from your selected pieces of literature.

Concluding thoughts

Through the brief overview presented in this chapter, we hope we have demonstrated that your experience of conducting literature reviews from within your own discipline and your experience of analysing the quality of sources provide a good foundation for reviewing a particular strand or theme within the educational literature. As an academic, you will be familiar with much of the broad content in the chapter, and we hope that it has encouraged you to have the confidence to adopt a similarly scholarly approach to searching and reviewing this potentially new area of literature.

As we have highlighted, the role of a review is not just to establish what has been found, it is also about making links between your own findings and the work of others and so to help to provide a sound pedagogical basis for future teaching activities undertaken within your field. If you are planning to publish your educational enquiry project you will, we are sure, find it very gratifying when others draw on your own work as they undertake a similar review of literature in a given topic area. Finally, you may also find it useful to think of how undertaking a review can form part of your own professional development as an academic, or as Hart notes, 'an expert in the field' (1998: 1). You only need to think back to work you have undertaken in your own disciplinary area to remind yourself of the role that literature has played in helping you develop your disciplinary expertise.

Suggested further reading

Name of journal	Description (from journal website)	Review policy	Website
Academic Exchange Quarterly	'Dedicated to the presentation of ideas, research, methods, and pedagogical theories leading to effective instruction and learning regardless of level or subject.'	Anonymous peer-review process	http://rapidintellect.com/AEQweb/
Active Learning in Higher Education	'For all those who teach and support learning in higher education and those who undertake or use research into effective learning, teaching and assessment in universities and colleges.'	Anonymous peer-review process	http://alh.sagepub.com/
Assessment and Evaluation in Higher Education	'Publishes papers and reports on all aspects of assessment and evaluation within higher education … aimed at all higher education practitioners, irrespective of discipline.'	Anonymous peer-review process	www.tandfonline.com/toc/caeh20/current

(Continued)

Figure 3.1   (Continued)

Higher Education Research and Development	'Publishes scholarly articles that make a significant and original contribution to the theory, practice or research of higher education.'	Anonymous peer-review process	http://www.tandfonline.com/toc/cher20/current
Innovations in Learning and Teaching International	'Contributions to the Journal [should reflect and promote] innovation and good practice in higher education through staff and educational development and subject-related practices. Contributions are welcomed on any aspect of promoting and supporting educational change in higher and other post-school education, with an emphasis on research, experience, scholarship and evaluation, rather than mere description of practice.'	Anonymous peer-review process	http://www.tandfonline.com/toc/riie20/current
Innovative Higher Education	'Presents fresh ideas in higher education in a straightforward and readable fashion … [and] publishes diverse forms of scholarship and research methods.'	Anonymous peer-review process	www.springer.com/education+%26+language/higher+education/journal/10755
International Journal for Academic Development	'[Aims] to enable academic/educational developers in higher education across the world to exchange ideas about practice and extend the theory of educational development, with the goal of improving the quality of higher education internationally.'	Anonymous peer-review process	http://www.tandfonline.com/toc/rija20/current
International Journal for the Scholarship of Teaching and Learning	'an open, peer-reviewed, international electronic journal published twice a year … to be an international vehicle for articles, essays, and discussions about the scholarship of teaching and learning (SoTL) and its applications in higher/tertiary education today.'	Anonymous peer-review process	http://academics.georgiasouthern.edu/ijsotl/

Journal of Higher Education	'Publishes original research reporting … the main functions of higher education and the dynamic role of the university in society. We seek to publish scholarship from a wide variety of theoretical perspectives and disciplinary orientations.'	Anonymous peer-review process	https://ohiostatepress.org/ index.htm?journals/jhe/ jhemain.htm
Studies in Higher Education	'Welcomes contributions that seek to enhance understanding of higher education policy, institutional management and performance, teaching and learning, and the contribution of higher education to society and the economy.'	Anonymous peer-review process	http://www.tandfonline.com/ toc/cshe20/current
Teaching and Learning Inquiry	'A new journal from the International Society for the Scholarship of Teaching and Learning which aims to 'publish insightful research, theory, commentary, and other scholarly works that document or facilitate investigations of teaching and learning in higher education.'	Anonymous peer-review process	http://www.issotl.org/TLI.html
Teaching in Higher Education	'Addresses … teaching, learning and the curriculum in higher education … to explore and clarify the intellectual challenges which they present. The journal is interdisciplinary and aims to open up discussion across subject areas by involving all those who share an enthusiasm for learning and teaching.'	Anonymous peer-review process	http://www.tandfonline.com/ toc/cthe20/current

Figure 3.1 Selection of higher education journals that include a focus on pedagogical research and/or learning and teaching

Name	Description	Website
Higher Education Empirical Research Database	The Higher Education Empirical Research (HEER) database comprises summaries of the latest published research on a range of topics related to higher education. It is intended for use by policy-makers, academics and researchers in higher education. The HEER database is fully searchable by theme, publisher and date and is free to register.	http://heer.qaa.ac.uk/pages/default.asx
Cochrane Collaboration	The Cochrane Collaboration is a large international network (drawn from over 28,000 people in more than 100 countries). The network seeks to help healthcare providers, policy-makers, patients, their advocates and carers, make well-informed decisions about healthcare, by preparing, updating, and promoting the accessibility of Cochrane Reviews. Over 5,000 reviews have been published online in the *Cochrane Database of Systematic Reviews*, which form part of *The Cochrane Library*. Cochrane Reviews are systematic reviews of primary research in human healthcare and health policy. They investigate the effects of interventions for prevention, treatment and rehabilitation.	http://www.cochrane.org/cochrane-reviews
Campbell Collaboration	The Campbell Collaboration (C2) helps people make well-informed decisions by preparing, maintaining and disseminating systematic reviews in education, crime and justice, and social welfare. The Collaboration is an international research network that produces systematic reviews of the effects of social interventions. The organisation has a number of Coordinating Groups which are responsible for the production, scientific merit, and relevance of the systematic reviews. The groups provide editorial services and support to review authors.	http://www.campbellcollaboration.org/
EPPI-Centre	The Evidence for Policy and Practice Information and Co-ordinating Centre is based at the Institute of Education, University of London, and carries out systematic reviews and develops review methods in social science and public policy. The Centre states that it is 'dedicated to making reliable research findings accessible to the people who need them, whether they are making policy, practice or personal decisions'.	www.eppi.ioe.ac.uk/cms/

Education Resources Information Center (ERIC)	The ERIC website describes the resource as 'an online digital library of education research and information' which 'provides ready access to education literature to support the use of educational research and information to improve practice in learning, teaching, educational decision making and research'. The database is sponsored by the US Institute of Education Sciences and Department of Education. Access is by subscription and may be obtained through your institutional log-in.	www.eric.ed.gov
British Education Index (BEI)	The BEI was developed around 50 years ago and aims 'to support the professional study of education by facilitating the identification and use of specific reading matter and event-related information'. Access is by subscription and may be obtained through your institutional log-in.	www.leeds.ac.uk/bei/ index.html
Thomson Reuters 'Web of Knowledge' (includes Web of Science)	Described as a 'research platform' that provides access to the leading citation databases. The service covers the sciences, social sciences, arts and humanities, and encompasses a wide range of other databases including the Social Science Citation Index. A number of databases can be searched simultaneously. Access is by subscription and may be obtained through your institutional log-in.	

Figure 3.2 Useful research databases

CHAPTER 4

WHAT ABOUT ETHICS AND SAFETY?

Elizabeth Cleaver, Maxine Lintern and Mike McLinden

Learning outcomes

By the end of this chapter it is anticipated that you will:

- Understand why considering the ethical dimensions of educational enquiry is essential to undertaking 'good' research;
- Identify the particular ethical considerations that need to be taken into account when undertaking educational enquiry within higher education; and
- Recognise the close relationship between ethics and safety within educational enquiry.

Introduction

This chapter will be of value to anyone who is thinking of undertaking educational enquiry that directly involves human participants. Many of you will be experienced at putting research proposals through your own faculty or school ethics committees, but the focus of these committees may have been generic: *is there any potential negative impact on society or particular groups of people as a result of the research?*; or research-team specific: *are there any potential harms to those involved in undertaking the research?* Making other people the subjects of your research, or as is increasingly popular or expected,[1] actively involving such individuals in the process of the research, thereby making them not simply research participants but also co-researchers, adds a new dimension to the research ethics process. Once you involve other people directly in your research it is likely that you will need to consider the potential impact of their involvement on both themselves (their welfare), other research participants and researchers that they may come into contact with (others' welfare), your own welfare and the credibility of your research outcomes. As this indicates, issues of safety and welfare are irrevocably tied up with ethical considerations. To this end, this chapter combines discussions of ethical and safety considerations when undertaking educational enquiry.

Before we explore these aspects of the educational enquiry process in more detail, it is important to stress that taking ethics and safety into account in your enquiry should not be seen as an onerous task; concern about ethics should not in itself lead to you avoiding involving other individuals in your research and turning instead to a focus on inanimate artefacts, data and texts. To do this would be to limit the potential sources of information available to you. As Cousin rightly notes,

> [t]here are at least two good reasons for having a strong ethical framework for a research project. Firstly, it has a protective function both for the researcher and for the researched ... The second good reason ... is that it is facilitative. An ethical orientation supports the thoughtful conduct of the research process and the eventual credibility of the report. (2009: 17)

In short, considering the ethical dimensions of your enquiry is essential to undertaking 'good' research.

---

[1]Many teaching and learning research and development grant proposals, including those written in response to recent Higher Education Academy funding calls in the UK, are now expected to include students as active participants in the research process and not simply as the subjects of enquiry.

Ethical practice, whether research practice or other professional practice, cannot be divorced from broader questions of morality and 'the need to act with due care and regard towards all those who are involved in ... research, and at all stages of the research process' (Heath et al., 2009: 21). In the case of educational enquiry conducted by higher education lecturers with their students, all of whom are likely to be over sixteen, the ethical considerations are somewhat different to those which are needed when working with those who are still legally minors. Heath et al. in their text *Researching Young People's Lives* (2009) provide a full and useful discussion of ethical considerations when involving young people under the age of sixteen in the research process and we encourage any of you who are likely to have contact with this younger age group in your educational enquiry projects to read Chapter 2 of their text.

For the majority of you, perhaps the most perceptible ethical dilemma that you may face is that of involving the students that you teach directly, and whose work you mark and grade, in an educational enquiry project. From our experience, the main concern of both academic staff and students in this context is the need for a clear message that students' choice to participate or not in a given project will have absolutely no bearing on the outcomes of their studies. While we as academics may feel that it is obvious that there is no connection between these two things, and may indeed feel some level of personal affront that our integrity appears to be under question, it is important to understand why students may worry in this way. Many students may not understand the rigorous ways in which their assignments are marked, moderated and in some countries, particularly in the UK, how the marking process is overseen by an independent external examiner from another institution. This therefore provides a clue to the nature of the messages that need to be communicated to students when gaining their informed consent for project participation or non-participation; something to which we will return in more detail later in the chapter.

Recognising the ethical (and moral) complexities of involving our students in our educational enquiry projects rests on an understanding of the importance of some of the key strands of ethical practice in social research more broadly – informed consent; anonymity and confidentiality; the use of incentives; subjectivity, positionality and power; and researcher and participant wellbeing – all of which will be explored in greater depth in this chapter. However, before we move into a more detailed discussion of these strands, it is useful to consider some extant procedures, codes of practice and protocols through which such strands are likely to be considered.

Governance and procedures

Institutional governance and procedures

Most of your home institutions are likely to have their own research ethics policy, code of practice and procedures and you should, in the first instance, always adhere to the expectations outlined in these documents. Such governance and procedures have been agreed by your employing institution and will clearly set out the standards and conduct expected of employees of the institution engaged in research and other forms of enquiry in order to protect the integrity of the research, the institution and its workforce.

In many larger higher education institutions such protocols and procedures are dealt with at the devolved faculty or school level where they are informed by the particular types of research undertaken, and the requirements of any professional or funding bodies directly connected to each disciplinary field of study. Examples include the UK's Royal Academy of Engineering and the Engineering Council's *Statement of Ethical Principles* (Royal Academy of Engineering, 2013a) and the American Psychological Association's *Ethical Principles of Psychologists and Code of Conduct* (APA, 2013).

With this in mind, if your own faculty or school's ethics committee is not conversant with the ethical protocols surrounding studies that involve people as participants in research, or students as co-researchers, you may wish to discuss with the chair of the ethics committee whether the provision of additional guidance for committee members, when considering any educational enquiry projects, would be helpful. Indeed this may be something that the ethics committee may approve and take ownership of. Alternatively you may find that applying to an alternative faculty ethics committee (for example, in social sciences or education) may ensure that your application for ethics approval is considered by those who have a good understanding of the approach and type of enquiry you are undertaking. It is important to stress, however, that we do not wish to encourage you to ask for something of which your own institution would not approve; nor would we encourage you to shop around in order to find an ethics committee that will agree to your proposal due to a lack of understanding of what your project entails. Before approaching another faculty, please do check your own local procedures and protocols and speak with the chair of your own institutional or faculty ethics committee.

It is also worth noting a point made by Cousin (2009) that we have discussed at length with our own students (early career academic staff) who are undertaking small-scale research projects as part of institutional higher education teacher development programmes (in the UK, predominantly at the Postgraduate Certificate level). The use of data collected for other purposes (for example student feedback collected via module evaluation questionnaires and student module results) may not need ethical review if the project is explicitly aligned with normal programme monitoring and development procedures. These procedures may be classed as audits or evaluations rather than research. However, the dividing line between audit, evaluation and research is not always clear. Moreover, conducting some types of audit or evaluation can raise ethical concerns. It is therefore wise to write a short summary, about half a page, of what you plan to do and consult with the chair of your local ethics committee first.

Some supra-institutional ethical codes of practice for educational enquiry

This section presents some relevant examples of ethical codes of practice from international professional associations whose members have a good understanding of the ethical and safety considerations associated with educational enquiry. The list is not comprehensive and you may wish to refer to other codes which are more resonant with your particular home country and discipline. However, these are well established and well regarded codes of practice and it may be worth considering at least one of them in the early stages of your research design and planning.

Common to all of the codes discussed in more detail below are key ethical principles which cover the rights and responsibilities of research participants and researchers. These include (but are not limited to) the importance of maintaining the welfare and dignity of participants and researchers, of ensuring that the purposes of the research are justifiable and honourable and that all individuals participating in the research are fully informed about the research (including its purpose, who has funded it, its potential outputs and its likely outcomes) and provided with opportunities to withdraw at any point in order to retain their autonomy.

The British Educational Research Association (BERA) *Ethical Guidelines for Educational Research* (BERA, 2011)

This code, published in a revised format in 2011 is somewhat shorter than the AERA ethical code (see below) standing at 11 pages in total. Its underlying principles are on the whole similar to those in the two other codes presented here, that educational research should be conducted within an ethic of respect for:

- The person
- Knowledge
- Democratic values
- The quality of educational research
- Academic freedom.

It goes on to state that it guides researchers in their conduct within this framework with regard to responsibilities to:

- Research participants
- The sponsors of research
- The community of educational researchers and
- Educational professionals, policy makers and the general public.

Australian Association for Research In Education Code of Ethics (AARE, 2013)

This code of practice is presented as a web page and is written for members of AARE to guide their behaviours and to ensure that the needs of the research and participants are put above those of sponsoring institutions or bodies. It covers both the subjects of research as well as those undertaking research. It argues that its principles should not be breached 'except where failure to do so would cause significant harm'. It is based around four basic principles:

1 The consequences of a piece of research, including the effects on the participants and the social consequences of its publication and application, must enhance the general welfare.
2 Researchers should be aware of the variety of human goods and the variety of views on the good life, and the complex relation of education with these. They should recognise that educational research is an ethical matter, and that its purpose should be the development of human good.
3 No risk of significant harm to an individual is permissible unless either that harm is remedied or the person is of age and has given informed consent to the risk. Public benefit, however great, is insufficient justification.
4 Respect for the dignity and worth of persons and the welfare of students, research participants, and the public generally shall take precedence over self-interest of researchers, or the interests of employers, clients, colleagues or groups (reproduced verbatim from AARE Code of Ethics: see http://www1.aare.edu.au/pages/page72.asp).

American Educational Research Association, Code of Ethics (AERA, 2011)

This extremely comprehensive code (156 pages in length), states that it covers the ethical principles and standards that govern the professional work of 'education researchers' (not just those who are members of AERA). AERA states that 'it is intended to provide guidance that informs and is helpful to education researchers in their research, teaching, service, and related professional work'. As such many of the guidelines relate to working with children in schools who are still

(Continued)

(Continued)

legally minors, and may not be directly relevant to your own research which is likely to be with adult respondents. The Code is underpinned by five key principles:

Principle A: Professional competence
Principle B: Integrity
Principle C: Professional, scientific and scholarly responsibility
Principle D: Respect for people's rights, dignity and diversity
Principle E: Social responsibility.

Any one of these codes will provide you with an excellent framework on which you can build an ethical approach to educational enquiry, so we do recommend that you look at them in parallel with any other institutional and other ethics protocols that you currently use. As a starting point we would recommend one of the shorter protocols (BERA and AARE) and move where necessary into the more in-depth discussions and considerations which are covered in the AERA Code of Ethics.

Ethical issues and dilemmas

Informed consent

BERA defines informed consent as 'the condition in which participants understand and agree to their participation without any duress, prior to the research getting underway' (2011: 5). However, it is both interesting and important to note that the origins of informed consent lie in *The Universal Declaration of Human Rights*, first published in 1948 (see United Nations, 2013) which, itself, arose out of the atrocities of the Second World War. Informed consent, in short, ensures that the integrity and autonomy of all who take part in research is maintained throughout the research process.

At this point you may be thinking 'but what has this got to do with me undertaking research in my classroom? If I ask students or other members of staff to take part in my educational enquiry project surely their very agreement to take part implies consent?' In one sense you are absolutely right; by agreeing to take part participants are consenting to be part of the enquiry process. However, how far this translates into informed consent depends on a number of factors: how much information you have provided for your participants about who has funded the project; what the enquiry entails; what will be expected of them if they participate and what will happen to any information they provide for you. This usually takes the form of an informed consent form or letter in which you detail all of this information and ask participants to sign to signify their consent to participation.

As you would doubtless expect in the academic world, the idea of informed consent is not a simple unchallenged one. For example, one key criticism is that it assumes that all participants bring personal and social decision making competencies to the research process (see Heath et al., 2009: 24). Moreover, how far researchers are able to communicate the true essence and reality of a project to others is an issue. Factors such as gender, age and cultural background may affect individuals' expectations of participation, their knowledge and understanding of social research processes and their willingness to take part. To this end, it may be necessary to tailor participant information sheets and informed consent forms for each subgroup of participants to take account of their particular needs. Burton et al. (2008) highlight the importance of this in terms of language, layout and font size as well as colour.

A useful study into the specifics of how researchers negotiate informed consent in practice funded by the UK Economic and Social Research Council (Wiles et al., 2007) highlights the importance of 'process consent': a term used to describe consent as an ongoing concern within a research project (see also Usher and Arthur, 1998). Participants need to remain informed as the project develops and have the opportunity to withdraw their consent and participation at any point without having to specify their reasons for this. For example, as part of this 'process consent' you may wish to return your initial analysis (and interpretation) of any raw data collected as part of your educational enquiry project to participants for their review and comment. As Walford (2001) rightly states, asking participants to confirm what they said in a transcript is very different to asking them to check your interpretation of what they said. Even if you have quoted a respondent's words verbatim, they may have meant it to have a very different meaning to that which you have given it within the context of your analysis.

When considering informed consent you will also need to provide information about data protection issues: how will data be collected and stored, who will have access to the data and how will you ensure confidentiality? In line with legislation, Denscombe (2010) provides some guidance on this issue, stating that the best way to avoid becoming embroiled in data protection legislation is to ensure that data are stored anonymously and cannot in any way be connected to individuals or institutions. This may include anonymising all transcripts of interviews, which can be tricky as you may have transcripts held alongside letters of invitation and/or a database of contact details of participants. One potential way to overcome this is to ensure that your data are kept separately from any letters or participant lists and cannot be connected directly to the details of participants. However, we strongly advise that you check with your own institutional data protection policies as these will reflect the national legal context within which you are working. Denscombe (2010), in Appendix 2: 'Data Protection a Practical Guide', provides an excellent overview of the UK's legislation on the storage of personal data for research purposes.

If you send any audio recordings away for transcription (outside of the immediate project team and your password-protected drives) you may also need to ensure that the transcribers adhere to your ethical framework and agree to maintain confidentiality at all times as often transcripts (before they are anonymised) can include institutional and personal details. Remember also that emailing documents may reduce their security; the more servers an item passes through, the more this can be a problem.

Confidentiality and anonymity

Our discussion around confidentiality and anonymity has already begun in relation to informed consent, but we feel it is worth dedicating a few further paragraphs of this chapter to this particular issue. It is important to stress here that in relation to the educational enquiry process, both confidentiality and anonymity relate directly to the ethical principles of non-maleficence; that is, the avoiding of harm to others which may occur through disclosure or the misuse of data.

First we will consider confidentiality. We have often been asked, by early career academics in particular, about the nature of confidentiality in their roles as personal and academic tutors. There appears to be significant confusion amongst such colleagues about the general nature of confidentiality in their professional sphere; an understanding is often assumed but rarely explicitly discussed. The important distinction that we have drawn in the past in discussions with academics is between confidentiality and privacy. Privacy of information indicates that the exclusive access to information rests with the person to whom it is disclosed unless there are legal obligations to disclose the information: for example where there is risk of serious harm to identifiable individuals or to society at large. Confidentiality, conversely, implies that the information provided will only be shared with those who 'need to know' this information and only for the purposes for which it was provided. For example, the British Medical Association (BMA) states that confidentiality includes 'an exchange of information amongst members of the healthcare team providing care and treatment to the patient. Clinical audit undertaken by a member of the team providing care to the patient is also considered part of direct clinical care' (2011: 4) and precludes secondary uses such as 'commissioning, risk stratification, financial and national clinical audit, healthcare management and planning, research and public health surveillance' (2011: 2). Data shared for secondary reasons must either have the consent of the individual in question or must be anonymised. This is a useful starting point for us as professional teachers with a duty of care to our students and colleagues.

 ## Activity 4.1　Confidentiality

A first year student comes to see you in your capacity as a personal or year tutor to declare that they are struggling to attend classes in the morning due to personal childcare problems resulting from an impending divorce. They state that they do not wish their tutors or classmates to know of their situation as they feel it is a sensitive and difficult subject for them at present and they would rather not discuss it more widely.

How will you communicate this to your colleagues whilst respecting the confidentiality of the student?

Suggested solution: it would be acceptable within the bounds of confidentiality to alert other staff, who come into contact with this student in morning classes, to the fact that the student is likely to be missing, and to indicate that this is due to personal circumstances outside of the student's control at present. You could state that any concerns about their participation on specific modules should be referred back to the personal tutor rather than being raised directly with the student. The full details of the student's situation (i.e. the divorce) would normally remain undisclosed to other staff unless it was deemed absolutely necessary to share this information or the student gave consent to do this.

The general principles outlined in Activity 4.1 also apply to your relationship with students and other staff as part of the educational enquiry process. As a first principle, your ethics application and your informed consent statement for participants should include reference to the fact that any data collected will only be viewed by members of the project team and will only be used for the purposes of the project in line with data protection legislation.

Turning now to the issue of anonymity, this can be viewed at two levels: first, as described earlier, it can relate to the way data are stored to ensure that your project complies with data protection legislation. However, secondly, and arguably more importantly for your participants, it can be applied to any reporting of your data in order that the exact source of the information presented is not recorded or identifiable.

Activity 4.2   Anonymity

You observe that female architecture students seem to be doing less well than male architecture students in their final year and that this gap widens over the three years of study; first year results are much the same across genders. Your educational enquiry project involves a longitudinal study of one cohort of female architecture students through their degree to explore some possible reasons for this.

How would you describe your sample in any publications or dissemination materials that you create for the project?

Suggested solution: rather than stating that your sample consisted of one cohort of female architecture students at a particular university in the UK who began their degrees in 2008, you could simply state that it consisted of a cohort of female architecture students in one university in the north or south of England, Scotland, Wales or Northern Ireland, depending on where you are based. The pool of potential participants therefore grows and the likelihood of individuals being identified directly reduces.

Case Study 4.1 provides one example of how, despite best intentions, promises of anonymity have the potential to be thwarted by others. It explores how considerations around the ethics of ownership of data and the protection of anonymity may emerge and alerts us to the issue that any findings that you discuss (whether with the press or at a conference) have the potential, inadvertently, to provide clues for others to reveal information that could reduce levels of research sample anonymity. It is important to stress that this is an unusual case, but as with all aspects of ethics and safety in research, an awareness of potential outcomes (however rare) can help us to develop robust research approaches which can, in turn, help to design out such eventualities as far as is possible.

Case Study 4.1   Considering collateral impact: some unwanted outcomes of conversing with the press

When completing the first phase of my doctoral study, a national professional journal published a call for people to share their views about the subject I had been investigating. I contacted the journal, had an informal conversation, agreed to submit a short summary of my findings so far and accepted an invitation to write a paper for future publication. A few of my comments appeared in the next edition of the journal and, initially, I was delighted. However, several weeks later, I found out that the Freedom of Information Act (HM Government, 2000) had been invoked to request similar information from a range of organisations. While I had taken great care to avoid disclosing any of my sources, the field was not very large and consequently it appeared that organisations were being asked for information that they had already given to me, but without the safeguards I had set in place as part of the research process. One person contacted me to ask if the Freedom of Information request was actually me in disguise and I became worried that the second phase of my doctoral study would be jeopardised; potential participants might feel less inclined to continue contributing if their anonymity was potentially threatened, albeit by a third party.

The use of incentives

It is becoming increasingly difficult to recruit research samples in the current climate of regular consultation and survey contact, accompanied by a growth in the general unwillingness of individuals to take part in activities that do not result in direct perceivable benefits (see Heath et al., 2009; Sturgis et al., 2005). This is something that is often acknowledged at the institutional and national level in UK higher education where we talk about our students getting 'survey-fatigue' through the expectation that they will participate in the National Student Survey (NSS), module and programme-level evaluation surveys, participant focus groups and, increasingly, mock in-house NSS surveys (Porter et al., 2004; Feldman, 2012).

In part, as a result of this recognition, and the acknowledgement that it is important to recompense people for the time that they take in participating in research in some appropriate way, it is now increasingly common to offer some form of material benefit in return for participation. This may, if your research is funded by the institution or an external funding body, simply be manifested as remuneration for student involvement in the project, or a prize draw for all who participate. Incentives for participation, in the form of prize draws, are now offered by most universities in the UK in relation to the National Student Survey. The University of Hull, for example, offered undergraduate students who participated in the NSS in 2013 an opportunity to win graduation photography packages.

Some universities have offered course credits for students in return for participation in research studies. However, there is a growing evidence base that this may not act as an incentive for participation in the way that has been assumed in the past (see Elicker et al., 2010; Padilla-Walker et al., 2005). As such, participation for credit is often found within the context of psychology research modules, where undergraduate students are expected to participate as an experiential module component.

The jury is still out as to whether it is ethically sound to provide incentives: what for one may be seen as a token and thank you, for another may be perceived as a bribe (Heath et al., 2009). While a small amount of remuneration can be a clear signal that the participation of an individual in the research process is valued, overly compensating in a particular way may lead to a skewed sample or a sense of coercion. For example, if you regularly use tablet computers in your teaching sessions and offer a tablet as an incentive for participation in an educational enquiry study, students who do not have tablet computers of their own may feel obliged to take part in your study as this will clearly help them with participation in your teaching sessions. It is therefore important to consider these issues if and when you decide to use incentives within your educational enquiry work. However, it is also important to note that it is now extremely acceptable (if not expected), with the trend to engage students as 'co-researchers' on projects, to pay for this work with fair remuneration.

Researcher positionality and power

We come to each project we undertake, whether a project seeking out new ideas and information or an evaluation of activities that have already happened, with a set of prior assumptions. We often have hunches or expectations as our view of a particular subject is coloured by our past experiences or the experiences of others that we know. Awareness of these subjectivities is the first step on our road to limiting their effects. These subjectivities are not only affected by our experiences but also by our *positionality*. This is a term taken from the social sciences which infers that *who you are* both shapes what you know about the world and what the world knows about you. As Takacs states, the perspectives from which you view others 'have been crafted by your own unique identity and experiences in the world. We live much of our lives in our own heads, in a reconfirming dialogue with ourselves' (2003: 27). Your positionality can therefore be affected by your background, your gender, your job, your ethnicity and so on and describes both your unique perspective on the world and how others view you.

Power is also a term that is used frequently in the social sciences and refers predominantly to the ways in which one group can exert control over another. Control may take on many forms in society at large, but given the particular focus of this text, we are concerned here with the power that tutors can potentially assert over their students. As stated earlier, the main issue that appears to arise here is the fact that tutors are the markers of students' work and the arbiters of their academic achievements. Whilst the idea that tutors would abuse this powerful relationship in any way is anathema to any of us, students may not feel that they can decline our requests to take part in educational enquiry projects; by opting out, or saying something inappropriate, they may feel that this will negatively impact on their tutor's perception of them, which in turn may directly or indirectly impact on their education. Key then, to researching our students, is an acknowledgement of the potential power that we may be viewed as holding. We need to ensure that we are explicit to students about the integrity of the marking process and that the research is not part of their programme of study and will not affect it in anyway.

There is extensive discussion in the broader social science literature about the impact of researcher (and funder) positionality and power and the associated contexts within which research takes place – each of which may impact on research experiences, outputs and outcomes (see Letherby et al., 2013 for a recent discussion of these issues). In short, any research should always be understood as a product of the broader context in which it is situated and the decisions that have led to particular methods being adopted (see Devine and Heath, 1999; Hammersley, 2000). And while we cannot always design subjectivity, positionality and power out of our educational enquiry, we can recognise their potential impact and try where possible to limit their effects through self-awareness, reflection and consciously confronting any personal values that could affect our projects.

One way around this issue is to involve students as co-researchers rather than as passive research subjects. There is now a wide recognition of the potential for active involvement of research participants within the research process, in part a reflection of broader policy and social shifts which reflect current human rights agendas and an associated growth in the importance of consultation, participation and voice (see Cleaver et al., 2007 for an overview of this changing context). The rise of this phenomenon is further documented by Heath et al. (2009), who provide a useful overview of the various ways in which students can be involved in educational enquiry projects: in the research design, collecting the data, interpreting the data, disseminating the findings and in some cases leading the research (peer-led).

However, involving students in a tokenistic way can in itself be unethical. To ensure that any project which involves students actively in the research does so with integrity, it is useful to reflect upon a series of questions (originally from Heath et al., 2009: 70–74) which we have adapted and augmented:

- Whose voice is being heard? Are you selecting or prioritising a certain type of 'voice' from amongst your students?
- Is student input tokenistic? Are you restricting the part that students can play?

- Who holds the power? Are you using students as a conduit through which you improve your understandings of their world for your own publications and personal gain?
- Are you enabling students, by providing training and facilities, to function as full members of the research team?
- Are students paid as team members and, where relevant, will they be involved in any presentations and publications?
- Have all students had an equal opportunity to take part in the project?

The 'insider' researcher

Hutchings' analysis of issues connected with making educational enquiry public – 'the ethics of bad news' (2003: 29; see also Hutchings, 2002) – forms the starting point for this section of the chapter. In short, it is not simply individuals within higher education who are affected by the outputs and outcomes of educational enquiry about higher education. When we undertake our enquiries we do so on the understanding that our academic freedom[2] will allow us to interpret and analyse any data that we collect for the purposes of wider dissemination and knowledge transfer. In researching fellow academics and students, both within our own institutions and beyond, we ask both higher education institutions and their faculties and departments to trust in the integrity of our research and that certain information will necessarily remain confidential (or at the very least anonymised) to protect each institution's reputation and commercial interests, as well as the safety and reputations of their staff and students. However, do beware of the 'contact information conundrum' in journals and other publications. If you are an 'insider' researcher any indication of your institutional affiliation may effectively let the cat out of the bag.

In some instances, of which we have past personal experience, institutions or government departments may embargo the wider dissemination of research which uncovers issues or concerns that they do not wish to 'air in public' or may be perceived negatively to affect them by association. Power can therefore cut both ways and could, in extreme circumstances, result in the outcomes of any enquiry you undertake being restricted or even deleted (see also Cousin, 2009: 22). A useful text which can help you to think through some of the politics of undertaking educational enquiry

---

[2]Academic freedom is enshrined in UK Law as part of the Education Reform Act 1988 which states that higher education institutions have a duty 'to ensure that academic staff have freedom within the law to question and test received wisdom, and to put forward new ideas and controversial or unpopular opinions, without placing themselves in jeopardy of losing their jobs or privileges they may have at their institutions' (HM Government, 1998: section 202(2)[a]).

projects (and the power relations that these may entail) is *Researching Your Own Organisation* (Coghlan and Brannick, 2010). While this text focuses purely on one approach to research: the action research project, the chapters which cover 'Preunderstanding, Role Duality and Access' and 'Managing Organisational Politics and Ethics' may prove useful stimuli for your own thoughts in this area. In particular the authors highlight some of the difficulties associated with being an 'insider' researcher (difficulties that may also relate to students who become co-researchers on educational enquiry projects), with crossing role boundaries (between tutor, colleague, student and researcher) and with managing the politics of an organisation where you may end up challenging the status quo.

In relation to these points, we return briefly to a discussion of 'power'. Norton (2009) highlights the importance of being aware of any differences in power between yourself and other colleagues. Whilst she acknowledges that power differentials are less likely to have the same impact on colleagues as they will on students, it is important to recognise that your position within a department, school or faculty may impact on colleagues' willingness to become involved in your enquiry project or, conversely, to say no. This may also be influenced by cultural expectations within the workplace and the spoken or often unspoken view that educational enquiry is somehow less worthy than other forms of research and scholarship (Norton, 2009). Two early career academics that we met during our time leading higher education teacher development programmes highlighted this issue. One spoke of the 'snorts of derision' encountered when engaging senior staff in thinking about learning and teaching developments in the department and another spoke about engaging in educational development work as a 'guilty pleasure'. This notwithstanding, across our careers we have found that many colleagues are extremely supportive of educational enquiry projects and it is important to recognise this when planning your projects; you are not alone! Most importantly, we encourage you yourselves not to fall into the trap of being unsupportive to others who are focusing on educational enquiry, however unintentionally this may happen.

Researcher/participant wellbeing (risk, safety and responding to emotion)

In recent years there has been a growing recognition of the importance of considering researcher and participant wellbeing in projects that include human participants. When considered in the past, this was an area that was most likely to focus on the wellbeing of participants, particularly when sensitive subjects are being addressed (see for example Brannen, 1988) or the wellbeing of researchers when dealing with dangerous substances or working in dangerous social or physical environments off site and often out of hours (see for example, Williams et al., 1992). These concerns remain, but paralleling a growth in concern about employee wellbeing more generally, and calls for a change in higher education's approach to the safety of social researchers (Kenyon and Hawker, 1999; Paterson et al., 1999), there is now increasing awareness of social research as an activity which has the potential to impact physically or emotionally on the researcher (Dickson-Swift et al., 2009). This becomes ever more salient when we begin to involve our students in research projects as co-researchers.

When Kenyon and Hawker (1999) undertook a small-scale research project in 1998 it was in response to the fact that, as part of two separate UK Economic and Social Research Council-funded projects, they were undertaking research interviews out-of-hours, sometimes in respondents' homes, and sometimes alone. One particular uncomfortable experience led the authors to consider who would know, and indeed what would happen, if something occurred during these field visits. At this time, no known protocol appeared to exist in the UK around lone working for researchers and, in part stemming from this and other parallel calls at the time (Paterson et al., 1999), the UK's Social Research Association (SRA) began the process of creating a Code of Practice for the Safety of Social Researchers in 2000 (SRA, 2013).

The SRA Code of Practice is still referred to by a number of Universities on their dedicated research safety web pages and institutional protocols and has become the starting point for a range of later national UK protocols and codes in this area (see for example the Universities Safety and Health Association and Universities and Colleges Employers Association, 2011). If you are working with students off-site when collecting data for educational enquiry projects then you will find these various publications of use alongside other risk-assessment guidance related to your particular discipline. These more focused disciplinary documents are likely to deal with the physical and emotional risks that students may encounter when learning within your own particular discipline (for example, distressing case studies in health and social care disciplines or physical hazards such as exposure to radiation or adverse weather conditions in the physical and environmental sciences).

While it is unlikely that the kind of projects that you will design and conduct as part of your educational enquiry work will directly or consciously deal with highly sensitive issues or involve lone working off-site outside of university teaching fieldwork trips, it is worth being at the very least aware of these issues as a precaution. As a first step you must follow your own institutional procedures and complete a risk assessment to ensure that you have fully considered any hazards that you and your co-researchers may face during the project. And if lone working (for staff and or students) is involved, in addition to your own institution's guidance, we would recommend that you refer to the guidance provided by the Suzy Lamplugh

Trust, a not-for-profit organisation set up to promote the personal safety of those working alone (see http://www.suzylamplugh.org/).

Concluding thoughts

This chapter has set out to provide an overview of some of the key ethical considerations associated with undertaking educational enquiry projects, where your own students are either the subjects of the research (in the form of existing data sets, as direct participants in a change initiative or as respondents to research data collection instruments such as interviews and questionnaires) or are co-researchers. Key to ensuring that any educational enquiry project is conducted appropriately, is an adherence to your institution's research ethics policies and procedures. To adopt such an approach is essential to establishing the validity and integrity of your research, in the eyes of your students, your institution and the higher education sector at large.

Finally, it is worth remembering that change, in any form, may be worrying to those involved. This is perhaps one of the lesser considered ethical dimensions of any interventions or changes in learning and teaching practice that can result from educational enquiry or development projects. In short, some students may find the fact that they are actively (or passively) involved in experimental or innovative change projects around learning and assessment stressful, particularly if they perceive that changes might negatively affect their module results. We should be alert to this and be aware of ways in which we can reassure any students to alleviate their concerns.

Suggested further reading

Miller, T., Birch, M., Mauthner, M. and, Jessop, J. (2012) *Ethics in Qualitative Research* (2nd edition). London: Sage.

Ransome, P. (2013) *Ethics and Values in Social Research*. Basingstoke: Palgrave Macmillan.

Sieber, J.E. and Tolich, M.B. (2013) *Planning Ethically Responsible Research* (2nd edition). Thousand Oaks, CA: Sage.

CHAPTER 5

WHAT KIND OF DATA SHOULD I COLLECT AND USE?

Maxine Lintern, Mike McLinden and Elizabeth Cleaver

Learning outcomes

By the end of this chapter it is anticipated that you will:

- Recognise the range of data types that can inform educational enquiry;
- Be ready to plan how you will generate or access appropriate data as part of your own educational enquiry activities; and
- Have reflected on how gathering or employing such data can both improve your understanding of your teaching and provide an evidence-based rationale for change.

Introduction

If you are to conduct any kind of enquiry into your teaching or your students' learning, you are likely to need to identify and obtain some form of empirical data on which to base your analysis. In Chapters 2 and 3 we considered the two overarching research paradigms – positivism and interpretivism – that arguably underpin a great deal of the evidence that you are likely to encounter as part of an educational literature review. In this chapter we take the discussion we began in Chapter 2 further, with a particular emphasis on the types of primary data that your own educational enquiry projects might generate or use and a brief consideration of the approaches you may wish to take to capture this data.

What we cannot do in the space available here is provide a comprehensive 'how to create research instruments' guide. This will require further thought, training and planning. For example, developing a 'good' questionnaire requires a number of stages including piloting it to ensure that questions are not leading, biased or unclear. There are many existing texts that offer sound advice on compiling research instruments and you may wish to undertake further reading in this area (see for example, Cohen et al., 2011; Bryman, 2012; Robson, 2011).

Finally, the chapter moves on to consider the importance of 'usefulness' or 'impact', and how you can work towards any educational enquiry you undertake resulting in clear benefits for a range of end users (yourself, your colleagues and your students).

What is data in an educational enquiry context?

Pedagogical research takes many forms and, as we maintain in this book, may constructively hail from any subject background. Unsurprisingly, then, what constitutes 'data' is also variously defined and may mean different things to different people. For the purpose of this chapter, we could start by defining 'data' as being: any information that has been collected in a purposeful, controlled and systematic manner, which can be analysed to produce meaningful ideas, hypotheses or theories, and could be used to positively impact on educational development and, in turn, the student experience.

Of course, this definition is in itself value laden: if information is not collected systematically is it any less true? Can data always be collected in a 'controlled' manner? Can you ignore the comments of one student because all the others disagree? These uncertainties mean our initial definition of what constitutes data immediately becomes blurred around the edges.

While for some of you this lack of clarity may appear challenging, we think it is worth reflecting on the potential opportunities that adopting a more interpretivist approach allows.

While this approach is likely still to be 'systematic', what this means in practice may look very different to activity you would normally associate with systematic data collection from within your own disciplinary research. In particular this approach may provide greater flexibility, range and scope as to the data you can use to help develop your ideas. In Chapter 3 we explored how the narrative approach to reviewing the literature could open up the variety of information that you could include, offering scope for the incorpo- ration of the wide range of educational literature and ideas, including policy documents and expositions of theory. However, the successful inclusion of a range of literature types rests on the assumption that knowledge can be con- structed from multiple perspectives, and that their juxtaposition in a review will work just as long as qualitative and quantitative differences in the data are expected, recognised and identified. If this approach is taken, then edu- cational enquiry can benefit from being able to productively use a wide range of literature gathered from a range of sources.

Applying a similar approach to data collection indicates that data can range from, at one extreme, numerical representations of every grade that each student has achieved during their programme of study and, at the other extreme, verbatim records of discussions with a small self-selecting group of students about their perceptions of these grades. Ultimately, the usefulness of each type of data depends not only on the quality and rich- ness of the information collected, but also the research approach under- taken and its associated values and interpretations of meaning.

This may all feel a little daunting right now, so in the spirit of this text, we recommend that you take as your starting point the research approach you are most familiar or comfortable with from your own disciplinary research experiences, and your choice of data and data collection methods will follow. The disciplinary-focused chapters in the second half of this text will help you to begin this process and provide you with some suggestions as to how to move forward. While educational 'purists' may claim that your home discipline might not offer the most suitable starting point to address the research question you are asking, we would argue that as a first port of call it is highly appropriate and will help you to 'have a go' without having to learn about or shift into a completely different mode of thinking or data collection.

As noted in Chapter 2, it is also important to remember that your chosen approach to research neither necessitates nor negates any particular data- gathering procedures; if you decide once you begin your educational enquiry project that your disciplinary research methods are not providing you with enough data or data of the right quality to address the research questions you posed, you can always add new methods to 'triangulate' and/or extend your data set. To do this you will need to be aware of the benefits and limitations of your own particular disciplinary research approaches for gathering educational data, and consider how a complementary or indeed alternative approach may add value to your enquiries. Ultimately it can be argued that there are no 'right' or 'wrong' types of data: only those which are useful, less useful or not useful at all depending on the focus of the research questions you wish to answer or the research problem you wish to solve. We explore this further in the next section of the chapter.

What types of data can I use and how might I collect them?

As discussed earlier, data fall very generally into two broad categories: quantitative and qualitative. Generally speaking, academics from STEM (science, technology, engineering and mathematics) subjects, medicine, and some health science areas are likely to draw upon a quantitative approach to data collection (as part of the positivist approach to research that we considered in Chapter 2). In contrast, it is more likely that some social scientists and those from the arts and humanities may be more at home with qualitative data (including for example, artefacts for interpretation such as texts, performance, images and sound). In the existing literature (and in Chapters 7–13 of this text) you will find discussions of a range of data collection methods, from very controlled purposeful sampling, followed by power calculations and detailed statistical analysis, to more discursive reflections on conversations with students, or close reading and analysis of textual information.

What is important to recognise is that all of these different types of data can be of 'good' or 'bad' quality and that this does not solely depend on pre-held assumptions about the 'rigour' of the methods used. Data can be of greater or lesser value depending on the purpose and aims of the enquiry underway and irrespective of the mode by which they were collected. Ultimately, most data collection methods in educational enquiry, however objectively pursued, can only collect the ideas that participants (or researchers) come up with during the data collection period, thereby providing a limited 'snapshot' of people's views, perceptions and ideas. This issue is exemplified well if we think about another very different but relevant situation: you will all have come out of an interview or an exam with the feeling that you have forgotten to say something or could have said something in a better way.

To illustrate these ideas further Case Studies 5.1 and 5.2 provide examples of educational enquiry taken from recent peer-reviewed journal publications. Each article is explored in relation to its research focus, the broad paradigm in which it sits and its associated research data collection methods. In addition, a commentary is provided which considers how a different or additional approach to gathering data may have helped to expand the conclusions of the study.

Case Study 5.1   The meaning of prompt feedback: a study of students' understanding of concepts and practices rated through the National Student Survey (Mendes et al., 2011)

Recognising that student satisfaction on feedback is notably lower than for other aspects of the student learning experience, this study explored three cohorts (first, third and fourth years) of chemical engineering students' understandings of the terminology and questions used in the UK's annual National Student Survey (NSS) questionnaires.

The study used a questionnaire to identify key factors that might influence NSS scores on feedback. This data collection method was chosen as it allowed for a large number of responses to be gathered and had the flexibility to collect responses using closed (with predetermined tick-box answers) or open (with free-text response boxes) questions. Due to the focus of the study, four of the five questions included in the questionnaire invited open-ended free-text responses, with the final being a multiple-choice question with predefined tick-box answers. The predominance of questions that allowed for open-ended responses was influenced by the fact that the study is exploring students' perceptions and understandings; neither of which is easily quantifiable or measurable.

Despite the open-ended nature of the questions, this study largely sits within the positivist paradigm; perhaps unsurprising given the disciplinary origins of the projects' first two authors – engineering. Within this paradigm the study brought together inductive and deductive approaches to research design and qualitative and quantitative approaches to data collection and analysis. The questionnaire items (questions) were predetermined and bias from the researchers was controlled by ensuring that respondents completed the questionnaire anonymously without researcher input or influence. Moreover, the themes that emerged from the open-ended responses were counted, and results are reported as percentages and bar graphs to provide a quantitative representation of student perceptions and understandings. Finally, comparisons were made between different groups within the study (males/females and international/UK domiciled students) by using descriptive statistical techniques (cross-tabulation) in order to identify any non-instructional factors that correlate with particular responses.

As the questionnaire used by Mendes et al. included both pre-set question answer categories (codes) for students to choose and free-text response options, it provided students with some opportunity to put their own views and interpretations forward. Some questionnaires do not do this: you will all have filled in a questionnaire where you have wanted to answer 'none of the above' or add in a new category to the answer options. However, the approach did not allow for the use of further prompts, clarifications or additional questions that can be added immediately in face-to-face research settings such as interviews or later in follow-up questionnaires. As such, researcher interpretations of responses could not be checked or tested.

In using another additional data collection method, such as group interviews or focus groups after the survey questionnaire, Mendes et al. may have been able to undertake further analysis of the free-text responses. This approach is sometimes known as 'triangulating' the data; that is, using a range of different data types to contribute to the evidence base from which answers to a research question emerge. Alternatively, rather than including free-text responses, they could have generated a more comprehensive set of closed pre-coded question responses to all questions by undertaking pre-questionnaire interviews or focus groups to understand the range of answers that each question might generate and creating closed questionnaire items in response to these findings.

This said, the approach taken provides a relevant set of answers to the research questions posed which are able to be represented graphically, with some basic statistical analysis undertaken to address correlation between respondent groups and particular answers. The study clearly points towards confusion within the student body with regard to some of the terminology used in the National Student Survey and plays a valuable role in opening up this debate further.

Case Study 5.2   Use of generative interviews to explore disciplinary perceptions of enquiry-based learning (McLinden and Edwards, 2011)

Although reference was made to enquiry-based learning (EBL) in Chapter 1, the term itself can be considered to be a contested one, with many permutations and alternatives used to describe the various approaches that sit under the 'broad umbrella term' of EBL (Kahn and O'Rourke, 2004). This lack of agreement can be particularly challenging when trying to determine how EBL approaches are already being employed at a departmental or institutional level. This second example is used to illustrate how one University set out to survey staff across the institution in order to find out how a range of EBL approaches were being used to support student learning, and identify factors that may serve as barriers to developing an 'institutional culture of EBL' within the context of a new institutional Learning and Teaching Strategy.

(Continued)

(Continued)

An interpretive approach was used in Phase 1 of the broader project to 'generate' key themes that would be drawn upon when deciding on the content and format of a pilot questionnaire prior to running a large-scale survey. This phase included the use of 'generative' interviews as part of a survey design stage. The individual interviews took place with invited stakeholders from within the institution who had responsibility for supporting student learning across different disciplines. During the interviews participants were invited to respond to a series of open-ended questions that were directly concerned with their views on the definition and use of EBL within the context of higher education and their own practice. Opportunities were provided for interviewees to offer additional comments of relevance to each question, or to the project focus more generally. Each interview was recorded and a verbatim transcript of the discussion was generated. Transcripts of the interviews were then used as the basis for coding key themes that were then used to structure a pilot survey tool.

Unlike the previous example (Mendes et al., 2011), McLinden and Edward's (2011) study sits broadly within the interpretivist paradigm. As noted by Cohen et al., such a paradigm begins with individuals and sets out to 'understand their interpretations of the world around them. Theory is emergent and must arise from particular situations; it should be "grounded" on data generated by the research act' (2011: 18). The questions used in the interviews were suitably open-ended to allow further prompts, clarifications and additional questions to be drawn upon as appropriate. The interviews were recorded verbatim and a summary of the transcript returned to each interviewee to verify its content prior to qualitative data analysis being undertaken. The findings of this phase suggested that perceptions of how EBL approaches are conceptualised differed across different disciplines/ activities and as such helped to frame the particular examples that were drawn upon when developing the pilot survey.

While being rooted in the interpretivist camp, this study recognises that the data generated through the interviews, despite being very rich, do not allow for the generalisation of results across groups of the population. As such, a questionnaire was developed which drew on the answers gathered during the qualitative data collection phase to provide this more generalisable data. However, many of the arguments which we introduced in relation to the previous case study still remain relevant. The initial sample was a purposive sample – that is a sample selected by virtue of knowledge of a population and the purpose of the study. The researchers could therefore not be certain that the sample represented the views of the broader academic community to whom the final questionnaire would be sent. How valid, therefore, were the questions generated by this approach and might a random sampling approach have been more fruitful?

As noted above, another issue to bear in mind is the amount of work that needs to be undertaken in order to generate a questionnaire. In addition, do not underestimate the time needed to listen to and make notes on an interview, let alone the time it takes if you wish to transcribe these interviews verbatim. This should, of course, not be seen as a reason not to undertake qualitative data collection, but should certainly be taken into account when planning your enquiry project.

As these two case studies demonstrate, the data collection methods you choose will be dependent on what you wish to find out about, the tools and resources at your disposal (including the tools you are familiar with), the size or scope of the research you want to undertake and what you want to do with the results in the end. Questions that may be useful to you in making a decision about this may include:

- Do you want to know more about your students; their likes and dislikes about the learning experience they are involved in? (This is likely to need a more qualitative approach to data collection.)
- Are you interested in measurable performance indicator outcomes such as examination pass marks, programme completion and drop-out rates? (This is likely to need a more quantitative approach to data collection.)
- Do you want to understand better the effectiveness of a particular type of educational approach or teaching intervention? (This would benefit from a mixed methods approach.)

Ultimately there is one underlying question that you need to ask yourself at every stage of your educational enquiry project (at the design stage, the data collection stage and at the analysis and reporting stage): will the quality of the data be good enough to provide the evidence I need to address my research question(s) and to support any developments that I want to make as a result of the project? If the answer to this is 'no' then your data collection may need to be extended to include a further stage or a different method.

Quality and types of data?

You would probably agree that using the exam results from a small sample of students out of a cohort of hundreds to justify a new teaching approach is not particularly robust, whereas a focus group with the same number of students discussing their experiences may give a more detailed understanding of what that approach has meant to their learning. Other anecdotal information, either quantitative or qualitative, may spark a particular burning question in your mind and lead to further research activity, but in itself is probably not substantial enough to stand up to external scrutiny.

Thus although the starting point of your educational development projects may not be 'robust' per se, you do need to consider what you want to use the information for in order to be able to spread the word about a successful outcome. Often you will need to generate data to evaluate the effectiveness of something: a new module or change in curriculum or mode of delivery. Much of the educational development that occurs as we go about our day-to-day jobs, updating our teaching approaches and curriculum content, is not evaluated systematically. This is a shame and often results in re-invention of the wheel multiple times across a range of institutions as well as within just yours!

To help to overcome this, below we consider a range of different types of data that could be collected or used as part of your own education enquiry project.

'Ready-made' data

A great deal of data are generated via the usual business of running university programmes and this often remains in databases or student record systems unexplored and underused. It is extremely appropriate to use this already gathered information for the purposes of improving your teaching and students' learning; indeed many institutions, as part of the move from quality assurance to quality enhancement, now expect module and programme leaders to include analysis of data collected from and about students in their end of year reports. However, if this is the limit of its use, it is a waste, as many useful insights can be generated from looking at this kind of 'everyday' information differently. It is also important to note that while such data are formally collected, they may not be collected using a robust research design framework: you get as many end of module evaluations as you get and this is not the same as recruiting a certain number of subjects to a study based on power calculations. That said, if you are honest about the potential and the limitations of the data and think carefully about how it might be supplemented or triangulated, it can provide a very rich starting point for your educational enquiry project.

And while some may criticise this data for being passive and retrospective – often nothing can be done to alter the outcomes for the students involved in the data generation – perhaps of equal importance is the fact that the data are not time-limited. The data set is already there, it is not going anywhere and you can go back and look at it at any time (depending on the data protection rules that are applied to it). Examples include:

- Pre-entry information: A level grades or UCAS (Universities and Colleges Admissions Service) points or equivalent; application rates; whether the institution was first, insurance or clearing choice for an entrant; or entrants' gender, age, BME status, and other socio-economic factors (see Case Study 2.1 in Chapter 2 for an example of using this kind of data in a study);

- Programme life data: attendance patterns; student attrition and retention information; completion-on-time rates; final grades; direct teaching (contact hours) per module or programme; and hours spent in the laboratory, studio, rehearsal room, lecture theatre or classroom. Much of this data will be published in the UK via the *Key Information Sets* (KIS) on the Unistats website (http://unistats.direct.gov.uk/) or will be part of the business information that institutional analysis managers use to track the performance of particular subject areas and programmes. Often external validating bodies will want to see this kind of data too;
- Past assessment data: previous cohort grades for module assignments or exams; marks distribution across different assessment types; or retrospective analysis of teaching interventions; and
- Module data: past evaluation scores; pass/fail rates; or optional module choice patterns.

Many of these 'data sets' can be compared to and correlated with each other, for example: pass rates for each gender; attendance patterns in mature versus 'young' students; or entry grades compared to final degree results. But care must be taken when diving into all this data that you do not overestimate any apparent linkages or introduce your own bias by looking for what you want to find, or finding what you want to look for.

'Current student opinion' data

This is the kind of data that is often routinely collected during and at the end of blocks of teaching such as a module or placement rotation. In the past this may have only been used in a superficial manner and the full richness of the information may not have been used proactively to develop curriculum design or the student experience. However, as stated earlier, many institutions are now using such data for quality enhancement purposes. It is important to recognise, however, that the quality of this information may depend on how good the collection method is or the kind of 'tool' that has been used to capture the data. An end of module evaluation questionnaire that does not ask robust, well thought out questions will not give you a true picture of students' thoughts on their experience. However, this kind of data, if collected correctly, can give a great deal of insight into the student experience. Some examples include:

- Module/block evaluation: Likert-type scales (for example, five-point scale from strongly agree to strongly disagree with a series of statements to be rated); numerical scoring of statements; free text comments; or simply students 'voting with their feet' gathered through attendance and/or engagement records;

- Online forums: using Moodle, Sakai, Blackboard or another formal virtual learning environment (VLE) or learning management system (LMS) or general chat/comments or responses to specific questions using social media tools such as Facebook or Twitter;
- Individual feedback and group discussions: between invited students or open to all; World Café discussions; course representative feedback; feedback at Boards of Studies; review meetings or quality days; and interviews (structured, semi-structured or open-ended); and
- Personal response feedback: low-tech paper-based notes or electronic in-class voting systems, used to generate or check subject understanding data within the class but also for session/module/course evaluation. These can be open-ended (What one thing would you change about today's lecture? Write one thing you've learned today on a 'post-it™' note) or more sophisticated closed data capture to ensure that learning has taken place. Any data captured electronically can be made instantly available to the cohort through online polling systems and feedback forums.

These kinds of approaches can generate quantitative and qualitative data and can tell you much about how students feel about particular aspects of their course or overall experience. If it comes at the end of the module or block you can only make any changes that might arise from analysis of the data for the next cohort of students. If data can be generated midway through, then you may be able to react to the information to address issues, problems or concerns for the cohort in hand. It is important to stress, however, that care should be taken not to use these avenues just to identify problems or what is 'wrong' with a course. They can also help to identify what is good or going well, what students are enjoying or to find out what helps to improve their learning and understanding. Doing more of what is good rather than cutting out what is bad can be a more effective way of developing a module!

'Observational' data

This is information generated by 'watching' what your students (and potentially your colleagues) do, which can give you an insight into engagement, attitudes, experiences and competencies. It can be gathered in a range of ways including:

- Awareness in the teaching environment: what are your students doing while you teach them? Have you reflected on how you respond to them?
- Peer observation: most HEIs have some sort of system in place, whether formal or developmental, where you can watch colleagues teach in a number of different ways which will teach you a lot about your own approaches to teaching. Watching how the students react/interact when others teach them can be just as enlightening;

- Abilities and competencies: can the students physically do what you require them to do? This can come from watching students interact with equipment and materials in a laboratory setting, a workshop, an art studio or a clinical skills suite. This may also form part of your programme's summative assessments such as musical recitals or objective structured clinical examinations (OSCEs);
- Personal attributes or 'soft skills': can you observe students growing in confidence, building their communication and leadership skills, or learning to work well in a team?
- Reflective activities: do you ask students to keep learning logs, or post reflective pieces online or as part of a development portfolio which provide narratives of learning in progress?

Often this kind of data can form the starting point of recognising that you want to know more about something; particularly when you observe an activity or get an anecdotal 'feel' that something is going well or needs improving. You may then want to take a more robust approach to collecting data to give weight and validity to your 'hunch'. However, it is important to note that without this initial observation you may never have asked the important research question in the first place.

'Big data sets'

This type of data consists of the large scale formal questionnaires usually based around the notion of 'student experience'. Often they are based on Likert-type scales and may or may not have free text sections. Access to this kind of data is sometimes restricted to certain groups of staff such as Heads of Department or course leaders, but some of it is in the public domain. Examples include:

- Local Faculty/Departmental investigations which focus on a particular aspect of the student experience;
- Cross-institution surveys: often a pre-final year version of the National Student Survey (NSS);
- The National Student Survey: the UK's annual survey of all final year students across almost all HEIs, which looks at a range of experiential factors from learning and teaching facilities, management of the course, overall experience to satisfaction with the Students' Union. Data can be split by course and the overall 'satisfaction score' is often used in course marketing. NSS data are published on the Unistats site so prospective applicants can compare programmes offered by different institutions. It also feeds into a number of university league tables. The NSS also has a free text component where students can offer their thoughts on their overall experience. Many subject teams use NSS data to develop their programmes of study further by responding to the feedback. Most Universities have targets and benchmarks relating to NSS scores; and

- PRES and PTES (the UK's Postgraduate Research and Taught Experience Surveys). These surveys are hosted by the UK's Higher Education Academy and are similar to the NSS but aimed at both taught and research graduate students. The survey data are only released to the participating institution and are aimed at internal enhancement rather than league table comparisons.

These big data sets can be incredibly useful as the data included are often quantitative and qualitative and uses recurring questions from year to year allowing ongoing longitudinal cross-cohort comparisons. This allows, for example, the exploration of trend changes over a number of years following an 'intervention' or change that has taken place. However, it is important to note that while the data are longitudinal, the sample is not. Changes that are noted across years may result from a 'cohort effect' and it is important, therefore, to ensure that the changes in results are consistent over a number of years before any firm conclusions are drawn.

If you do not normally get involved in the NSS analysis then you might wish to look at how your courses are doing and whether the data might provide a useful starting point for your educational enquiry project.

'Educational intervention' data

This kind of data may consist of any or all of the types described above but normally includes a before and after 'snapshot'. In effect *'something'* is measured about the education, an intervention or change takes place, and then the *'something'* is measured again to see what difference it has made. Many things can fall into this category so here are just a few suggestions:

- Comparisons of assessment scores, before and after a change in teaching approach;
- Reflections from students on their perceived confidence to do something (perhaps a clinical skill) before and after a training/simulation session;
- Year-on-year analysis of NSS data for a course as the curriculum is developed;
- Feedback on student engagement following a shift to an enquiry-based rather than a didactic course delivery approach;
- Changes in retention and completion rates following a focus on supporting struggling students.

Often there is a notional difficulty with these types of comparison (especially for those coming from a STEM background), which is the issue of comparing different cohorts. Groups of students are not inbred lab rats or cloned cells so often you are not comparing like with like. Even when the group or individual is their own control, their experience through the make-up of the cohort, the environment and even the time of year as well as a whole series of other influences that you may or may not be aware of or able to control for, may affect the results. You cannot be sure that the only variable that has altered is the variable that you changed. Social statisticians undertaking large-scale or whole population surveys have ways of controlling for such variations in influence, but when undertaking smaller-scale educational enquiry you may not be able to engage with such approaches. For example, last year's group is not the same as this year's group and if they do better in the exam following your 'new' tutorials can you be sure it was because of your intervention? The answer is probably no, not entirely, but as long as you can consider and account for other confounding factors as far as possible, you still have a reasonable chance that your intervention has made a difference. Certainly the fact that they did better in your module while perhaps achieving no better scores in the others would lend weight to your argument.

This is a difficult area and there are many opinions on how far you can reasonably take the 'effect of intervention' argument. This notwithstanding, we make changes to our teaching all the time and often do not try to elicit what the impact has been in a systematic way; so any evidence that can be gathered is arguably better than none at all. Case Study 5.3 provides one example of how evidence can be gathered and analysed to provide evidence for the success of an intervention.

Case Study 5.3   Smarter assessment = smarter students! The effective use of online quizzes in order to enhance the learning experience in children's nurse education (Harrison, 2011)

The delivery of a *Nursing the Acutely Ill Child in Hospital* module was augmented with a new set of online quizzes, coupled to an innovative interactive glossary. The module ran for six weeks and therefore six online quizzes were developed and made available on a weekly basis. This enabled the student to find out 'where they were at' in their learning: what they already knew and understood and, perhaps more importantly, what they did not know. The students completed the quizzes as and when they wanted to and based on their responses, individualised, instantaneous and detailed feedback was given. Embedded within this feedback were links to glossary terms and interactive activities which enabled the student to address any gaps in knowledge or understanding in a non-threatening environment. Increasingly though, the quizzes were

(Continued)

(Continued)

found to foster inquisitiveness, challenging students to find their own solutions to the initial problem.

Additionally, the online nature of the quizzes (and accompanying resources) afforded students the opportunity to control the frequency, intensity and, to a certain extent, the location of their learning. The consequence of this was that students were able to engage with these quizzes when they wished to, including during their time based in a practice environment. In this setting, students told us that they would task themselves to find out the answers in order to complete the quizzes, for example learning how to use the *British National Formulary* (a yearly publication that provides healthcare professionals with up-to-date medicine usage), thereby ensuring the further development of transferable skills.

The use of online quizzes has been extremely popular: whilst there were 54 students in the group, there were 657 attempts made in the six weekly quizzes – giving a group average of 110 attempts per quiz. This learning and teaching innovation appears also to have had a profound impact on students' summative assessment results. Student results after the changes improved with a 100 per cent pass rate in the exam and 94 per cent of the students receiving a mark of 70 per cent and above.

Many student testimonials attributed these outstanding results to their repeated use of the quizzes. They found the quizzes invaluable as they were challenging, thought-provoking, reassuring, engaging and fun. Indeed, one of the students stated 'the use of online quizzes has transformed my learning experience in a way I thought could not be

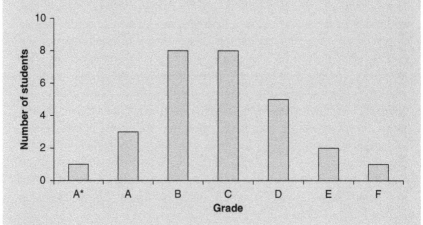

Figure 5.1   Results 'old' module

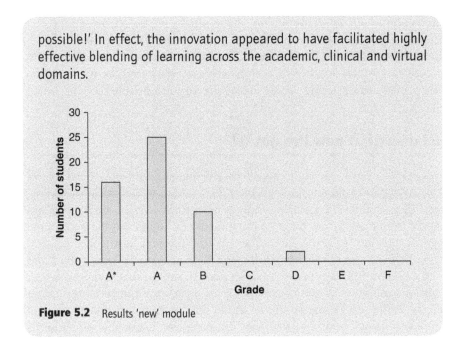

possible!' In effect, the innovation appeared to have facilitated highly effective blending of learning across the academic, clinical and virtual domains.

Figure 5.2   Results 'new' module

'Investigative project generated' data

It may be that once a particular question has been formulated about a learning and teaching issue, the plan to investigate it evolves into a full-scale research project. This may involve other colleagues and involve students as part of the investigative team. Such projects can be internally funded, perhaps as part of funded teaching enhancement activities or an NSS target improvement process, or externally funded as a 'normal' research project would be.

An example of this kind of funding stream is the current UK HEA series of Teaching Development Grants which are available at the individual, departmental and cross-institution collaborative level. Running a funded project often helps to 'legitimise' (if that is needed) the time spent on investigating your learning and teaching activity. It can also help to foreground the robust evidence required to bring about a change in the way particular subjects are taught. One recent example is a Teaching Development Grant Departmental Award which was won by the Law School at the University of Hull in 2012 to undertake a project to develop ways for students to gain legal and other key skills within undergraduate law programmes (see http://www.heacademy.ac.uk/resources/detail/teaching-development-grants/departmental-round-6/legal-skills).

Projects like this can be an excellent way of getting students involved in developing their own curriculum. This can result in really productive interactions with students where any course problems are couched as research problems which students are invited to help to resolve. However, do note that if you ask students to undertake this form of research, you should be prepared either to act on whatever they find, or to provide a strong evidence-based rationale as to why you are unable to.

What do I do with it now I've got it?

Imagine you have run your project or investigation and now have lots of data; educational enquiry projects often generate more data than you envisaged they would. The next question is what to do with it all? As you will expect from reading this book so far, the answer to this will depend on the type of data and to some extent the amount that you have collected. You need to decide the best approach to analysis to achieve the most robust and useful output. In this process you also need to ensure that you do not lose sight of what you set out to achieve. There is no point in running student questionnaires and focus groups to gather data on how a particular module should be developed, and then not reaching any actionable conclusions about how to do this.

Ultimately, your approach to the analysis and presentation of results is likely to be guided by the qualitative, quantitative or mixed data collection methods that you have used, but here are a few suggestions as to what you could do and how you can get the most useful information from your data. Do not be afraid of getting expert help if you are not sure you are doing the right analysis:

- Qualitative analysis: for example, discourse analysis, storytelling or thematic analysis.
- Quantitative analysis: for example, creating comparative tables, graphs, bar charts by using simple statistical techniques (mean, standard deviation) or more detailed statistics (ANOVA, t tests, power calculations). Of course this notional split between simple and more complex depends very much on the quality and quantity of your data as well as your personal experience, skill and confidence.
- Comparisons: for example, across intervention groups, cohorts and year groups, with regard to assessment scores, intake UCAS scores, retention and completion rates.

The next question is what do you do with your outcomes once you have them? If you have shown solid evidence for an improvement in assessment rates following a change in teaching approach, and have the student feedback to support how much they like it, what next? Well, if it is 'your' module or equivalent you have the authority and now the evidence to move in a particular way: this is curriculum development as it is meant to be! Many modules and courses will have ongoing development or action plans (often linked to the NSS outcomes) which you can feed your findings into to make sure they make a difference. Your findings could also be used to impact recruitment policy, develop student partnerships or relationships with the student union. It may provide robust support for student experience or engagement initiatives across departments of whole institutions. And depending on the size of your cohort and the robustness of the research approach, it could have an impact on current educational theory or understanding.

The point is that data generated as part of educational enquiry are meant to be useful; to have positive impact in a real sense on real students. You may have started out on a project as part of the assessment on an educational development qualification such as the Postgraduate Certificate in Academic Practice, but it will only really mean something if you act on your findings to improve the learning of your (or other peoples') students. In today's busy times with 'REF-able' outcomes being the most prized in most UK HEIs, work of this kind can often be overlooked. But we would argue that if teaching is a part of your day-to-day work, then developing it in a robust evidence-based manner, should be too.

Will anyone else care?

It is very difficult for others to care (including your students) if they are unaware that your educational enquiry has taken place! Disseminating findings of this kind may be something that is not a priority for you. You may think that what you have done is so specific to your circumstances or subject area that it does not have much transferable value. However, robust data showing how intervention X improved the essays written by a group of history students may be exactly the good idea an English Literature tutor is looking for. Your success in using problem-based learning with a cohort of 300 students may inspire someone else from a completely different subject area to give it a go. If you do not make your results public then others will not be able to build on your findings and are likely to end up re-inventing the proverbial wheel again and again. Imagine if we did not publish or share and challenge our subject research – nothing would ever move forward. Over and over again, as educational developers we have found ourselves connecting up individuals and teams from very different disciplinary settings to discuss similar interventions and to avoid duplication of action. While we are comfortable in our role as institutional and cross-institutional 'boundary spanners' (Williams, 2010) who make connections across different constituencies and groups (see also Wenger, 1998), we would also encourage you to ensure that others who are actively seeking ideas can find your results.

Generally, if you think a colleague in a similar position would find it useful to know what you have found out, then you should make it public! You can start small if you wish to – a departmental seminar or institutional learning and teaching conference is a good place to begin. Most subject areas have education meetings, or have a satellite section focusing on education as part of the main subject conference. Go along to a few and you will probably find yourself (as many of our colleagues have done) sitting there thinking 'I could have done that' or worse, 'I did that already, but didn't get my data out there'. To this end, Chapter 6 moves on to explore some ways in which you can disseminate your educational enquiry findings.

   Activity 5.1   Ideas to get you started

If you are not sure where to begin, this activity provides you with a few quick ideas to get you immersed in the data that are already around you and to help you to crystallise your thoughts:

- Spend an hour or two looking back at the standard module evaluation data that you and your colleagues have collected over the past few years. What does it tell you about student engagement and achievement?
- Arrange to meet with a group of students to discuss what they think about a particular module or learning style. Providing coffee and cake often helps with these kinds of meetings!
- Find out if any projects are already running in your department – can you get involved or extend an existing project further?
- Think about the bit of your teaching that you are never happy with (we probably all have at least one of these!) and devise a way to find out why it does not work as you would like and what you could do to improve it.
- Look at the educational development literature for your subject area – are there any evidence-based solutions or other good ideas that you could try to implement in your setting and record the results?
- What are the key areas of concern in your department or institution? Employability? NSS scores? Retention? Focus on identifying how you, from within your context, may be able to help to improve on or resolve these concerns. This may also be linked to corporate institutional plans or targets.
- Use minutes of existing meetings (for example, staff–student consultative committees, boards of studies) to identify areas needing development with your students and involve them in the solutions.

- If you are undertaking a teaching qualification, discuss mutual problems with other participants and see if they cross subject boundaries and could become collaborative projects.
- Raise the subject of educational development in departmental meetings: what do your colleagues do or wish to see done?

Concluding thoughts

If your educational enquiry projects are actually going to make a difference to what you teach, the way that you teach it and the learning experience of your students, then they must be based on robust and reliable data or information. This is true irrespective of your subject background. By producing and considering data in a way that you are familiar with (emanating from your subject-based research) you will be able to generate important insights that will help make that difference. But be prepared to recognise the limitations of any approach that you may adopt. We hope that this chapter has encouraged you to begin to think through ways in which you can triangulate any data that you collect. In practice, this may involve joining forces with someone, perhaps from another disciplinary area, who brings other research skills to the table or by thinking through ways in which you can develop these alternative skills yourself.

Suggested further reading

Corti, L., Van den Eynden, V., Bishop, L. and Woollard, M. (2014) *Managing and Sharing Research Data: A Guide to Good Practice*. London: Sage.

Olsen, W. (2011) *Data Collection: Key Debates and Methods in Social Research*. London: Sage.

Sapsford, R. and Jupp, V. (2006) *Data Collection and Analysis* (2nd edition). London: Sage.

Some links to resources or methods mentioned in this chapter

http://www.theworldcafe.com/method.html
http://www.thestudentsurvey.com/
http://unistats.direct.gov.uk/find-out-more/about-unistats/
http://www.heacademy.ac.uk/pres
http://www.heacademy.ac.uk/PTES

CHAPTER 6

WHAT ABOUT DISSEMINATION?

Maxine Lintern, Mike McLinden and Elizabeth Cleaver

Learning outcomes

By the end of this chapter it is anticipated that you will:

- Appreciate the role of dissemination in successful educational enquiry;
- Recognise the importance of building dissemination into educational enquiry projects from the very beginning; and
- Be ready to plan a dissemination approach and strategy.

Introduction

This final chapter of Part One considers the various avenues for the dissemination of educational enquiry. We argue that dissemination is a vital part of your own successful educational enquiry and wider teaching and learning development activities; not least as it can help you to ensure that any insights gained from your reading, syntheses of evidence, empirical enquiries or evaluation activities are shared with others. Over our own careers we have been astonished by the wide number of learning and teaching 'wheels' that are reinvented on an annual basis, even within and across faculties in just one institution! This is not only a waste of highly precious academic resource but, perhaps more importantly, does not follow the underpinning values and principles of good academic citizenship and the expectation that our original contributions to knowledge will be shared with the academic community and increasingly, with society more broadly (the impact agenda). However, in contrast to the dissemination of research findings that academics regularly and actively engage in, you may feel less comfortable with the idea of sharing teaching and learning materials, evidence and insights. We start the chapter by exploring this and other paradoxes which currently exist in the UK higher education system (and beyond).

Teaching: a private or public activity?

Teaching in higher education is often viewed as a private and personal activity. We can all identify with colleagues who have walked into a temporary post to take over teaching only to find that everything to do with the modules – books, administrative paperwork, lesson plans – have left with the previous occupant. With the advent of shared computer drives and virtual learning environments, creating often permanent records of resources and materials on them, and a growing sectorial change in attitudes towards the sharing of teaching materials, this is now, thankfully, much less likely to happen. In addition to the oft held view that teaching is a private activity, in many institutions, teaching resources are becoming incorporated into institutional Intellectual Property Rights (IPR) policies. This has resulted, in part, from growing institutional awareness of the market value of such resources as they become ever more complex, electronic and open to online dissemination. This clearly has implications as to what can be shared and by whom.

Yet as stated in Chapter 1, the importance of sharing our teaching experiences and discoveries is absolutely key to the purposeful development and improvement of our teaching and our students' learning. There is clearly a contradiction here, which is further compounded by the recent global movement towards openness in education. Academics are increasingly being encouraged to share openly both in terms of their teaching materials (Open Educational Resources or OERs) and in terms of their insights into teaching and learning (both *what* to teach as well as *how* to teach). Indeed, teaching and learning has been at the forefront of the open access movement, manifested most recently in 2012 with the OER Paris Declaration (UNESCO, 2012) and the development of Massive Open Online Courses (MOOCs) by some of the world's leading higher education providers. In the UK the government-funded Higher Education Academy (HEA), which supports a range of teaching development activities, holds as a prerequisite for funding, that applicants should be able to demonstrate the usefulness and impact of any funded activity beyond the host institution. While this is, in part, driven by a wider UK public sector accountability agenda (in that the HEA must demonstrate the impact and benefits realisation of the public funds that they distribute), it also rests on the principles of social justice and the recognition of the role that education can play in addressing global inequalities.

Here we have uncovered one of the key dilemmas facing us in the UK higher education sector at present. More than ever, the sector is being viewed less as a public service and more as a market-driven sector where individual institutions are required to maintain themselves as viable businesses. Yet at the same time, 'openness' and social justice are growing as global and national higher education agendas. Those of you who are party to some of the conversations that are happening at the highest levels in UK institutions will be aware of a range of ways in which your own institutions are attempting to make sense of this paradox and to negotiate a middle ground between maintaining intellectual property rights and sharing open resources. How this will develop over the next few years remains to be seen. The year 2012 saw the advent of MOOCs, developed and provided by some of the top Ivy League institutions in the United States and other leading institutions internationally. Coursera, recognised as one of the leading forces in the development of MOOCs, has recently announced that its global community of Universities is providing free educational resources for 2.7 million students across 4 continents (Coursera, 2013).

It is important to stress, however, that while MOOCs are open to anyone with an internet connection to sign up and study on them on an individual basis, they are not interchangeable with OERs. OERs are increasingly covered by Creative Commons licensing tools (Creative Commons, 2013) which enable the free reuse and often the repurposing of resources and materials within different educational contexts providing the activity is not for profit or personal gain. And while MOOCs may contain OERs, many do not and their materials remain the copyright of their host institutions. So while the tide is now turning towards 'openness' in education, it is currently manifesting itself in a range of ways. It is important that you check your local policies and ensure that any dissemination plans are in keeping with institutional and, if appropriate, funder expectations.

When should I disseminate?

Having acknowledged this wider context, we now return to points made in Chapter 1 and, in particular, Healey's (2003) argument that the scholarship of teaching and learning should comprise Boyer's first three types of scholarship: the scholarships of discovery, integration and application (Boyer, 1990). As we stated in Chapter 1, this conceptualisation helps us to move forward in our quest for an approach to the enhancement of teaching which draws upon academics' existing skills-sets: the skills of higher-order thinking, scholarship and research. As Brew reminds us, this approach is key to our teaching remaining relevant 'in the 21st century society [where] the capacity to adapt and change teaching and learning in continually shifting circumstances is critical for the future of the discipline' (2011: 3).

It is important to note that there are likely to be some key similarities, but also some important differences, associated with the process of dissemination for educational enquiry when compared to the types of scholarly and academic dissemination that you are more familiar with. Similar to other areas of academic work, it is extremely important to share our findings in order that approaches to teaching and learning (across institutions and across countries) can benefit and move forward based on developments that take place. It is also important to gain peer feedback and review of our work to ensure its quality.

However, one of the key differences that you may feel less comfortable with, is the point at which dissemination can, and is encouraged to, occur. Academics are encouraged to share their teaching and learning research and enquiry with others *during* its development and its implementation as well as at the end of the project or development process. This is viewed as an important part of the project process: gaining feedback at all stages and particularly at a point when a change of plan could make a crucial positive difference. In this context, we view dissemination as part of a change cycle whereby we actively seek to influence the practice of others as part of our teaching development work, and actively seek the feedback of others as our own teaching development enquiry projects are formed, developed and put into practice.

This is exemplified clearly in the Australian Learning and Teaching Council (ALTC) funded D-Cubed Report (Hinton et al., 2011), which encourages readers to think about dissemination as something that should be planned for and integrated into projects from their very beginning, and not simply viewed as a 'bolt on' at the end. This ensures that findings and recommendations from the work are shared at the earliest opportunity. Many teaching and learning conferences (including your own institutional events) will encourage 'work-in-progress' reports and workshops which can be used to invite peer feedback and engage peers in the early findings or insights of your project. A key benefit of this approach is learning about what other people are doing which is similar to your own work and sharing ideas, literature searches and conclusions which together add to the richness of your own and others' projects. In short, this approach helps us to avoid reinventing the wheel quite as often as we do when we develop our teaching practice and resources in the privacy of our offices and classrooms. And given current pressures on academics' workloads in the higher education sector, we are certain that this approach will have the added benefit of saving you time!

You may find it helpful therefore to think about planning your dissemination activities as part of your project from the very outset. As stated above, this approach is advocated as good practice by Hinton et al. (2011) who, drawing on the work of Rabin et al. (2008) and McKenzie and Alexander (2006), argue that the impacts of dissemination can be greatly improved if dissemination is viewed as a series of successive phases rather than a one-off event, as a planned strategy rather than a collection of atomistic activities and as an ongoing two-way process aimed at bringing about change. Two useful planning tools that you may find helpful when planning for dissemination are further described below.

The D-Cubed 'Planning a Dissemination Strategy' resource (Hinton et al., 2011: 37)

This resource is designed to support you in developing a dissemination strategy which spans the lifecycle of your educational enquiry project. It will help you to map your dissemination strands, plans and activities against five different project stages:

- proposal development and project planning;
- early phases;
- later phases;
- project conclusion; and
- post-project phase.

The resource provides examples of possible steps that you may wish to take as part of each phase of your project (in relation to potential adopters, identified stakeholders, the existing evidence base, planned deliverables and encouraging uptake) and gives examples of appropriate dissemination activities associated with each step including:

- using email lists, discussion forums and other social networking tools;
- supporting sub- or spin-off projects within and beyond the institutional setting;
- creating online repositories or adding resources and guides to open-repositories;
- attending and holding conferences, workshops and showcase events; and
- mentoring and participatory dissemination.

The 'Agency for Healthcare Research and Quality Dissemination Planning Tool' (see AHRQ, 2013)

This resource explores six elements of dissemination that will help the translation of research into practice in the healthcare field. Many of the insights are extremely practical and transferrable to the educational practice setting:

1   Identifying what it to be disseminated;
2   Identifying the roles of the target audiences (what will they be using it for);
3   Identifying dissemination partners through whom end users can be reached;
4   Identifying the best ways to convey research outcomes to the different audiences;
5   Identifying how to evaluate the dissemination process and channels; and
6   Planning dissemination activities.

As outlined in both of these examples, key to ensuring that dissemination has impact is identifying *who* you wish to disseminate to and in *what format*, a subject that we explore further in the next section.

What kind of dissemination should I engage in, and for whom?

If you feel most comfortable starting with a tried, tested and accepted approach to dissemination then, given the focus of this book, you may wish to think about disseminating at a disciplinary teaching and learning conference. Indeed, many of you may feel that this is the most appropriate first step as it will be given more kudos in the current academic worlds that you inhabit. A number of disciplinary research conferences (particularly those in the USA) have a teaching and learning stream as a standard part of their annual events; others have dedicated teaching-focused conferences. The American Sociological Association includes a 'Teaching and Learning in Sociology' strand as standard in its annual meeting programme, while other disciplines have well established independent teaching-focused conferences. For example, the International Conference on Chemistry Education holds its twenty-third annual meeting in 2014.

More local to home, many of your own institutions will have their own teaching and learning annual conference or similar events at which staff from different disciplines can present and share projects, ideas and experiences. Those of you in larger institutions may also have discipline or faculty-level events. Ultimately, your decision about which conference to present at will depend on a range of factors specific to you and your project: the stage your project is at, what conferences are available to present at, who you think the dissemination will be most useful for and importantly, whether you have any funds to pay for event fees and travel.

In recent years in the UK many university teaching and learning conferences have been used to showcase work that has arisen from academics taking part in early-career development programmes such as Postgraduate Certificates in Academic Practice or Higher Education in the UK. However, resulting from a strong central investment of resource and funding from the Higher Education Academy, institutions in the UK are increasingly developing academic continuing professional development (CPD) frameworks which are aligned to the UK Professional Standards Framework for Teaching and Supporting Learning in Higher Education (UKPSF) (HEA, 2011). One key element of the UKPSF (Area of Activity A5) is the expectation that academic staff will 'engage in continuing professional developments in subjects/disciplines and their pedagogy, incorporating research, scholarship and the evaluation of professional practices' (HEA, 2011). This involves not only taking into account the work of others in a scholarly way, but also a recognition of the importance of evaluating (both formally and informally) your own practice, and developing this practice using the methods of critical reflection and research. Indeed, as CPD frameworks continue to become embedded within the higher education sector in the UK (and beyond) it is increasingly likely that the role of educational enquiry in meeting institutional and sector-wide CPD standards will grow, providing a rich source of evidence and practice for future conference presentations and workshops.

In addition to conferences, you may wish to disseminate through the growing number of disciplinary-focused peer-reviewed learning and teaching journals. Some have a long history; for example, the *Journal of Chemical Education* has been published in the USA since 1924, *Medical Education* in the UK since 1966 and *Teaching Sociology* in the USA since 1973. Others in the UK are newer, many arising from the establishment of the Higher Education Academy Subject Centres in the early 2000s. Examples include *Bioscience Education, Engineering Education Journal* and *ELiSS* (*Enhancing Learning in the Social Sciences*). Whilst most of these journals involve peer review, some are actively focused on practitioner evaluation and enquiry projects and others on traditional larger scale pedagogic research findings. You will need to spend a little time in your own subject area looking at the journals available and at the kind of research that they include, and then plan your own dissemination approach accordingly. On the way, we are certain that you will find some very interesting ideas and evidence which will help you to reflect on and change your own teaching practice. We also hope that for those of you who are not social scientists, the earlier chapters in this book will help you navigate some of the more formal social science research approaches that you may encounter in some of these journals.

Although sharing and dissemination in academia is often associated with the more familiar and conventional channels described above (conferences, books and journal articles), we also encourage you to consider new avenues for sharing. These are growing in popularity within the learning and teaching field (and beyond) and may offer opportunities to reach new audiences, possibly outside the academic community, and to disseminate in different ways.

Technology-enhanced approaches to dissemination, built around user-generated content and online communities, are now increasingly popular. Social networking sites, vodcasts and podcasts, wikis, blogs and Twitter feeds can be a positive way to engage with the development and findings of others' educational enquiry projects and to disseminate your own. However, a slight word of caution needs to be expressed here. Many institutions are currently developing social media policies which may affect the kind of dissemination you can undertake within your own institutional setting. As with the institutional IPR policies we referred to above, we encourage you to explore and familiarise yourself with local policies around dissemination of information using social media and other web tools.

Another useful tip for any activities that involve sharing information over the web is to discuss your plans with web-developers or technology-enhanced learning experts in your institution. Just posting an item on the web does not mean it will be found, read or commented upon. You will be aware, when you undertake your own web searches, that certain pages seem to be prioritised at the top of the search list. The process by which this happens is similar to the process by which references are listed for you when you use academic search engines in citation databases (as discussed in Chapter 3). However, academic databases, which have strict protocols for data storage and presentation, use keywords, dates of publication or authors as the basis for searching; all items within the database will consistently include information in these different search fields. Because data on the web are not produced using a coherent format, web search engines cannot use this approach. Instead they read what is termed the *metadata* associated with a web resource and use this to rank the source against the search terms. Metadata is 'information about information' (so the equivalent of keywords or authors' names) but there is no web-standard approach to adding metadata to web resources. This therefore makes the results gained from web searching reliant on two key things: first the searcher knowing what key words to use in relation to the metadata available to search from and secondly, the authors of web resources knowing how to ensure that metadata is correctly incorporated into the resource. The reality is that many web resources lack metadata and a number of search engines are not able to recognise certain types of embedded metadata fields or 'tags'. Finally, like printed resources, web resources date and the impact of dissemination can be limited if project pages are not kept up to date after a particular project concludes.

Adopting technologically enhanced modes of dissemination may also offer you an opportunity to disseminate to, and gain feedback from, groups who have traditionally been excluded from discussions about pedagogy: your students. In creating a project wiki or blog you can invite your students, not simply those who may be actively engaged in your educational development project, to provide feedback and to contribute to its development. In this way, a range of students can be actively engaged in the co-construction of the curriculum, by playing a part in a project that will develop your teaching practice and/or the content and format of their studies. There is growing interest in students as co-creators and co-producers of curricula (see Bovill, 2013) and this provides just one way that you may be able to engage students in a meaningful way in this process. To help with this, McVitty challenges us to avoid hiding the reasons for our peda-gogical choices from students, too many of which still remain 'tacit' (2012: 16). In short, unless students are actively engaged in understanding peda-gogy and the evidence base for decision making, they are unlikely to be able to make fully informed contributions to curriculum development.

How will I know that my dissemination has been successful?

In the contemporary higher education environment simply informing the academic community about your work is now viewed as only the first step of the dissemination process. As stated earlier, the 'impact' agenda has taken hold in the higher education sector within the UK, greatly affected by the government's calls for greater accountability in the spending of public money. Whether you have been successful in obtaining external or internal funding for your educational enquiry project or whether you are simply using some of your academic core-funded 'research and scholarship' time, you are likely to be required either by the funding body or your institution, to show how their investment (of funds for your salary) has produced a return for yourself and, where relevant, has had an impact on the wider sector.

While the journey from start to finish of a project may not be linear or predictable, it is now recognised as good practice to ensure that whatever results you have found are shared with those for whom there will be some benefit. Addressing the impact of the findings of your enquiry on others is not always easily done, but there are some relatively straightforward ways in which you can plan for and measure impact. These include:

- the number of visits to a web-resource or results gathered from a web feedback-tool (which may be a link which allows the user to send simple feedback which is collated into an Excel spreadsheet or may be some-thing more sophisticated such as a feedback questionnaire);
- the handing out of a brief feedback questionnaire at events which asks people to reflect on how they might take insights from your project into their own workplace;
- the number of spin-off or sub-projects that grow out of your initial project. An example of this process in action at the national scale is the TESTA (Transforming the Experience of Students through Assessment) project. The project initially arose out of a £200,000 HEA National Teaching Fellowship Project Grant in the UK which involved collaboration between four UK universities: Bath Spa, Chichester, Worcester and Winchester. However, fol-lowing the success of the initial project, the TESTA team are now supporting a range of other UK and Indian universities (following successful bidding for a British Council grant) to adopt the TESTA approach (see TESTA, 2013).

While your initial funding may not be as large as the TESTA funding, we would encourage you to take a similar supportive approach within your own institution to help others within and beyond your immediate teams to build on the insights of your educational enquiry project. The three activities presented at the end of the chapter could be helpful for this purpose.

 Some activities to help you to plan for and execute your dissemination approach

The following three activities have been adapted from an excellent resource (Harmsworth et al., 2000) which has garnered the experiences and insights of over 100 educational development projects that were funded in the UK during the 1990s. Although the original PDF resource may be regarded as slightly dated due to the fact that it pre-dates many of the fast-changing modes of dissemination discussed above, its key principles and insights remain valuable.

 Activity 6.1   Planning for dissemination (adapted from Exercise 1, Harmsworth et al., 2000: 5–6)

Ask yourself and/or each member of your project team to write down:

1   A description of the aims and purpose of the project for someone outside of the team;
2   What they believe the project has to disseminate and to whom.

As a group, complete the table in Figure 6.1.

Handy hints

- Try to distil your collated ideas into no more than ten key points.
- Even if you are not working as part of a formal research team, use the exercise yourself to clarify your understanding of what the project is setting out to achieve.
- When you have completed the exercise, share it with colleagues and students to check the language that you have used is clear to everyone.

(Continued)

(Continued)

Our project is about:	
Our project aims to:	

Our project will be disseminating the following:	To whom?
1	
2	
3	
4	
5	
6	
7	
8	
9	
10	

Figure 6.1   Planning for dissemination

Activity 6.2   Meeting the needs of stakeholders (adapted from Exercise 3, Harmsworth et al., 2000: 9)

Key to a strong approach to dissemination is an assessment of the needs of the audience(s) that you wish your work to resonate with, and be of value and use to. Identify the key problems or issues that your project will help to address or overcome and to which stakeholders these apply. As each stakeholder group is likely to view these issues and problems from different perspectives you may also need to think about altering your 'message' to suit. For example, at one end of the spectrum, if you wish the Vice Chancellor of your institution to take note of the findings of your project, you are likely to need to consider the ways in which its outcomes help to fulfil the strategic aims of the institution. Alternatively, at a practical everyday level, your students are probably more likely to be interested in the immediate impact of your educational enquiry work on their own learning experiences. The table in Figure 6.2 is provided to help you to plan for the best approach to dissemination for each issue and each group.

Handy hint

- If you do not know what each group's needs and priorities are likely to be, explore this with members of that group or with colleagues who might be able to provide some insight. Never assume that your own priorities are the same as those of others.

	Issue or problem	Target audience or group	Dissemination format and key messages
1			
2			
3			

Figure 6.2   Meeting the needs of stakeholders

 ## Activity 6.3   Measuring dissemination success and return on investment (adapted from Exercise 10, Harmsworth et al., 2000: 31–32)

As a team or individually, think about your dissemination aims and plans and how you will measure their success. Add a fourth column to the table that you have already completed as part of Activity 6.2 to address success in dissemination (see Figure 6.3).

Handy hint

The following questions may prove useful in this process:

1   What will success look like in relation to each stakeholder group (including yourself)?
2   What evaluation methods will help you to measure or account for this success?
3   How will you communicate this success back to each stakeholder group?

	Issue or problem	Target audience or group	Dissemination format and key messages	Success measures
1				
2				
3				

Figure 6.3   Measuring dissemination success and return on investment

Concluding thoughts

This chapter is the last chapter of Part One of this text and has explored the importance of disseminating your educational enquiry outcomes. What you disseminate, when you disseminate it and to whom, will necessarily depend on the nature of your enquiry. However, even if the enquiry is small in nature or focus, it is still worth getting it out there as a soon as possible. The benefits are twofold: you will have an opportunity to reflect on and develop your enquiry as it progresses and others will have the benefit of your early thoughts and ideas with the potential benefit of preventing that wheel from being invented yet again!

We hope in reading this chapter, and the previous five chapters of Part One, that we have inspired you to reflect on why undertaking educational enquiry is important and to recognise some of the key factors that need to be taken into account when planning and executing an enquiry project. The key purpose of this text is to encourage you to draw on your own existing disciplinary research, scholarship and higher-order thinking skills to undertake educational enquiry, set within a broader understanding of the norms and conventions of existing educational research. The remaining chapters of this text (which together form Part Two) are designed to help you in this process and to support you to begin your own educational enquiry journey. Each of the seven discipline-focused chapters that follow explores how the disciplines can bring new and helpful methodological and conceptual resources to the process of educational enquiry.

Suggested further reading

 Becker, L. and Denicolo, P. (2012) *Publishing Journal Articles*. London: Sage.
Case, J. (2013) *Researching Student Learning in Higher Education*. Abingdon: Routledge.
Levin, B., Qi, J., Edelstein, H. and Sohn, J. (2013) *The Impact of Research in Education: An International Perspective*. Bristol: Policy Press.

PART TWO

ENQUIRY IN THE DISCIPLINES

CHAPTER 7

ENQUIRY INTO LEARNING AND TEACHING IN THE PHYSICAL SCIENCES

Helen King and Tina Overton

Learning outcomes

By the conclusion of this chapter it is anticipated that you will:

- Be able to identify key topics for educational enquiry in physics, chemistry and geoscience;
- Recognise analogies and synergies between your science research and educational enquiry; and
- Evaluate and choose a preferred research methodology for studying a topic of interest in your academic practice.

Introduction

If you are an academic in the science disciplines, you will be very familiar with the way research is planned and carried out. If you imagine that you are moving into a new area of experimental research then there are key activities which you would expect to be doing: a literature review of what has already been done, planning to collect some data, making observations, analysing data, drawing conclusions and disseminating outcomes. If you are planning to move into the area of educational enquiry then an effective way to start is to use exactly this same approach:

- you do some background reading and find out what has been done before;
- you plan an 'experiment' or some intervention, gather data and observe what happens;
- you analyse your data and draw some conclusions;
- you plan to disseminate your findings in publications of various types and contributions to meetings and conferences.

Using this approach, educational enquiry is not so very different from scientific enquiry and for many areas of learning and teaching practice that you may wish to evaluate or study, process and practice can be transferred from your own research field with reasonable ease. As Chapters 1 to 6 in this text have shown, an evidence-based approach is equally applicable to educational enquiry as to science research. As academics you will already routinely read the literature in your chosen scientific field in order to keep up to date and to stimulate your ideas and this can be carried over to your teaching and learning activities. There is already considerable discipline-specific literature in many areas of educational enquiry which will provide you with opportunities to learn from what has gone before (what works, what does not, useful methodologies and so on).

One difference that you may notice from reading the literature on educational enquiry is that it appears perfectly acceptable to repeat and publish a study carried out elsewhere. We would never do this in scientific research yet it is quite a common occurrence once academics start to investigate what happens in the classroom. This is because, in educational enquiry, we are researching something with an extremely complex set of variables associated with it – people and their activities. So what works in one context or institution may not be applicable to another; repeat investigations are important to draw out commonalities and identify findings that seem to correspond across diverse settings. As such, one good way to start your educational enquiry activities is to begin by going to the literature and to build upon what has gone before.

Getting started

You may find the educational literature a little daunting at first due to unfamiliar terminology. All disciplines have their own jargon and it always takes time to get up to speed with the language. This is not intended to make subjects exclusive or inaccessible; it is just a short cut and something that you will practise in your own disciplinary contexts. In the learning and teaching literature you may encounter new or familiar words being used in different ways (for example case study, coding, convenience sample, ethnography, grounded theory, phenomenology and so on; see http://www.dictionaryofeducation. co.uk for a useful glossary). This can be challenging at first, but getting used to new ways of describing such terms can be a useful skill, particularly if you are likely to become involved in interdisciplinary science research.

Research questions

Formulating research questions in science is something that academics are skilled at. Articulating an education-related issue that is 'researchable', however, is something that you may find more challenging. For example, you may want to investigate your fieldwork activities with students, how students solve problems, or some aspect of students' laboratory work. These in themselves are not research questions and are not directly researchable. Your research questions must be tightly framed and be worth asking. An example of such a question in relation to fieldwork activities might be 'How do students' attitudes to learning change as a result of attending a residential field course?' While we stated above that it may be useful to replicate an existing study in your own setting, be careful that you do not end up reinventing the wheel and answering a question that has been addressed many times before across a range of disciplines. For example, is it really worth asking whether a student-centred approach is effective when there is an extensive evidence base that argues that it is? As an alternative you could investigate the effect of a particular student-centred intervention on, for example, conceptual understanding, retention of knowledge or attitudes to learning that would help to extend our understanding of discipline focused student-centred learning. Some examples of research questions from a collaborative geoscience fieldwork research project (HEA GEES, 2003: see www.gees.ac.uk/projtheme/pedres/pedresfw/pedresfw.htm) include:

'What was the impact on the learning and teaching experience of the removal of fieldwork from academic programmes in geography, earth and environmental sciences?'

'To what extent does current practice in fieldwork reflect Biggs' constructive alignment model (Biggs and Tang, 2011)?'

'What types of information technologies are used to support fieldwork and what is their impact on student learning?'

Just as with science, these overarching research questions need to be broken down in order to be effectively addressed. This is explored in an example taken from the Higher Education Academy Subject Centre for Geography, Earth & Environmental Sciences 'Researching Fieldwork' project (Fuller et al., 2003). A broader research question – *What was the impact on the learning and teaching experience of the removal of fieldwork from academic programmes in geography, earth and environmental sciences?* – was broken down into three related questions for the purposes of ascertaining student perceptions:

In the light of any previous field experiences

1. How could fieldwork have made this unit better?
2. How could fieldwork have made this unit worse?
3. What impact do you think the loss/withdrawal of fieldwork had on your experience of the unit and understanding of the subject?

Gathering data

Data acquisition is key to any successful empirical investigation. Ultimately the methods used to gather data will be determined by what you are trying to discover and the normative approaches of your subject discipline. Scientists are used to gathering reproducible, high quality (however that may be defined) objective data. If you start educational enquiry from a scientific standpoint then you are likely to want to gather large sets of data and analyse them statistically. As discussed in Chapter 2 in relation to the positivist standpoint in research, this is an entirely reasonable approach which will lend itself to addressing many research questions. However, people are more variable than most physical systems; it is difficult to carry out controlled experiments on people in social situations, and very difficult to control all of the variables. Laboratory scientists may be unused to this because reproducible, quality data defines an acceptable experimental method, whereas geoscientists used to doing fieldwork in less controllable settings may be more comfortable with this variation. As such, be prepared for more variation and potentially more anomalies than you may be used to in your discipline-focused research activities.

Large sets of quantitative data can provide a feeling of security and can be very good at giving an idea of *what* is going on in the learning environment. However, we often want to follow up the '*what?*' with '*how?*' or '*why?*' Although this chapter is about using the research paradigms of the scientific disciplines within educational enquiry, it is helpful here to mention qualitative research. Some scientists who begin educational enquiry start with quantitative, statistically rigorous studies but then evolve towards qualitative methodologies in order to provide insights that cannot be obtained through quantitative data alone (see Case Study 2.2 in Chapter 2). This shift may mean learning about how to use new research tools (open-ended questionnaires, focus groups and interviews) and new analysis tools and methods (transcription, open coding and thematic analysis). Such approaches necessitate a re-evaluation of the value of small sample sizes and qualitative research approaches, which may be quite foreign to the researcher from a positivist background. It is helpful, therefore, to use an analogy which will resonate more closely with your own disciplinary experiences: just as a geoscientist might be content to analyse a physical environment by plotting selected points and extrapolating between them, so an educational researcher may be content to interview a limited number of participants and draw conclusions based upon this sample.

Role of the researcher

Good scientific method assumes that the results obtained are independent of whoever carried out the research. You may want to assume this is true in educational enquiry. However, this is seldom the case and you should be aware of the role of the researcher and your possible influence on the outcome. A useful analogy here might be the role of the observer within quantum physics; for an electron to be detected it must interact with a photon which has an effect on the path of the electron. Furthermore, in educational enquiry you may not be an *independent* presence in the research as it may be in your own interest for your study to have a positive result. After all, none of us implement changes that we expect to make learning worse! You should also bear in mind the well-known Hawthorne Effect (Franke and Kaul, 1978). This describes the phenomenon observed when subjects improve or modify an aspect of their behaviour being experimentally measured in response to the fact that they know they are being studied. The Hawthorne Effect is an example of the 'self-fulfilling prophecy' or 'Thomas Theorem' (Merton, 1948; see also Thomas and Thomas, 1928). In short, you should think carefully about whether your students know they are subject to an investigation and be aware that this may affect their performance and may also result in positive outcomes.

Geoscience enquiry sources

Enquiry into learning in the geosciences has increased considerably over the last decade or so. Whilst recognised globally through bodies such as the International Geoscience Education Organisation (IGEO: http://www. geoscied.org/), the majority of the research has taken place in the USA. This is due, in part, to the sheer size of the country and the number of higher education institutions but is also a result of significant funding from the National Science Foundation. Geoscience education research has become a mainstream aspect of conferences such as the Geological Society of America (GSA), with the total number of abstracts submitted to these conferences increasing from less than 10 in 2001 to nearly 100 in 2010 (Stokes, 2011a). By 2009, there were 12 US graduate programmes dedicated to geoscience educational research (Libarkin, 2009). In the UK, interest is developing and a number of geoscience researchers are expanding their fields to include enquiry into learning and teaching, as illustrated by the emergence of the new Higher Education Network of the Geological Society of London in 2011   (http://www.geolsoc.org.uk/gsl/groups/hen).

In the US, and also increasingly in the UK, the term 'geocognition' is being applied to enquiry into learning. Geocognition is a multidisciplinary area of research involving people and processes from areas such as cognitive science and psychology, as well as geoscience, in order to investigate how geoscience is learnt and understood. Areas of research include:

- Learning, teaching and assessment (in the classroom, laboratory and, most importantly, the field); issues of equality and diversity; and the importance of the affective domain;
- Geoscience knowledge (misconceptions, sticking points, barriers to learning, complexity and uncertainty, the geoscience research paradigm, and the transfer of knowledge from other sciences);
- Ways of thinking and practising geoscience (geological time, spatial visualisation, novice–expert continuum) (King, 2008).

Physics and chemistry enquiry sources

There have been lively physics and chemistry education networks in the UK for some years, supported largely through the Institute of Physics and the Royal Society of Chemistry. The advent of the Higher Education Academy (HEA) subject centres and the Centres for Excellence in Teaching & Learning (CETLs) initiative helped to bolster these activities. Pedagogic research in these disciplines is in a fairly fledgling state but interest is growing and small research groups are starting to emerge. Beyond the UK, pedagogic research is showcased in Europe via the European Conference for Educational Research in Chemistry and the Groupe International de Recherche sur l'Enseignement de la Physique (GIREP). However, this activity is more mature in the US where research groups and graduate programmes can be found in the most prestigious universities. As within geoscience this is due in large part to the availability of funding via the National Science Foundation.

Examples of research projects

The best way to get an understanding of the range of research projects undertaken in education in the physical sciences is to browse some of the journals and magazines listed in further reading. The online articles available in the *Journal of Geoscience Education* or *New Directions in Teaching and Learning in the Physical Sciences* provide good starting points. Some projects disseminated in these journals are small-scale research studies that investigate or evaluate student learning in a particular setting such as a single lecture class, laboratory, field course or module. Others seek to explore learning and ways of thinking in an entire discipline such as Titus and Horsman's (2009) study of how well students visualise objects in three dimensions, or Samarapungavan et al.s' (2006) exploration of chemistry students' beliefs about the nature of science. Both of these approaches are equally acceptable. If you have the experience, time and funding you may be able to run a large-scale project. In contrast you may wish to focus on a smaller review, for example of the students' learning in your first year laboratory class, if the research is unfunded or attracts small scale institutional funding.

The projects outlined below as examples give a flavour of some of the various methodologies that might be employed. They also illustrate how educational enquiry can be made directly relevant to the physical sciences. Some are on a larger scale than you may feel ready for right now but they are intended to inspire, not to intimidate!

Examples from the geosciences

The idea of geocognition has led to an innovative range of educational enquiries in the broadest sense: from investigating students' conceptions of geoscience (Stokes, 2011b), to exploring visualisation skills. One such example is of a large-scale project which used GPS tracking and other methods to investigate how people with a range of expertise go about mapping in the field (see Case Study 7.1).

 ## Case Study 7.1   Mapping a field (Petcovic et al., 2009)

The rationale for this research was based on a number of prior studies around the nature of geoscientific expertise. It was noted that there had been very few investigative studies that explored expert and novice

(Continued)

(Continued)

behaviour in the field environment. Hence a pilot study was devised, using a mixed methods approach, to investigate the different approaches to mapping a new field area. Quantitative and qualitative data were gathered at the same time, yet independently, to provide a richer understanding of participants' behaviours. The methods included self-reports of prior geological experience, field maps created by the participants as part of the study, GPS navigation data indicating their travel-times and pathways as they negotiated the field area, audio logs as they spoke aloud their thoughts, and follow-up interviews. These methods were selected so as to explore how the participants moved around the field area and how their understanding of geological systems and processes influenced their decisions on where to go and at which sites to spend more time.

Participants were selected to represent a range of expertise and the 'self-reports' provided data to verify this. Seven participants were used in the pilot to test the methodological approach. The GPS data and participants' maps were analysed quantitatively to compare between experts and novices. The audio logs and interviews were examined using qualitative, content analysis.

Analysis of the GPS tracks indicated that experts had more economy of movement compared with novices, illustrated by simpler paths and less backtracking. It was also noted that the novices were more likely to have difficulties determining their location, identifying rock types and features, and shifting between the map and landscape. In addition, they were less likely to develop a mental model of the area or to test a model against further observations. However, it was found that the experts exhibited a range of approaches and behaviours, making it hard to recommend a single strategy to novice mappers. In conclusion, the researchers suggested that, in addition to teaching mapping techniques, students should also be helped to develop their meta-cognitive (thinking to think) skills in order to enhance their problem-solving abilities.

The approach described in Case Study 7.1 was a collaborative endeavour between colleagues at two Universities with funding from a number of sources. Their main intention was to explore geocognition in itself, with less emphasis on the implications for learning and teaching. The example in Case Study 7.2 is of a smaller-scale project, focused on using educational enquiry to inform and evaluate curriculum design.

Case Study 7.2   Mineralogy and curriculum design (Boyle, 2003)

This educational enquiry project was based on a lecturer's teaching experience and feedback from his students about mineralogy. The students had reported the subject to be boring and difficult, but the lecturer felt that this was due to the teaching methods employed rather than anything inherent about the subject area itself. To test this, he identified a number of relevant learning theories from the literature to inform his curriculum design (including aligning the aims and outcomes of a module to its learning, teaching and assessment methods and learning-style preferences) and then introduced new approaches to his teaching incrementally over a number of years. Each time he ran the module he gathered data from the students in the form of qualitative feedback and quantitative assessment scores. This data was used to inform the further development and enhancement of the curriculum design.

   This project was highly practical and applied, having a direct influence on the lecturer's practice and his students' learning experiences. Educational enquiry was used to both inform the curriculum and project design (through garnering evidence from the educational literature) and to evaluate the changes made (through gathering and analysing data).

Examples from physics and chemistry

Concept inventories are popular research tools in the physical sciences and can be used to probe students' misconceptions. They are typically used in large-scale quantitative studies and there are a number of well validated and tested inventories available. One of the most well validated is the Force Concept Inventory, or FCI (Hestenes and Wells, 1992). The FCI probes students' understanding of Newtonian mechanics and comprises multiple choice questions covering kinematics, Newton's three laws, kinds of forces and superposition of forces, from which a taxonomy of student misconceptions has been derived. It has been widely employed by physicists across the world and there are many examples of the use of the FCI as a pre- and post-intervention instrument in physics education (see Case Study 7.3).

Case Study 7.3   Peer interaction and Newtonian mechanics (Hake, 1998)

In a large quantitative study involving over 6,000 students, Hake investigated the effect of peer interaction in lectures on conceptual understanding of Newtonian mechanics. The FCI was used as a pre- and post-instruction test on students studying the subject in two very different ways: traditional lectures with recipe-based laboratories and algorithmic problem solving and in sessions where students were involved in active learning, hands-on activity and discussion with peers and tutors. The study reports percentage learning gains through recording improvement between the pre- and post-instruction FCI results. The results showed a positive percentage gain for both teaching methods, indicating that the average performance on the FCI had improved after instruction. The normalised gains for each method showed that the interactive teaching method was about twice as effective in enhancing conceptual understanding as the traditional lecture-based approach.

This study stimulated much debate in the literature about the role of interaction in lectures and about the nature of the FCI and what it is assessing (Huffman and Heller, 1995; Savinainen and Scott, 2002). Critics of the FCI point out that it uses multiple choice questions which favour certain types of learners and that some students who score well on the pre-test may have difficulties answering free response problems covering the same material. That aside, this is an example of a paper that has had a major impact on physics education and on other disciplines.

Large quantitative projects of the type described in Case Study 7.3 draw on a positivist research paradigm that produces statistically significant outcomes which can provide researchers with a view of what is happening in the classroom. However, they do not necessarily provide any insight into *why* or *how* things are happening. For that it is necessary to use qualitative research methods, often drawing data from relatively small populations. Case Study 7.4 is an example of how a qualitative approach can be used to gain insight into how students solve chemistry problems.

Case Study 7.4   Problem-based learning in the chemistry lab (Kelly and Lovatt, 2012)

This paper describes a small-scale qualitative investigation into the processes used by undergraduate students whilst engaging in problem-based learning chemistry laboratory activities. The qualitative data were collected through observation and semi-structured interviews. Students were selected for the study to give a broad spectrum of previous chemistry experience. Their initial meetings and final presentations were videoed and the laboratory sessions were observed. Students worked in groups of six on a problem over a two-week period. A structured observation template was used during the laboratory observations and enabled the observer to detail events in the activity, such as student interactions, questions asked and answered, focus of discussions, time spent on calculations and linking theory to practice. Nine students were selected for individual interviews based on their level of engagement (high or low) with the problem-based learning (PBL) activity.

The data showed that groups adopted either 'novice' or 'expert-like' behaviour. Novice behaviour included using materials supplied and organising their knowledge around the obvious features of the problem. Expert-like behaviour included features such as relating results back to the original problem, discussing results and bouncing ideas off others. It was also found that students who displayed novice-like approaches to solving the problem also had surface approaches to their learning whilst those with expert-like characteristics had a deeper approach to learning and were more successful in solving the problem.

Case Study 7.4 gave some insight into the challenges students face when tackling PBL activities. The study enabled tutors to recognise that students need differing levels of support and scaffolding through PBL activities if they are going to be able to succeed regardless of their previous chemistry knowledge. For further information on surface and deep approaches to learning see Marton and Saljo (1976).

Case Study 7.5   Mission to Mars group project (Moran, 2011)

This project was a relatively small-scale initiative which aimed to address the transition from secondary to tertiary education and, in particular, to develop independent learning skills in physics undergraduates. A project-based learning activity was introduced into the first week which aimed to give students experience of working in a

(Continued)

(Continued)

team, to settle into higher education, enable students to meet other students and academic staff, and to learn how to use a range of information sources. In the first year of implementation, teams of students were given project-based scenarios in which they had to produce a brief for a government minister on the reduction of carbon dioxide emissions. The activity was assessed by a poster and written report. Evaluation of the activity showed a lack of enthusiasm for the topic from students. It was thought that students' previous experiences at secondary school meant that many of them were already very familiar with the issues of climate change which led them to take a superficial approach to the project and to stray away from science into the field of politics. It was also clear that students wanted to be engaged in more overtly physics-focused activities. The evaluation led to the conclusion that the introduction of an initial project was sound but that a more physics-focused activity would be more effective at keeping students engaged and that more structure was needed. A new activity was developed for the subsequent year called Mission to Mars. This was clearly more directly related to physics and greater structure was introduced by dividing the activity into five interrelated sub-topics: mission length and trajectory, mass management and launch, communications and life support, radiation and heat shielding, and landing craft and re-entry. Students worked in small teams to short deadlines and longer-term goals. They used authentic resources, such as NASA documents and selected research papers. Assessment was by an oral presentation. Evaluation of the activity showed higher levels of positive feedback from students compared to the previous year and it was clear that they appreciated that the activity helped them to develop skills and to settle into university life.

The project described in Case Study 7.5 was very practical and was developed to address a real classroom problem. The outcomes had a direct influence on the lecturer's practice, the first year curriculum and the students' learning experience. Educational enquiry was used to both inform development of the new activity (through garnering evidence from the educational literature) and to evaluate the changes made (through gathering and analysing data).

Challenges and opportunities

Any new research can be challenging; particularly if you are exploring new territory, trying out new methods or suggesting new ideas. However, it is also really exciting to find out how the universe works: educational enquiry enables us to expand our knowledge of the physical universe and to better understand how its occupants behave and interact. This joint understanding of both the physical and the human world can enrich your teaching and motivate and enthuse your students. Having a better understanding of how the humans in our classroom learn science, and sharing this knowledge and interest with them (and with your colleagues), makes them not only more effective learners but also partners in the learning process and possibly in your research. There are a number of challenges that are particular to educational enquiry that you may not have come across in your discipline research. None of these are insurmountable but are worth bearing in mind when you embark on this type of work.

Funding is a potential issue if you want to undertake large-scale work employing research staff or using technical equipment. In the USA the National Science Foundation sponsors big research projects in physical sciences education and there are now a number of established research groups. In the UK, smaller-scale funding can be obtained through sources such as the Higher Education Academy and university teaching development funds. However, you do not necessarily need additional money – your classroom can serve as the equivalent of your laboratory and is fit for a variety of different approaches. It is also worth considering how such research can support you to meet your institution's expectations to enhance the quality of your curriculum and teaching. Such investment in the teaching side of your academic practice will be beneficial in terms of informing this quality enhancement; and if you can get funding then that is an added bonus!

As with all research projects, careful planning is important, and this can be more difficult when working within the confines of the academic year. The rhythms of the timetable mean that you have to be well organised in order to maximise data collection. Missing the start of a module can sometimes mean the loss of a whole year's data set, especially if you are collecting pre- and post-intervention data. If you are considering researching what happens in your classroom, laboratory or field course then you need to plan to run the research at the right time; if you miss a window of opportunity you may have to wait another six months or a year before you can do it again.

Longitudinal studies that follow a cohort of students throughout their university career can provide interesting data (see for example, Zeegers, 2001), and are perhaps one of the most useful approaches in terms of the application of research findings. A well-known large-scale longitudinal study of the understanding of science concepts in school children followed a sample though twelve years of schooling and demonstrated the effectiveness of concept maps in developing conceptual understanding (Novak and Musonda, 1991). Studies of this scope are not always possible for those of us working with undergraduates. One of the main risks with this approach is that of attrition, so you need a large cohort to start off with. Another drawback of this and other large-scale projects is the amount of data you collect which will take time to input and analyse. Projects with smaller cohorts will generate a more manageable data set but will be restricted in breadth; these are ideal for in-depth-type qualitative approaches. Cross-sectional studies can be a useful alternative to longitudinal studies. For example, students from across all years within a degree programme could be simultaneously sampled in order to explore changing attitudes or skills across the programme, although it is important to recognise the potential impact of 'cohort effect' (see Chapter 5).

In educational enquiry projects it can be easy to get carried away and to lose focus. Some interesting data may reveal tantalising new insights that you want to follow up or another colleague might be investigating something similar, so you adapt your research to include their approach as well. However, it is important to articulate clear research questions to help keep you on track. Whilst interesting diversions can be noted for the future, try not to get led too far away from your original purpose.

Perhaps one of the biggest differences between research in the physical sciences and educational enquiry is the object (or subject) of the research. Once your research involves people a whole new set of challenges arise. It can be hard to generalise from a small sample but the information you get from that sample can be incredibly rich. An analogy here might be with borehole analysis. You can dig down and get a detailed picture of the stratigraphy in a very localised area. You might be able to extrapolate between multiple boreholes in different locations but you cannot be certain that these are entirely representative of the whole area, let alone the continent. It is interesting to note that the development of geology was hindered for many years by the belief that the layers found in the Alps were continuous around the globe, removing the need for fieldwork outside Europe.

Another challenge with conducting research with people is that it can be very difficult to take an entirely objective view or to completely isolate yourself. As one physics colleague noted '*you are a perturbation in the system*', and you can have an impact on what is being observed. In particular, you may have preconceived ideas about what you want to find out or expect your participants' responses to be, which could then bias your observations or interpretations (see Chapter 2). These are challenges that need a different way of thinking and emphasise the need to keep records of your approach to the research. When you come to write up for publication these various factors need to be declared so that the reader is clear about how the research was conducted.

Finally, educational enquiry in your discipline can be a lonely activity. It is possible that only one or two other colleagues in your department will be interested in your work and others may disparage it. It is important therefore for you to identify and connect with the wider community (see suggested further reading). Many science research conferences now also include education sessions, so connecting with like-minded colleagues is becoming easier and can be done in tandem with disciplinary networking. You may find that education sessions are very different from your discipline sessions and are focused around sharing ideas and building a community, rather than defending territory. Although the physics, chemistry and geoscience education enquiry communities are growing they are still relatively small and offer a great opportunity for establishing your own niche and rapidly developing a strong reputation. Educational research journals (see suggested further reading at the end of this chapter), professional bodies and other organisations in the UK (such as the Institute of Physics, Royal Society of Chemistry, Geological Society of London, Higher Education Academy) and internationally (such as the Geological Society of America, Science Education Research Center [SERC], International Geoscience Education Organisation [IGEO], International Union of Pure and Applied Chemistry, European Physics Network, American Chemical Society, American Association of Physics Teachers and the European Science Education Research Association) provide useful starting points.

Ultimately, undertaking educational enquiry can introduce a new layer of academic rigour into your curriculum development work. You are no longer basing your practice just on your experience of being taught or on what you think works, but on a strong evidence base drawn from research by your colleagues in the discipline. Further, as explored in this chapter, educational enquiry does not have to be on a grand scale to be interesting and informative. Many universities now require students to complete module or programme evaluations; feedback is also gained through staff–student liaison committees and their equivalents. All of these approaches will produce data that you can use to inform your teaching (see Chapter 5 for other suggestions). However, as discussed above, these types of quantitative data do not always reveal exactly what is going on. The National Student Survey (NSS), for example, describes how satisfied the students are with various aspects of their learning experience but it does not explain the *reason* for their responses (Mendes et al., 2011).

Using a range of educational enquiry methods can help you to drill down further into the data to understand better what is going on; rather than simply counting all the stars in the sky you can start to understand the process when one goes supernova. It is only by understanding the behaviour or perceptions of students that we can usefully enhance our teaching practice.

Activity 7.1 provides some prompts to help you consider a suitable research question and the approaches you might take to answer it. A variety of methodologies for use in educational enquiry are discussed in Chapter 2 and in the remaining discipline-focused chapters of this text.

 ## Activity 7.1   Defining a research question and considerations for your research plan

It is important to have a clear, specific research question in mind when planning your educational enquiry. This activity provides some pointers to help you narrow your focus and offers some general issues to consider when planning your research project.

Defining your research question

- Is it specific enough?
- Can it be investigated?

Other considerations

Look at the literature:

- Has it been done before?
- Can you learn from others?

Develop your methodology

- Quantitative or qualitative methods or a mixture of both?
- Pre- and post-intervention study?
- Do you need to develop a tool, questionnaire or other instrument? If so, how will you pilot it?
- Can you use a tried and tested tool?
- What sort of data will you generate?

Plan your delivery

- How many students do you need?
- When will you gather data?
- Timing in the academic year?
- Do you need other people to collect data?

Analyse your data

- Make sure you go beyond the 'happy sheet'.
- Remember the possible influence of the researcher.
- Remember the Hawthorne Effect.
- Do you know how best to analyse qualitative data?

Disseminate your findings

- Apply to present at a conference.
- Investigate where you might publish your findings.
- Start writing your paper.

Feed back into your teaching

The outcome of educational enquiry should be more enjoyable teaching, better student learning, greater understanding and more effective graduates.

Concluding thoughts

Educational enquiry in the physical sciences is a relatively young and thriving research area. The individuals involved are highly motivated to enhance learning in their subject area in order to ensure the continued success of the discipline and the furthering of knowledge in science. Educational enquiry may still be seen as 'second class' research by some; however, this has led to active, supportive, collaborative and energetic international communities of researchers as they seek to meet and work with like-minded colleagues.

Educational enquiry provides you with opportunities to bring the two aspects of your academic practice (teaching and research) closer together and to use the learning derived from one to enhance the other. Conducting research into learning, however small scale, can provide a strong evidence base for your teaching and curriculum design, and provides an opportunity for professionalism in all aspects of your academic practice to improve the success of your students, and to enhance the experience of learning and teaching for all.

Suggested further reading

Feig, A. and Stokes, A. (eds) (2011) *Qualitative Inquiry in Geoscience Education Research*. Geological Society of America, Special Paper No. 474.
'This volume provides the first reference of its kind for geoscience education researchers to explore in-depth qualitative theory and methods, and to examine case studies documenting both the application of these methods, and the

contribution made by qualitative inquiry to geoscience education and geoscience cognition' (2011: 5).

Palmer, D. (2006) *An Annotated Bibliography of Research into the Teaching and Learning of The Physical Sciences at the Higher Education Level.* Available at: http://www.heacademy.ac.uk/assets/ps/documents/practice_guides/practice_guides/ps0067_annotated_bibliography_of_research_into_teaching_and_learning_of_the_physical_sciences_in_he_sept_ 2003_1.pdf

Gladwin, R (ed.) (2006) *An Annotated Bibliography of Research into the Teaching and Learning of the Physical Sciences at the Higher Education Level Update 2006.* Available at: http://www.heacademy.ac.uk/assets/ps/documents/practice_guides/Updates_bibliography_March_2007.pdf

These two publications summarise and discuss key publications in pedagogic research in physical sciences and discuss them in a language accessible to HE practitioners.

Piburn, M.D., van der Hoeven Kraaft, K. and Pacheco, H. (2011) *A New Century for Geoscience Education Research.* National Academies Board on Science Education Committee on the Status, Contributions, and Future Directions of Discipline-Based Education Research. Available at: http://www7.nationalacademies.org/bose/DBER_Piburn_October_Paper.pdf

'This review of research in geoscience education has been conducted at the request of the Board on Science Education of the National Research Council [in the USA]' (2011: 2).

Reid, N. (2006) *Getting Started in Pedagogical Research in the Physical Sciences.* Available at: http://www.heacademy.ac.uk/assets/ps/documents/practice_guides/practice_guides/getting_started_ped_research.pdf

A practical guide to the early stages of developing a pedagogic research project.

Bringing Research on Learning to the Geosciences. Available at: http://serc.carleton.edu/research_on_learning/index.html

The website states: 'Research on learning has many important lessons that can improve teaching in the geosciences. This site brings together resources for faculty, teachers and curriculum developers working in the geosciences.'

Journal of Geoscience Education. Available at: http://nagt-jge.org/

The journal website states: 'The *Journal of Geoscience Education (JGE)* is the premier peer-reviewed publication for geoscience education research and curriculum and instruction at the undergraduate and pre-college levels. Each issue contains Editorials, Commentaries, Papers on Curriculum & Instruction, and Papers on Research.'

Chemistry Education Research and Practice. Available at: http://pubs.rsc.org/en/journals/journalissues/rp

The journal website states: '*Chemistry Education Research and Practice (CERP)* is the journal for teachers, researchers and other practitioners at all levels of chemistry education.' It is published free of charge, electronically, four times a year.

New Directions in Physical Sciences Teaching. Available at: http://journals.heacademy.ac.uk/journal/ndir
New Directions focuses on new developments by practitioners in the field of learning and teaching. This is a good place to publish early studies without full research evaluation. Submissions are peer-reviewed.

Education in Chemistry. Available at: http://www.rsc.org/Education/EiC/index.asp
The journal website states: '*Education in Chemistry* provides support for all teachers of chemistry across the secondary, further and higher education sectors. It aims to strengthen the community by providing high quality, peer-reviewed content, tools and resources which promote the sharing of best practice and innovative teaching.'

Physics Education. Available at: http://iopscience.iop.org/0031-9120/
Published by the Institute of Physics, *Physics Education* is the international journal for everyone involved with the teaching of physics in schools and colleges.

Physical Review Special Topics – Physics Education Research. Available at: http://www.aapt.org/Publications/perjournal.cfm
Published by the American Association of Physics Teachers, the journal website states: 'the scope of the journal will cover the full range of experimental and theoretical research on the teaching and/or learning of physics'.

CHAPTER 8

ENQUIRY INTO LEARNING AND TEACHING IN MATHEMATICS AND ENGINEERING

Michael Grove and Joe Kyle

Learning outcomes

By the conclusion of this chapter it is anticipated that you will:

- Be able to discuss an approach to educational enquiry in the context of your disciplinary approach to modelling and solving problems;
- Be able to identify analogies and synergies between your disciplinary research and educational enquiry; and
- Be ready to apply the ideas and concepts discussed to develop an outline plan for an educational enquiry project based on a modelling and problem solving approach.

Introduction

Mathematics is one of the oldest academic disciplines, yet possesses no single widely accepted definition (Mura, 1993). Attempts to define its nature have varied over the ages and Courant and Robins (1941) provide a fascinating discussion of 'What is Mathematics' from its origins as a discipline in Babylonia around 2000BC, to its emergence as a science in ancient Greece around 400–500BC. Mathematics as a discipline has developed with the emergence of new fields of study (for example group theory in the nineteenth century) and the strength of its interaction with other disciplines has perhaps never been more important.

Mathematics can perhaps be best classified as two fields of study: pure and applied. This was a distinction first noted by ancient Greek mathematicians and one which generations of philosophers have sought to define more clearly. In pure mathematics there exists a desire to understand and prove what might appear abstract concepts, whereas applied mathematics involves the application of mathematical methods to model and solve real-world problems in science, engineering, business and industry. These fields do not exist independently; applications of mathematics to real-world problems have themselves resulted in the development of mathematical theories and techniques that in turn, have become the subject of pure mathematical study in their own right. For example, in 1970 Stephen Hawking and Roger Penrose published a paper on space–time singularities that required the development of new mathematical techniques to prove their theories.

Engineering also has its origins in ancient times with the development of fundamental inventions such as the wheel and the pulley. Indeed their development is consistent with a modern definition such as that provided by the Royal Academy of Engineering which defines engineering as:

> the discipline, art and profession of acquiring and applying scientific, mathematical, economic, social, and practical knowledge to design and build structures, machines, devices, systems, materials and processes that safely realise solutions to the needs of society (2013b).

Engineering is a broad discipline, and is more commonly classified in terms of four sub-disciplines: chemical, civil, electrical and mechanical engineering. Although engineers might at first receive training within one of these areas, the skills they possess and develop, much like a mathematician, enable them to work in multi- or inter-disciplinary settings.

At the core of both mathematics and engineering is the nature of rigorous systematic enquiry, in particular a desire to understand patterns and behaviours, identify solutions to problems, and make improvements. As disciplines they can be defined in terms of the types of problems they seek to under-stand or solve, the methodologies and techniques used to tackle these problems, and the results that are subsequently achieved. In essence, this underpins and defines the approach to enquiry in these disciplines: modelling and problem solving.

Approaches to disciplinary enquiry: modelling and problem solving

Modelling and problem solving are at the heart of mathematics and engineering and, although variations exist, the processes can be represented in a general sense by a cycle such as that presented in Figure 8.1.

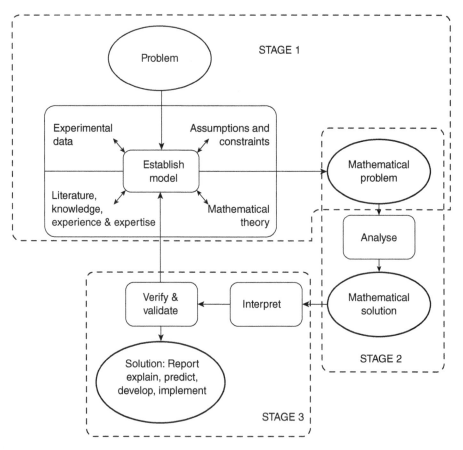

Figure 8.1   Modelling and problem solving in mathematics and engineering – the modelling and problem solving cycle (developed from the work of Savage and Williams, 1990)

The modelling and problem solving cycle contains what Savage and Williams (1990) term 'locations' and 'stages'. The 'locations' (shown as bold ovals in Figure 8.1) refer to specific inputs or outputs, such as a problem or its apparent solution, whereas 'stages' (dashed rectangular boxes in Figure 8.1) refer to specific processes within the cycle. Notice how each of the three 'stages' aligns with how we earlier suggested the disciplines of mathematics and engineering might best be defined, that is: the types of problems they seek to understand or solve ('Establish the model'); the methodologies and techniques used to tackle these problems ('Analyse the problem'), and, the results that are subsequently achieved ('Interpret and validate').

The starting point for the cycle is a problem which can be either real-world or mathematical. A real-world problem is one which exists within, for example, nature, business, or industry, but which has not yet been transformed, through modelling, into a mathematical problem, whereas a mathematical problem is already expressed in mathematical terms (Savage and Williams, 1990). The modelling process enables us to take a real-world problem, simplify it while retaining its essential features, and represent it through a mathematical description with a view to seeking a solution. For many problems, several possible solutions or approaches to achieving a solution might exist, and so a mathematician and engineer will need to interpret and validate these to explore their consequences and determine which is the most appropriate, if at all, for a given problem. Often the generated solution may be insufficient or inaccurate, and the modelling and problem solving cycle will need to be repeated. In addition, the process of solving problems can, in itself, give rise to new and unexpected problems.

So far our discussion of modelling and problem solving has been somewhat generalised. It is important to note that while a mathematician will engage with all three stages of the modelling and problem solving cycle, they will not necessarily follow all of the individual processes and the starting point on the cycle may vary. For example, one of the most famous mathematical problems of all times – Fermat's Last Theorem – states that no three positive integers a, b, and c can satisfy the equation $a^n + b^n = c^n$ for any integer value of n greater than two. Fermat's Last Theorem is already expressed in mathematical terms, and so the modelling process can be omitted entirely. However, consider the problem that fascinated a 17-year-old Galileo: determine the period of oscillation of a bronze lamp suspended from the ceiling of the cathedral at Pisa. Before attempting a mathematical solution, an appropriate model for the oscillation of the lamp needs to be established, including assumptions, which can then be represented in mathematical terms.

These two examples define a key difference between pure and applied mathematics; applying mathematics to a real-world problem requires the development of a model. Because of the processes that are followed, problem solving in engineering is very closely related to problem solving in applied mathematics, but strong links also exist with problem solving in physics as there may also be a practical or experimental element that tests or informs the model. This might include the construction of a physical, or scale model, that undergoes resonance or wind tunnel testing, or the testing of a material to confirm its load-bearing capacity.

Having discussed the modelling and problem solving cycle as a whole, it is now important to consider the process that takes a mathematical problem and yields a mathematical solution: this is the 'analyse the problem' stage (Stage 2 in Figure 8.1). This is, in itself, an important process of enquiry for any mathematician or engineer, and is essential for mathematical proof. George Pólya's seminal book entitled *How to Solve It* (1945), provides guidance on tackling mathematical problems through a logical and reliable four-step process:

1 *Understand the problem:* Is it clear what the problem is that needs to be solved? Is the problem well understood? Is there sufficient information to obtain an answer, or are there further questions that need to be asked?
2 *Devise a plan:* There are often many reasonable methods or techniques that can be used to tackle a problem; a strategy can be developed that brings together the mathematical tools and techniques required to tackle the problem in a logical manner.
3 *Carry out the plan:* The plan can be implemented ensuring each step is checked to ensure it is correct.
4 *Look back:* The solution obtained should be examined to check the result, arguments and mathematics processes utilised. Reflecting upon what worked, and what did not, can assist with solving future problems.

Pólya's approach can help us tackle a mathematical problem, but it by no means guarantees that a valid, or indeed any, solution will result. Pólya himself suggests that if you cannot solve a particular problem there may be an easier or related problem you can try to solve instead. Indeed Andrew Wiles, who provided the proof of Fermat's Last Theorem in 1995, had abandoned his initial efforts to solve this problem until another mathematician established a link between Fermat's Last Theorem and the Taniyama–Shimura conjecture.

At the beginning of the twentieth century, the German mathematician David Hilbert published a list of mathematical problems which, at the time, were all unsolved (1902; for a translated English language version and biography of Hilbert see Reid, 1996). These problems received significant attention by the world-wide mathematics community, although a few, as they were stated by Hilbert, are too vague to ever be described as 'solved'. Ten have an accepted resolution, seven a partial resolution and three remain unsolved to this day. Although the problem solving process does not guarantee the precise resolution mathematicians ultimately seek, in the case of the ten partially or unresolved problems, the activities of many individuals in attempting a solution have collectively enhanced our mathematical knowledge base and enabled progress towards resolution to be made. In short, an inability to secure a solution is not seen as a failure if something is learned from trying to do so.

Having set the scene, in the discussion that follows, we will now explore how a modelling and problem solving process as defined by Savage and Williams (1990) and Pólya (1945) can be adapted to enable enquiry into learning and teaching within mathematics and engineering.

Adapting disciplinary enquiry to educational enquiry

At the heart of both disciplinary and educational enquiry is the desire to better understand something which is not currently familiar in order to establish facts or generate new conclusions. In a disciplinary context this can be achieved through modelling physical scenarios and solving mathematical problems. Examples include trying to understand the flow behaviour of a thin film at a boundary interface or, in an educational context, seeking to understand why many undergraduate students within mathematics and engineering struggle to model and solve problems as they make the transition to university-level study.

Both of these examples constitute equally valid forms of enquiry and, if approached in a systematic manner, are legitimate forms of research. The modelling and problem-solving cycle of Figure 8.1 demonstrates the approach many engineers and mathematicians take to disciplinary enquiry, and this can be adapted to enable a systematic approach to educational enquiry within these same disciplines as shown in Figure 8.2.

Comparing Figures 8.1 and 8.2 reveals the strong similarity between the two cycles. Both consist of 'locations' (shown as bold ovals) that describe specific inputs or outputs, and 'stages' (dashed rectangular boxes) that describe specific processes undertaken. Not only can the overall approach for both disciplinary and educational enquiry be similar, the individual inputs and outputs can be both comparable. For example, the starting point for both cycles is the identification of some problem that requires further study or analysis, and their final output consists of some explanation or

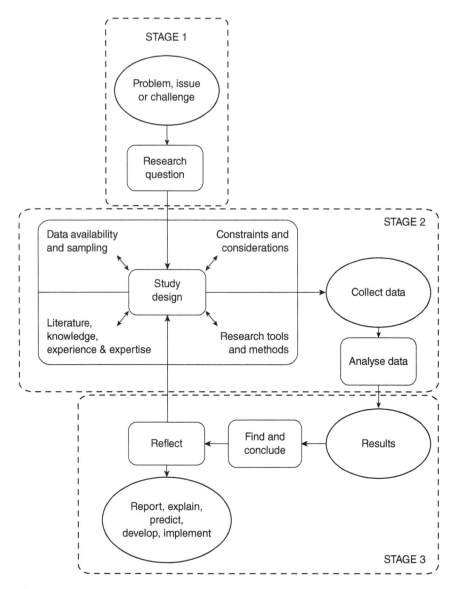

Figure 8.2   A complementary approach to educational enquiry cycle

increased understanding of this original problem or situation. A comparison of each 'stage' is shown in Figure 8.3.

Despite the potentially similar nature of the two cycles, translating the approach of modelling and problem solving to educational enquiry can be challenging as the skills of the researcher need to be applied in differing ways through what can initially appear quite different processes. For example, whereas both cycles involve formulating an approach or strategy towards

Stage	Disciplinary enquiry	Educational enquiry
1	**Establish the model:** Represent a physical situation in simplified terms but ensuring the essential features are retained.	**Define the research question:** Identify a specific question to focus the research undertaken and aid understanding of a particular situation or phenomena.
2	**Analyse the problem:** Formulate the problem as a series of mathematical expressions and work to establish a mathematical solution.	**Design study and collect data:** Identify and implement a methodology (qualitative, quantitative or mixed) to collect data and evidence to answer the research question including a piloting (and validation) phase for research tools and methods.
3	**Interpret and validate:** Explore the implications of the mathematical solution (in physical terms) and test validity. Refine and repeat as appropriate.	**Interpret and reflect:** Identify key findings from analysed data and generate conclusions. Reflect upon implications of findings and refine and repeat as appropriate.

Figure 8.3   A comparison of the stages of educational and disciplinary enquiry

understanding a problem that requires analysis, the nature of the assumptions, simplifications and how the problem can be represented will vary.

Consider, for example, if we were seeking to understand the spread of a communicable disease (such as influenza). We might reasonably commence our investigations by developing a model that divides the population into three distinct groupings: those who are susceptible to the disease, those who are infectious and can spread the disease to others, and those who have recovered from infection and can be assumed to be immune. We can then formulate differential equations that describe the numbers within each group and explore how they vary over time. Already it can be seen that this is a simplification: after all, it cannot be assumed for all diseases that, once individuals recover, they automatically become immune. Moreover, the transmission characteristics (that is, the number of secondary cases caused by one infectious individual within a susceptible population) of a disease may vary as a result of factors such as age, location or gender. While such a model may not be perfect, it allows us to identify potential infection patterns of a new strain of influenza.

Compare this with, for example, a study to determine how a department of mathematics or engineering might increase student engagement within a particular programme or module of study. While this might be a noble overall aim, multiple steps are required before changes can even be identified, let alone implemented. The first stage in tackling such a problem is to identify what we actually mean by 'student engagement', in itself a very broad area (for a wide-ranging discussion of this topic see Trowler, 2010). Adopting a broad approach will be time-consuming and perhaps not entirely appropriate for a single-discipline area, and so we may, quite reasonably, choose to reduce the problem to something more relevant in response to a specific issue or concern. For example, we may want to increase student engagement with formative problem or homework sheets within an introductory mathematics course. Equally, we may decide to concentrate upon a sub-set of the student cohort, for example male or female students or those arriving with non-traditional educational backgrounds. In effect, we have simplified our original problem to something that remains meaningful, but which is more manageable in our attempt to generate increased knowledge and understanding.

Before we can attempt to increase student engagement with formative mathematics problem sheets by trying a new approach, we need to understand why students do or do not engage with such learning opportunities. We need to develop an understanding of what we observe among the student cohort so that any subsequent intervention can be implemented in an evidence-informed manner. To do this, we design a study that collects data and evidence from the identified student cohort, and use this to develop evidence-informed ideas and hypotheses that can be tested with students to generate conclusions.

In both cases, we will have developed what might be a simplified model but one that has helped contribute to our increased understanding of the original problem. There may be further work to be done, but we can now develop these initial models by incorporating other factors (refinement) in order to make them more representative of the real-world situation or problem. In developing this comparison, we have stumbled upon two important aspects of educational research that require explicit consideration: defining a research question and designing a research study.

The nature of evidence

In mathematics we are usually very clear about the nature of the mathematical object or problem being studied. For example, a theorem is a mathematical statement that has been proved beyond all doubt using vigorous mathematical reasoning, and an axiom (such as one of Euclid's five postulates) is assumed to be true without proof and forms the foundation upon which all theorems are based. While we may first have to construct a model in mathematics and engineering to describe a particular physical situation or phenomenon, we typically do so in a manner that allows it to be presented in mathematical terms. This involves applying mathematical theorems and identities to form a series of equations, which we then strive to solve using a range of mathematical and computational methods.

Within educational enquiry, the situations being considered will usually be less well defined; they may be imprecise and far more ambiguous. The primary reason for such ambiguity arises out of the nature of the phenomena being studied. In educational research we will typically be studying social phenomena rather than physical phenomena and, further, we are studying the behaviour of individuals and how they react and respond to different situations and stimuli. Even when individuals are exposed to exactly the same situation, they may respond in differing ways based upon individual perceptions and prior experiences. As such, it should not be surprising that the factors affecting student engagement with problem sheets, for example, can be very different even across two cohorts within the same institution that may at first appear to be very similar.

While it is not surprising that individuals react in differing ways to an identical situation, this is wholly different to what we might expect when we solve (correctly) a series of identical mathematical equations which are solved in a uniform way. Here we would expect two different individuals, from differing locations and mathematical backgrounds to obtain identical, or at the very least mathematically equivalent results; any variation from this would challenge the very nature of mathematical proof and logic.

The variability encountered when undertaking educational enquiry can be uncomfortable for many mathematicians and engineers, leading to questions regarding the validity and reliability of the evidence that has been collected. However, as Figure 8.1 shows, solving a mathematical problem, using a set of well-defined processes and rules that build upon fundamental theorems, is not always the starting point; in engineering and mathematics we often have to first develop a model that translates a physical problem or situation into mathematical terms. In developing a model of the same physical situation, two individuals may make quite different assumptions or include different parameters and boundary conditions so that when the resulting mathematical model is solved the outcomes can be very different just as in educational research.

Let us return to the model developed by Galileo for a gravity pendulum. The time period (T) can be described mathematically in terms of its length (L) on the assumption that its maximum angle of displacement from the vertical (amplitude) θ_0 is small:

$$T \approx 2\pi\sqrt{\frac{L}{G}} \text{ assuming } \theta_0 \ll 1$$

This result tells us that the period of oscillation is independent of amplitude, and this is the reason pendulums are very effective timekeepers. However, such a model is ideal and can be refined in many ways to create a description that is more representative of what is observed within the real world (Nelson and Olsson, 1986). For example, correcting for larger amplitudes yields:

$$T = 2\pi\sqrt{\frac{L}{G}}\left(1 + \frac{1}{16}\theta_0^2 + \frac{11}{3072}\theta_0^4 + \dots\right).$$

Whereas we are quite happy to accept either of these results, we do so on the basis that we understand how they were obtained and more particularly the circumstances under which they remain valid. In this vein, if we consider educational enquiry on the basis that the initial model upon which the study is based may be different, we can be more accepting of some of the generalisations and conclusions that are reached.

A further issue often encountered when considering the outcomes from educational enquiry is not the issue of variability but of replicability. Solving the same mathematical problem correctly on multiple occasions should yield identical solutions; yet repeating the same educational study, even with the same group of individuals, can result in different conclusions. Again, such an outcome might appear to go against our disciplinary training, yet in engineering there are many results that cannot be readily replicated, both in theory and practice. For example, chaos theory considers the behaviour of dynamical systems, an area where small differences in the initial conditions of a system can lead to drastically different outcomes, thereby making long-term prediction and generalisation impossible.

Perhaps one of the flaws in the reporting of some educational research is that the models applied, and in particular the assumptions made, when the research approach was designed are not always made explicit to the reader. For example, a sample can be stated to be representative of a population when the reasons for such a significant generalisation are not always clear. The disciplinary training of mathematicians and engineers makes us well placed to make a meaningful contribution to educational enquiry by questioning the data and evidence presented and, when undertaking enquiry ourselves, by being explicitly clear about the validity of our models and assertions and the circumstances upon which results can be more widely generalised.

From problems to research questions

Before introducing the idea, and importance, of a research question as a starting point in educational enquiry, we first need to consider what we mean by a 'problem' be it real-world or mathematical. In both disciplinary and educational enquiry, a problem has many parallels. For example, we are not considering something that might be regarded as routine where the solution can be easily determined from a textbook or internet search; instead, we are seeking to generate new understanding, insight or knowledge to explain a specific phenomenon or situation.

In mathematics or engineering this does not necessarily have to mean developing a new theorem or proof, but could involve applying mathematics in a new context, for example, optimising the efficiency of a production process within an industrial organisation. Such a problem may have already been solved elsewhere previously, perhaps in a different company, but within the context of the industrial organisation now being considered this problem is new. Similarly for educational enquiry, we might be seeking to understand the local context (institutional) of a national phenomenon, for example student perceptions of the study of engineering at university.

Once we have identified a problem, we need to formulate this as a research question to help focus the line of enquiry that a study will follow. A research question is a vital fundamental first step in educational enquiry as it makes clear exactly what the study will attempt to explore, determine or learn about a particular phenomenon. It helps narrow the focus of the research to something that is achievable but still meaningful in the context of the original problem (consider the example of student engagement above), and perhaps most significantly, guides the structure, approach and data collection of the subsequent study.

Writing a research question can often be the most challenging aspect of designing an educational study, but there are some general principles that can be applied to aid this process that are valid for any form of enquiry. The research question should be *clear* in the sense that what is being asked is understood by both yourself, as well as other researchers in the area. It needs to be not only *focused* and *well defined* to ensure it is neither too broad nor narrow, but also to be *researchable* which requires the question to have an answer that can be obtained through the collection of data and evidence. This last point should not be taken to imply that a research question must always be 'answerable'. There are many mathematical and educational problems for which we continue to seek solutions, but a research question must be posed in such a way that we can make a meaningful attempt at answering it and in a manner that hopefully moves the collective knowledge base of the subject area forward.

Fortunately, mathematics and engineering as disciplines are not only about solving problems, but identifying and posing questions about problems in a way that helps make them solvable. They are also disciplines where precise and logical statements are made to provide clarity and avoid ambiguity. Applying a mathematical or scientific way of thinking to writing a research question is therefore highly beneficial as it enables the researcher to examine what might be a complex situation, identify the essential features upon which to focus, and determine the key questions that need to be asked. In doing so it helps simplify the original situation and reduces the approach to one that still allows the original problem to be explored in a meaningful way.

Consider Figure 8.4 which compares the research questions that might arise for a particular problem in both educational and mathematical enquiry.

Notice in both instances how the research question can be made more sophisticated to provide a greater understanding of the original problem, but in doing so, the complexity of the processes to collect data, evidence or seek mathematical solutions also increases, which has implications in terms of time and overall feasibility. Similarly, considering each research question in turn provides incremental progress towards what might be considered the 'ultimate outcome' and increases our understanding of the original problem. In the case of Fermat's Last Theorem these incremental steps were essential for Andrew Wiles' proof (1995).

The educational research questions outlined in Figure 8.4 are not without their issues. For example, what do we mean by 'interesting and enjoyable' or 'more likely'? However, this is not the problem it might seem, as we can apply another mathematical approach by *defining* precisely what we mean in each instance to ensure an unambiguous description. For example, 'more likely' might be defined as 'a probability greater than the overall national mean for students of an equivalent age'.

Formulating a research question is analogous to the first step (*understand the problem*) of Pólya's four-stage process for solving mathematical problems. In order to solve a problem, we firstly need to understand it, identify the relevant questions that need to be asked, and determine the information we need to solve it. Mathematics can also provide an alternative approach to educational enquiry which involves replacing the research question with a hypothesis, a statement that can be tested to determine if

	Disciplinary enquiry (Mathematics)	Educational enquiry (Outreach Interventions)
Problem	Fermat's Last Theorem	What is the impact of university-led interactions on the local school-age students who attend and participate in them?
Starting point ↓ Ultimate objective	Does it hold for $n = 3$? Euler's flawed proof for this case.	Did the school students have an interesting and enjoyable day?
	Special cases resolved by Sophie Germain and others.	How have the activities changed school student perceptions of STEM subjects and STEM study?
	Is there a link with elliptic curves? Shimura–Taniyama–Weil Conjecture	Are school students who attend outreach days more likely to study STEM disciplines in HE – do these activities have a causal effect?
	Can STW conjecture be resolved? During 1993–95 Wiles, after a few nervous moments, completes the proof.	What are the optimal interventions needed to encourage school and college students to progress to STEM subjects in HE?

Figure 8.4 Disciplinary and educational research questions

it is true, or perhaps even a conjecture, a statement which is unproven but which is believed to be true. For example, in the case of our outreach problem in Figure 8.4 our hypothesis might be: *School students who attend three or more outreach events in a six-month period are 25 per cent more likely to go on to study the STEM disciplines at university-level.* Once we have identified a research question or hypothesis we then need to go on and design studies that allow them to be tested and explored.

Developing and refining the model

Designing an educational study can have many parallels with developing a mathematical model. In both cases we can plan an approach that enables the original problem to be analysed and understood in a rigorous and scientific manner. In mathematics and engineering the model presents the physical situation in mathematical terms which can then be solved, whereas in educational enquiry a study methodology is designed which describes the data and evidence to be collected, the collection methods to be used, and how it will be analysed. In educational enquiry, a researcher will usually engage with all stages of the cycle (Figure 8.2), whereas in mathematics and engineering, we might have a problem that is already presented in mathematical terms and so Stage 1 (Figure 8.1), which involves designing the model, will be omitted entirely.

In developing a mathematical model of a physical situation, the researcher will include a range of inputs to inform its development. For example, there may be constraints, such as limits on the overall dimensions of a racing car or civic responsibilities when designing a building or bridge that will result in boundary conditions being applied to the model, and assumptions will be made to simplify the model to focus only upon the essential features of the problem. In educational enquiry, the problem may also be simplified and restricted to a narrower focus. For example, in trying to understand why some undergraduates struggle with problem solving, only engineering students might be considered and the population for the study restricted to such students in their first year of study within the UK. In both disciplinary and educational enquiry this then has implications for the generalisations or conclusions that can be made. Just as our mathematical model might only be valid under a specific set of conditions, for example at low velocities, so too if a study's sample population is restricted to first-year engineering students within the UK then the findings cannot be generalised to include first-year students on undergraduate physics majors within the United States.

In developing both a mathematical model and an educational study, the researcher will incorporate a range of knowledge and experiences generated by both themselves and others through prior activity. For example, the well-understood (exponential) model of radioactive decay might be modified to understand how a radionuclide behaves within the human body when it is administered during a medical treatment. Similarly, the methodologies used to collect data for an educational study in mathematics could be adapted from those that might have been used previously when investigating problem solving in chemistry. Such information will be gathered from a range of sources including other colleagues, research literature, of which a wide range is available in education, and experimental or prior studies. The following journals may provide you with a good starting point: *Engineering Education*; the *Journal of Engineering Education*; *Educational Studies in Mathematics* and *Research in Mathematics Education*. In both forms of enquiry, the researcher will first need to apply their skills to understand the nature of this information and use their judgement to determine its appropriateness for use within their studies, particularly in terms of its validity and reliability.

Mathematics and engineering are disciplines where researchers regularly question findings and conclusions to ascertain that they are robust and reasonable and, as such, researchers are well placed to apply this approach to educational enquiry. The importance of prior experience should also not be underestimated; mathematical modelling relies upon using prior experiences and judgements, for example in terms of deciding upon the assumptions that might be regarded as reasonable in order for a model to remain valid under a variety of conditions. While mathematicians and engineers might initially be uncomfortable with some of the approaches used in educational enquiry, through engaging with this as a field of study we can build our familiarity and begin to tackle ever more challenging problems; after all, this is not too different to how we approach our disciplinary enquiry. All mathematicians and engineers will have a fundamental training in calculus, yet when we first started out the integral of In x would have been a challenge; now, such a task is routine and has long been superseded by more challenging problems. We learn mathematics by doing mathematics, and similarly we can only gain fluency and familiarity in educational enquiry by reading about it and attempting it for ourselves.

One key difference that you may encounter when reading the educational literature is that an educational study is likely to be developed around two key research approaches: qualitative and quantitative methods, or a combination of both (see Creswell, 2008 and Chapter 2 in this text for a more in-depth discussion of these approaches). Briefly, quantitative research uses numbers and statistical methods to explore phenomena and test causal links and hypotheses with a view to obtaining an unbiased result from a sample that can be generalised to a larger population. In contrast, qualitative research captures words, images, observations and artefacts and their associated meanings as data, and provides interpretations of situations including the 'why?' and 'how?' of human behaviour; its focus is often upon a smaller number of cases and provides significant amounts of contextual information that can enrich a study.

As mathematicians and engineers we are entirely comfortable handling numerical information, and will naturally favour a quantitative approach to collecting and interpreting data. Furthermore, we will have typically received some prior form of statistical training either in a theoretical or experimental context and, failing that, we possess the mathematical skills to understand and apply a range of statistical methods and approaches to analyse and interrogate data. Many mathematicians and engineers, perhaps even the majority, are sceptical of qualitative approaches when they first begin to read the educational enquiry literature. However, qualitative research is an important methodology as it enables us to not only understand the reasons behind decisions and events, but is also often an important and essential precursor for designing a quantitative study.

To consider the importance of qualitative research, and why it is important not to dismiss it out of hand, let us return to our example of student engagement with formative problem sheets where our study focuses on a population that consists of first-year male engineering students from research-intensive UK universities. The hypothesis generated for the study might be: '*Less mathematically able male students don't engage with formative problem sheets until after the results from mid-semester assessment*', and while there is a need to clarify what we mean by 'less mathematically able' and 'engage', we ourselves can define these, and as such it represents a hypothesis that can be reasonably tested. But how might such a population and hypothesis have been decided upon? It is likely that the researcher will have formulated these from their own observations, experience of teaching, monitoring student homework submissions, or talking with students and other colleagues. Identifying this information involves dialogue, interviews, and observations; qualitative data has been captured and interpreted even if it is perhaps anecdotal, and has been incorporated into the design of the study.

In this context, formulating such a qualitative approach is similar in nature to the conversations we have with other colleagues about how we define and approach mathematical problems that then influence the ongoing revision of our models and ideas. For example, consider the problem that was posed to Pascal and Fermat around 1654 relating to the division of a stake between two players whose game was interrupted before it concluded. The resulting correspondence between the two (see Tannery and Henry, 1894) was fundamental in establishing what we now know as probability. Similarly, much as the results of computer simulations or experiments can inform the ongoing development of mathematical models, qualitative research can inform the overall direction of a study enabling rich data to be obtained that would not have otherwise been captured.

Case Study 8.1   Improving the mathematical modelling and problem solving skills of undergraduate STEM students

In 2010, the UK National HE STEM Programme established a project led by the School of Physics and Astronomy at the University of Leeds aimed at improving the mathematical modelling and problem solving skills of undergraduate STEM students as they make the transition to university study. In total the project involved 13 departments within 6 higher education institutions which each implemented an individually tailored approach relevant to their disciplinary area and needs of their institutions, but within a common framework. The project undertook a rigorous research-based evaluation (undertaken by the School of Education at the University of Manchester) aimed at demonstrating not only the impact of the intervention but also providing evidence-based feedback on how interventions might be developed in the future.

The first stage of the evaluation was to understand the aims of the intervention being developed. Discussion with the project lead and an analysis of the literature helped to identify the research questions which focused around the extent to which the (Leeds physics) students experiencing the intervention were, and might be, brought to genuinely solve problems using mathematical modelling, and as a consequence become (more) aware of modelling as a process.

The research study was designed and undertaken using both qualitative and quantitative methodologies. The intervention was studied in a quasi-ethnographic manner (qualitative methodologies to explore cultural phenomena) and informed by course documents, observations during teaching sessions on several occasions, examination of student coursework relative to learning objectives, and cross-checking of observation findings with interviews from five students and the project lead. Two instruments were designed, one building upon previous work, to measure the learning outcomes of students as a result of the interventions in a way that would enable comparisons to be made between disciplines and institutions. For the first, a Likert-type questionnaire instrument was constructed as a measure of 'disposition towards mathematical modelling and problem solving' (a measure of how positive the students feel about mathematical modelling and problem solving). The other instrument was labelled an 'awareness of mathematical modelling and problem solving' (in effect a measure of how aware the students are regarding the processes that the literature states are involved in true mathematical modelling and problem solving). Each instrument was validated, with the first being identified as a reliable and valid measure, while the latter, although promising, was identified as needing more substantial development.

A project report is available online (Pampaka and Williams, 2012) but perhaps the most significant point to note from this work is that despite using a quantitative approach with the development of research instruments, they acknowledge that the most important evaluation evidence has so far proved to be qualitative in nature.

Applying your disciplinary skills to data analysis

After collecting data from an educational study, it needs to be analysed. This is the equivalent of obtaining a mathematical solution for our problem having applied Pólya's four-stage process if needed. To aid the data analysis process, data from an educational study are usually sorted and coded. Coding condenses an extensive data set into a series of smaller units that are more easily analysed by organising it into categories and concepts derived from the obtained data. It is approached in a systematic manner and allows data to be presented in a form that allows analysis by computer software such as SPSS or NVivo. When analysing qualitative data obtained from the study of student approaches to problem solving, one of the categories might be where students make *assumptions*, another might be where they make *estimations*. However, it is important, when undertaking such 'inductive' analysis, that you do not make predictions or assumptions and that any coding emerges from the data you have collected. As mathematicians and engineers you will be skilled in spotting trends and patterns in data, and this will stand you in good stead when analysing and categorising data from both qualitative and quantitative studies.

 Activity 8.1   Planning your educational enquiry project in maths and engineering

Try asking yourself, and then answering, the following questions. Keep closely to the word limits to help focus and sharpen your thoughts. You may find them helpful when communicating your ideas to others, seeking

(Continued)

(Continued)

to develop collaborations, or looking for potential funding sources to support your educational enquiry:

- The problem or situation I am interested in exploring is ... [50 words]
- The particular aspects of this which interest me are ... [50 words]
- The authors/individuals/organisations who have previously explored this area are ... [30 words]
- They have found or concluded that ... [50 words] and have identified that further work is required on ... [50 words]
- The contribution I might make to advancing understanding of this area is ... [50 words]
- My research question or hypothesis might be ... [50 words]
- The population is ... [20 words] and the sample ... [20 words]
- The methodologies I might use are ... [50 words] and will allow me to collect the following data and evidence ... [50 words]
- Others I can talk to about my ideas include ... [50 words]
- My timeline for progressing this study is ... [10 words]

Concluding thoughts

Mathematicians and engineers are, on the whole, comfortable tackling interdisciplinary or applied problems, and when undertaking this analysis, will rarely do so in isolation. We routinely collaborate with other academic colleagues and research students within our disciplinary areas to define, discuss and explore problems. Given this (and the nature of the disciplines) it is perhaps unsurprising that mathematicians and engineers are increasingly involved in tackling global problems and challenges, for example in relation to health, infrastructure, and the environment, and do so in conjunction with those from other disciplines. As a consequence, new research groups have developed in areas such as mathematical biology and environmental mathematics. Working with others is a core part of our disciplinary nature, and while undertaking educational research for the first time can be daunting, we are sure you will find it far less so if it takes place in conjunction with colleagues who are more experienced in this area.

Mathematicians and engineers bring a wide range of experiences, perspectives and skills to educational enquiry, and as such, our participation is widely welcomed by those from other disciplines. The first step is for us to make a start on a journey of disciplinary enquiry and see just how well our skills and knowledge translate.

Suggested further reading

Brown, G. and Edmunds, S. (2011) *Doing Pedagogical Research in Engineering.* Edited by A. Crawford and J. Dickens. Loughborough: Engineering Centre for Excellence in Teaching and Learning (engCETL), Loughborough University.

Schonfeld, A.H. (2000) *Purposes and Methods of Research in Mathematics Education*, Notices of the AMS, June/July 2000 pp. 641–649. [online]: http://www.ams.org/notices/200006/fea-schoenfeld.pdf [Accessed 21 August 2013].

The American Statistical Association (2007) *Using Statistics Effectively in Mathematics Education Research: A report from a series of workshops organized by the American Statistical Association with funding from the National Science Foundation.* [online]: http://www.amstat.org/education/pdfs/UsingStatisticsEffectivelyin-MathEdResearch.pdf [Accessed 21 August 2013].

CHAPTER 9

ENQUIRY INTO LEARNING AND TEACHING IN THE LIFE SCIENCES

Helen Barefoot and Mark Russell

Learning outcomes

By the conclusion of this chapter it is anticipated that you will:

- Recognise the benefits of undertaking educational enquiry within the life sciences;
- Have reflected on potential barriers to, and enablers for, educational enquiry within the life sciences context; and
- Be ready to plan your own educational enquiry within the life sciences.

Introduction

This chapter is timely as the teaching of science is currently under analysis globally. In 2012 the UK House of Lords Science and Technology Select Committee conducted an inquiry into Higher Education STEM subjects (Science, Technology, Engineering and Mathematics; see Science and Technology Committee, 2012) and in 2011 the American Society for the Advancement of Science set out a call to action in terms of the need for vision and change in biology undergraduate education (Brewer and Smith, 2011). The call recognises a need for teaching methods and curricula to become more student-centred with greater reference to, and reflection of, current biological research.

Many life science academics identify themselves as researchers within their discipline. Their educational training, their interests and their current roles (including targets associated with research output and grant funding) reinforce this sense of identity. In this context, educational enquiry may seem like an unnecessary requirement; an additional burden, or someone else's responsibility. However, in this chapter we argue that the skills and expertise associated with your own disciplinary research have the potential to be used for educational enquiry resulting in both greater enjoyment in teaching and improved learning experiences for students.

One of the aims of the UK Professional Standards Framework for Teaching and Supporting Learning in Higher Education (the UKPSF; see HEA, 2011) is to 'Demonstrate to students and other stakeholders the professionalism that staff and institutions bring to teaching and support for student learning'. Within each aspect of the UKPSF (areas of activity, core knowledge and professional values) there is reference to the importance of engaging with (and by implication, of undertaking) research into and evaluation of learning and teaching practices. This indicates that it is every academic's responsibility to develop and evaluate their academic activities so that they understand the effects of teaching on student learning.

Educational enquiry is often thought of as an activity which takes place within the realms of social sciences, and although some life scientists may be familiar with methods of research associated with social sciences (e.g. those from psychological and anthropological study backgrounds) for many, they are likely to appear less familiar. In contrast, in this chapter we argue that many of the ways of thinking about research and the methods of investigation and application used within the life sciences are also relevant for educational enquiry. For example, approaches to research within education, many of which may initially appear different to those in the life sciences, will in fact include considerations of validity and objectivity (Medawar, 1977).

We argue that if we acknowledge and understand the synergies between discipline-specific research and educational enquiry, many life science researchers may feel more encouraged and confident to research and evaluate their teaching and students' learning. To this end, we consider aspects of the scientific research process from the identification of a

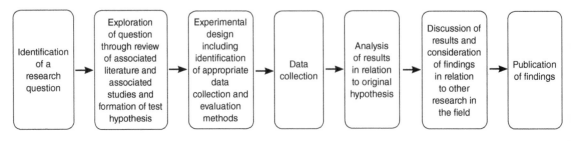

Figure 9.1   The scientific research process

research question and applying for funding to the publication of findings (see Figure 9.1) and discuss how this very familiar process translates into educational enquiry activities. In addition, we point to some of the possible limitations of narrowly applying a 'life sciences' approach to educational enquiry and explore some of the ways in which you might, with time, wish to take your own approaches to educational enquiry forward.

Life sciences research and educational enquiry: a comparison

If we compare the scientific research process as set out in Figure 9.1 to Glassick et al.s' (1997) suggestion that learning and teaching scholarship should demonstrate the following standards – clear goals; adequate preparation; appropriate methods; significant results; effective presentation and reflective critique – we can immediately see that there is not a great deal of difference between the scientific enquiry process and that of educational enquiry. In short, a clear hypothesis, appropriate methods for data collection and analysis, consideration and presentation of results are all crucial within both spheres. As such, there is certainly no reason why educational enquiry should not be held accountable to expectations of rigour and reliability in the same way that traditional scientific studies are. What may be less familiar to you are some of the different interpretations and constructions of rigour and reliability that underpin some aspects of more interpretivist educational enquiry (an issue which is explored in Chapter 2 of this volume).

What are the origins of an enquiry project?

If we consider the process in more detail, educational enquiry within the life sciences, as with much other life sciences research, is often stimulated by a specific issue that has arisen or been observed or an idea which theoretically may provide answers to, or developments in, our understanding of a phenomenon. In the world of education this could be, for example:

- Reductions in interactions in class created by increased student numbers;
- Diverse student needs within a single classroom setting;

- Limited contact time between staff and students;
- Reduced attendance at lectures;
- A lack of engagement in study activity outside of class;
- Difficulties in assessing and/or providing 'satisfactory' feedback.

The clear goal of the enquiry – the research question, and its expected outcomes – will, as with your own disciplinary research, be dependent on the identified challenge and associated questions that arise.

Can I use familiar methods?

The nature of any enquiry or intervention (to be evaluated) will, of course, be dependent on the particular research questions posed, but many educational enquiry projects can usefully include quantitative methods such as comparisons of student performance values (comparing means and standard deviations of exam or coursework grades) and an analysis of scores from student feedback questionnaires (see also Chapter 5 of this text). This quantitative approach is one that you may feel more comfortable with adopting as it broadly aligns to methods that you will be familiar with using in the life sciences: observing and measuring change before and after an intervention and looking for statistically significant results that can be reported on. Further examples of this process in action are provided in Case Studies 9.1 and 9.2 presented later in the chapter.

One immediate challenge that you may encounter if you employ the more quantitative data collection and analysis approaches outlined above, relates to the difficulty of undertaking research with matched control groups and the difficulty of accounting for uncontrollable variables when studying any development, change or intervention in learning and teaching (see Chapter 5 of this text for further discussion). However, these are certainly not reasons enough to avoid educational enquiry. As Dolan (2007) points out in our own subject discipline, ecologists and evolutionary biologists often study phenomena which they are unable to control or predict and for which they are unable to characterise all the variables involved. This is arguably very similar to research in learning situations in which student cohorts vary, staff members change and curricula can evolve during the time of study. Indeed, a discussion of these changing learning contexts and variables can act to enhance and enrich, rather than detract from, any educational enquiry findings as they help to develop the validity of the enquiry.

In this world of uncertainty, a more qualitative approach to enquiry may prove useful. Qualitative methods can help you to explore *why* things are occurring in your practice in the context in which a problem or something you have observed has occurred; something that may be more difficult if you are simply measuring trends in performance or student satisfaction scores. In exploring the use of open statements on student questionnaires or data gathered from unstructured or semi-structured techniques such as individual in-depth interviews or focus group discussions, you will be able to develop ideas and hypotheses *inductively* as the research unfolds. This can, for example, involve exploring trends in opinions and perceptions using a thematic approach to the analysis of qualitative data (see Elgie et al., 2012). O'Loughlin (2006) also suggests examples such as considering if the complexity of student writing has increased, or reflecting on whether a greater frequency of students asking higher-order learning questions occurs during or following an intervention. Qualitative analysis of an intervention may not be limited to student opinion and could also take into account staff attitudes, for example to find out about the ease of implementation, the degree of effort required, the ease of transference to other modules etcetera.

How do I assess the field and prepare for dissemination?

Similar to your normal disciplinary practices, in preparation for any educational enquiry work, it is useful to review the practice of others. However, you may feel uncertain about how to search for relevant literature in an unknown field, when over 20,000 education enquiry articles are published each year (Mosteller et al., 2004), and which educational conferences to attend. We would recommend that you start with specific life science education conferences and events such as the UK Higher Education Academy's (HEA) workshops in the biological sciences, and focus initially on pedagogic literature published in discipline specific journals (some examples include *Bioscience Education, Advances in Physiology Education, Journal of College Science Teaching, Biochemistry and Molecular Biology Education*). Journal articles and presentations not only provide results and evaluation of others' studies but also often present clear guidance on how to implement new teaching or assessment activities; something that is particularly useful if you are planning to implement a new teaching and learning initiative within your own context and wish to avoid reinventing a few wheels.

Reading these articles and attending these events will also provide you with the experience and confidence to disseminate your own educational enquiry work to others. Further insight is offered by Michael (2006) who provides specific guidance for publishing life science education research, and lists a number of things that should be reported when submitting for publication (none of which should look particularly surprising to you as they equate to similar types of information that you might be required to discuss in a disciplinary research paper):

1. Clear indication of the hypothesis being tested;
2. Characteristics of the student population involved in the study;
3. Characteristics of the course in which the intervention took place;
4. The nature of the intervention and methods of 'control';
5. Outcomes that occurred as a result of the intervention.

Can I get funding for educational enquiry?

Although grants for educational research may not be as large as some discipline-specific research grants, opportunities do exist to apply for grant funding for life science-focused educational enquiry projects. For example, the Higher Education Academy in the UK will award over £1.5 million for teaching development funds throughout 2012–13 (HEA, 2013b) and the Joint Information Systems Committee (JISC) awarded £5.4 million for technology related projects in 2011 (JISC, 2011). Within the life sciences there are numerous opportunities for discipline-related pedagogic education with past research funding including individual awards from the American Society for Plant Biology (2012) (up to $30,000) and the UK STEM project funding from the Higher Education Academy (HEA STEM, 2012) of grants up to £30,000. Many institutions also have learning- and teaching-related funding for small-scale projects to enhance teaching.

It is worth noting that due to the fact that most educational enquiry grants fund development work that will be of direct benefit to an academic's institution, many external awards in this field do not cover full economic costs and often require institutions to commit to some form of 'match-funding' for the grant (although very rarely do they require 100 per cent match funding). Match funding, in these circumstances, is often recorded as academic 'time commitment' to a project (funding in kind). Gaining permission to apply for educational funding may be challenging for you if your own institution is not supportive of this type of research and committing academic time to it.

Knowing how, where and when to apply for funding can also be an initial barrier for those new to life sciences education research. As with any grant application knowing what is available and when to apply is imperative. We would recommend that your first port of call is your institutional Educational or Academic Development team, who will be aware of the various funding opportunities currently available. You could also talk to your HEA subject lead regarding areas of interest that have funding available and you could contact colleagues who have published funded work to ask how they got started. However, we would stress that your existing skills of putting together research grant applications will stand you in very good stead in relation to any educational enquiry applications that you make.

What if there is no culture of learning and teaching research in my institution?

In some HEIs, particularly those with a significant strategic research focus, a culture for learning and teaching research may not be well established. With research targets associated with high impact publications and grant awards, academic staff may need to, or feel they will only be rewarded if they focus time and energy on discipline-specific research activity. Without a culture of educational enquiry it is difficult for individual staff members to initiate projects and allocate time to learning and teaching research. An option here is to play the numbers game; connect with other staff in a similar position to work together to create a critical mass. Organise workshops or meetings to discuss teaching issues and devise ways of addressing them. Heads of departments are increasingly under pressure to meet teaching-related targets and an offer of a specific project that will help meet one of those metrics may be what is needed to get learning and teaching on the map. Again your educational or academic development team may be able to connect you up with like-minded colleagues who wish to explore, or are already exploring, similar issues to you.

Following on from the point above, if there is no culture of learning and teaching research, individuals who do engage in educational research may feel undervalued compared to those engaging in discipline-specific research and may also be hindered if there are no reward and recognition routes associated with learning and teaching practices. A recent Higher Education Academy (HEA) publication on reward and recognition (HEA and Genetics Education Networking for Innovation and Excellence, 2009) demonstrated that most academics feel that teaching and learning is undervalued and that promotion criteria which include learning and teaching are often inconsistent, absent or not always implemented in contrast to those around research (see also Ramsden and Martin, 1996; Parker, 2008).

However, there is some evidence that progress is being made regarding the reward and recognition of staff engaging in educational enquiry (Chalmers, 2011; Vardi and Quin, 2011), and in recent years a number of institutions have developed clear progression routes for staff engaging in research in learning and teaching. Furthermore, many students' unions in the UK are now implementing student-led teaching awards to complement those also offered by institutions. Within the life sciences, external recognition is also available via the UK's Society for Biology's Bioscience Teacher of the Year award, which recognises outstanding learning and teaching practice and the BioSciEdNet Scholar scheme in the United States.

Even if your own institution is not one of the more 'progressive' ones in this respect, all is certainly not lost. The current UK interest in league tables, and your own institution's position within these, may prove helpful here. Measures such as teaching quality scores and National Student Survey (NSS) satisfaction scores form part of many league table calculations and can make a big difference as to where your institution sits. The recent increase in the fees students pay in the UK has also shifted focus to the quality of teaching, perhaps as never before. In this context, expectations about developing teaching in an evidence-based manner are growing and the opportunity to win external funding to support teaching projects can only help in moving educational enquiry into the mainstream of your department's activities.

Ethical approval

As explored in Chapter 4, educational enquiry typically involves human participants and this brings with it a whole new set of ethical considerations for many life science academics who are used to undertaking experiments involving animals, plants or non-living organisms. Some institutions may have ethical protocols which cover reflective practitioner developmental work or projects, recognising that as a part of good academic practice. Depending on the nature of your enquiry, your study may be covered by such protocols; however, specific ethical approval may also be needed. You will need to make an informed judgement, depending on the focus of your study, in order to determine the type of ethical approval required and apply for it in accordance with your institution's regulations and protocols. Remember that you are not alone. If you are unsure of where to begin then perhaps you could approach a colleague with experience of working with human participants from within the life sciences or a cognate area (in psychology or nursing perhaps) to discuss your ideas and gain confidence in applying for ethical approval.

Some benefits of undertaking education enquiry in the life sciences

We hope you have already begun to see some of the key similarities between your own current disciplinary research practices and those associated with educational enquiry. While you may encounter a few obstacles along the way (for example, unfamiliar research practices) we hope that these are eclipsed by some of the benefits and rewards of undertaking educational enquiry, not only in terms of improving the student learning experience, but also for the development of your own teaching practice.

Enhancements in student experiences, skills and performance

Chickering and Gamson (1987) identify 'faculty and student contact' as one of their seven principles of good practice in undergraduate education. Engaging in educational enquiry provides an ideal opportunity to work directly with students on developing their learning experiences. Many educational enquiry projects involve student feedback and discussion via focus groups or individual interviews. Directly involving students in research, and in some cases as co-researchers, demonstrates to them the importance of educational research and provides insight into research processes, curriculum development processes and how learning, teaching and assessment activities can be enhanced through evidence-based enquiry. Within life science disciplines the inclusion of students in educational research may also introduce them to qualitative approaches to research which may not have been explored within disciplinary modules on research methods. The process of educational enquiry can provide opportunities for staff members and students to work together and can model the kind of collaborative working that is an important skill in itself for a life scientist. This, alongside an opportunity to be involved in research and curriculum development first-hand, may also help you and your students to meet some of the key requirements of your professional, statutory and regulatory body (PSRB). For example, healthcare science and biomedical science students must demonstrate an awareness of a range of research methodologies, and are required to reflect critically on their performance and practice in order to meet the requirements of the Health and Care Professions Council (HCPC) and the Institute of Biomedical Science (IBMS).

Whether educational enquiry in the life sciences is related to assessment (Falchikov and Goldfinch, 2000), classroom or laboratory activities (Gliddon and Rosengren, 2012) or careers development (Willmott, 2011) the ultimate aim is to enhance the student learning experience. Developing and then evaluating teaching strategies and initiatives within the life sciences which result in improved student understanding and student performance is extremely rewarding for the educator and can of course be directly beneficial for the students.

Opportunities for collaboration

Educational enquiry with the life sciences presents opportunities for collaboration within and beyond the discipline. At the classroom level, Allen and Tanner (2005) consider the benefits of co-teaching including peer feedback and the time to discuss and deconstruct what happened during a teaching session. Attending internal and external teaching and learning events, such as the American Society of Cell Biology and the Society of Experimental Biology's annual education events, can provide you with opportunities to share with and learn from colleagues who are also undertaking educational enquiry within life science disciplines. Such meetings will not only help to stimulates ideas and identify 'hot topics', but may also lead to collaborative projects and bids to funding bodies.

One key benefit associated with undertaking educational enquiry is that collaboration may, and often does, occur beyond the discipline. Consideration of teaching and assessment methods within life sciences may be compared with teaching and assessment methods within other disciplines, resulting in new ideas and a shared understanding. This can further lead to opportunities to build on the research expertise of others (perhaps qualitative?) which can, in turn, help to overcome the need for you, or your students, to learn a whole new set of research skills. Working with these colleagues or peers, and recognising their understandings of and approaches to research, will in itself be developmental for both yourself and your students.

Examples of educational enquiry in practice

To place our discussion so far into context, Case Studies 9.1, 9.2 and 9.3 demonstrate some different approaches to educational enquiry within the life sciences. We hope, through these, to provide you with some real examples of how life scientists have begun to engage in educational enquiry.

Case Study 9.1   Peer assessment and laboratory reports (Barefoot et al., 2011)

The laboratory report is a widely accepted and commonly used assignment within the life sciences to assess students' understanding of experimental results and scientific writing ability (QAA, 2007a). Despite writing a number of laboratory reports throughout the first year, bioscience students were not demonstrating improved performance on subsequent laboratory reports. The research asked whether peer assessment could support student learning as evidenced in improved performance on subsequent laboratory report assignments. The interest in peer assessment as a potential solution was stimulated by attendance at an HEA Bioscience Subject Centre event where this approach was discussed. Consideration of the benefits of peer assessment both at the event and subsequently through the review of relevant literature provided a research-informed approach to the problem and ideas about how to implement the change.

Since 2007–08 at the University of Hertfordshire, peer assessment of a laboratory report has been carried out within a large 30 credit-point first-year module taken by all biology students (between 140 and 225 each year). As well as analysing student performance on the laboratory report in comparison to previous years when the assignment was tutor marked, the performance on subsequent laboratory reports was also considered and shown to be improved (Barefoot et al., 2011). The results corresponded with other research within the field which reported benefits to student learning associated with peer assessment.

As a process of continued enhancement, the peer assessment activity was developed to help students to reflect further on their learning. An

(Continued)

(Continued)

online reflective questionnaire was introduced to the peer assessment process during the 2009–10 academic year, and was distributed via a web-based application. The questionnaire enabled better staff understanding of students' perceptions of the peer assessment exercise and enabled students to explicitly reflect on their learning. The questionnaire contained 27 questions, some of which used a five-point Likert-type scale (Strongly Agree; Agree; Neither Agree Nor Disagree; Disagree; Strongly Disagree) and some of which used radio-buttoned closed-choice questions. Using Likert-type questions can help to produce quantifiable data from what, at face value, may seem to be unquantifiable: student ideas, perceptions and understandings. In addition, the inclusion of some open-ended questions enabled students to provide free-text qualitative comments to supplement the pre-coded quantitative options (Barefoot et al., 2011).

The questionnaire thus enabled the staff to carry out some quantitative analysis on the results of the intervention. For example, 82 per cent of students engaged in the reflective questionnaire (*n* = 148) and 83 per cent of those indicated that they felt better prepared for their next laboratory report as a consequence of the peer assessment activity (Barefoot et al., 2011). The reflective questionnaire also provided useful feedback for the project team as to which aspects of the laboratory report students found most challenging (see Figure 9.2).

Most challenging section of report	Percentage of students
Abstract	4
Introduction	17
Methods	1
Results	14
Discussion	58
References	6

Figure 9.2   Student perceptions of the most challenging aspect of the laboratory report

However, the mixed method nature of the project helped to ensure that more qualitative insights into students' perceptions of the peer assessment process were gathered to help to explore *why* the approach was working. As one student stated: *'I felt that [understanding] the marking scheme and even reading other people's work made me reflect upon what I was good at and what I could work on/add to in my report and future reports'* (Barefoot et al., 2011).

In short, the peer assessment activity supported student learning and helped students to reflect on their own understanding of their learning. Information from the reflective questionnaire has also guided the staff that teach on the module. They now talk more explicitly with students about what is required within each section of a laboratory report and provide more detailed guidance on what should be included within the discussion section.

We hope that Case Study 9.1 has illustrated to you how educational enquiry can accommodate some of your existing research practice, preferences and skills. What at first may seem unquantifiable experiences, concepts or understandings can, through using particular approaches to data collection, be quantified for analysis and reporting purposes. Ultimately, for those who are used to dealing with numbers rather than words, this may feel a more comfortable and familiar approach.

Case study 9.2   Regular low stake assessments using Electronic Voting Systems (EVS) (Barefoot and Russell, 2012)

Engaging over 100 biology students in large lectures can be particularly challenging and it can be difficult to design tasks which encourage student interactivity. This study identified a way to improve student engagement in lectures and to stimulate study behaviours throughout semesters to avoid students focusing primarily on high stake summative assessment tasks.

Electronic Voting Systems (EVS) or 'Clickers' had already been used in other disciplinary areas at the University of Hertfordshire (for example, within engineering and radiography) to enhance student learning. Evidence from the literature also suggested that they could be used effectively in large teaching classes to gauge student understanding (and misunderstanding) of core science concepts (Brewer, 2004). Staff within the Bioscience department applied for institutional funding to buy handsets for first-year students so that use of EVS could be incorporated into their teaching.

In 2008–09 all first year Bioscience students were given an EVS handset unique to them and staff teaching on first-year modules began to incorporate formative questions into their teaching. The formative questions

(Continued)

(Continued)

emphasised a learner-centred approach in that students were able to gain instant feedback on their understanding of certain topics. In line with the findings of Linsemneier et al. (2006), this also brought beneficial changes to the teaching approaches of many of the module lecturers and facilitators; staff were able to review concepts and address misconceptions immediately, ensuring the better understanding of complex topics.

The project also enabled the EVS to be used for regular low stake assessments within modules. For example, within a large cohort first year human physiology module, a progress test which used to take place in semester B (worth 10 per cent of the module mark) was replaced by 10 EVS drop quizzes which took place throughout semesters A and B. The top six marks scored within the quizzes counted towards 10 per cent of the module mark. The quizzes could be held during lectures, workshops and practical classes ensuring interactivity in each learning environment. They not only helped to improve the overall mean mark for the module but also improved the spread of marks within the module by helping students to measure their own understanding of physiology concepts and to self-regulate their own learning. It is interesting to note that prior to the drop quizzes being part of module assessment approach (2008) 44 per cent of students achieved a third class mark for the module. Introducing the EVS drop quizzes (which was the only change within the assessment diet) saw the percentage of students achieving a third class mark being reduced to 18 per cent (2010). The percentage of students achieving a first or upper second score also increased from 7 per cent (2008) to 32 per cent (2010).

In short, the random issuing of the drop quizzes helped students actively to engage with the physiology material throughout the semesters rather than focusing study effort only at high stake summative assessment points. The success of personalised EVS use has spread throughout the School of Life Sciences and all Level 4 (first-year undergraduate) bioscience modules now include regular low stake drop quiz assessments. Further, the strategic use of personalised EVS has also been rolled out to many other parts of the institution.

In effect, the researchers in Case Study 9.2 introduced a change to a population and then measured the impact; in this case improved attainment by the students when compared to the previous year's cohort. Thus there were very clear metrics to work with – the 2008 scores compared to the 2010 scores in terms of both mean and spread and only one change in approach, the use of the clickers. When reduced down in this way you can see how this is a simple hypothesis driven experiment to test the effect of a single factor; a model very familiar to every life scientist.

Case Study 9.3   Developing career opportunities in biological sciences (Willmott, 2011 and Molleman and Barefoot, 2009)

As well as researching teaching and assessment activities, educational enquiry has also been carried out into employability and careers education within the life sciences.

The UK's Destinations of Leavers from Higher Education (DLHE) survey (2010–11) showed that only 67.5 per cent of biological science graduates were employed within a job related to their subject. Out of 19 subject areas identified this was the 7th lowest percentage nationally (HESA, 2013). In an increasingly difficult job market, one of today's challenges is to consider how employability and guidance on employment opportunities within life sciences can be provided within, and beyond the curriculum.

At the University of Leicester the 'Careers After Biological Science' (CABS) programme has been developed to provide employment advice and support for undergraduates. The programme focuses on two key elements. First, former biological science students are invited back to the University to describe their current role and offer practical advice to undergraduates who may be considering moving into a similar discipline. Secondly, social media resources (for example Facebook and LinkedIn) are used for the organisation and promotion of careers events as well as providing a repository for career profiles and a wealth of useful resources. The alumni sessions are extra-curricular activities providing insights into the diverse range of jobs that biosciences graduates may enter. Evaluation of the programme indicated that the students and staff identified the importance of the programme and it has now become an integral part of careers provision for Bioscience students (Willmott, 2011).

Industrial (sandwich) placements play a very important role in terms of employability within the life sciences yet the number of students engaging with sandwich years is in decline. When asked, students gave a number of reasons as to why they did not wish to do a sandwich placement including:

- Not wanting to be at university for four years;
- Not wanting to increase their debt;
- Concerns about losing friends whilst on placement;
- Fears about entering the workplace; and
- For some local students, concerns about living away from home (Molleman and Barefoot, 2009).

(Continued)

(Continued)

To address this, at the University of Hertfordshire, the careers advice (which included guidance on finding and applying for placements as well as employability skills development), was moved from weekly optional drop-in sessions to a week-long event focusing on employability and work experience opportunities at the very beginning of the second year of study. All bioscience students attended the sessions and activities which included practical skills from developing a CV and considering interview techniques, to self-awareness exercises and talks from former students and employers. The practical aspects were seen by students as the most useful elements of the week and students recognised the importance of information regarding the sandwich placements. Following feedback from the students, the week-long programme has been continued with reinforcement activities and careers sessions facilitated throughout the second year via the personal tutor system and extra-curricular events.

The example in Case Study 9.3 illustrates how approaches to support students into employment can be developed iteratively following feedback from students. New activities (careers events, use of social media) were introduced and the students were asked how useful they found them. By responding to the feedback, staff were able to justify the use (and expense) of the activity and embed it into future offerings, further develop and refine it and expand it across the second year. This 'try–examine–develop–try again' model will be very familiar to any life scientist who has tried to identify the correct dose of drug to test or how long to incubate something for. Thus, once again we see how your well-honed skills can be re-purposed to explore and develop the educational environment around you.

 ## Activity 9.1   Identifying and attending a life sciences education conference or event

If you have not done so already, we recommend that you identify and attend a life sciences education conference or event. Many researched-based conferences have an education strand or may have a special symposium regarding education within the discipline. The Higher Education Academy in the UK has a Science, Technology, Engineering and Maths (STEM) annual conference focusing on teaching and assessment initiatives within the disciplines as well as many regular workshops and seminars for staff to attend. Speaking with, and learning from colleagues at such events is one of the easiest ways to consider and develop your own enquiry activity.

Concluding thoughts

Within this chapter we have considered the benefits and challenges associated with educational enquiry within the life sciences. The intrinsic benefits of taking a scholarly approach to investigating and enhancing our teaching are great. Such an approach enables us to consider questions such as 'how are my students really learning?', 'how can I make my teaching methods more effective for student learning?' and 'how can I improve students' experiences of assessment?' If we take a strategic approach to these questions, by applying our understanding of discipline-specific research to our educational enquiry, we can develop our teaching methods relatively easily to ensure that we achieve both a student-centred curriculum and a rewarding experience for both students and staff.

Suggested further reading

Shapiro, C., Ayon, C., Moberg-Parker, J., Levis-Fitzgerald, M. and Sanders, E.R. (2013) 'Strategies for using peer-assisted learning effectively in an undergraduate bioinformatics course', *Biochemistry Molecular Biology Education*, 41, 24–33.
We recommend that you take a look at one of the discipline-specific education-based journals mentioned in this chapter (for example, *Biochemistry and Molecular Biology Education*). In this journal, Shapiro et al.s' recent paper (2013) uses a combined quantitative and qualitative approach to investigate the benefits of peer-assisted learning.

Luckie, D.B., Aubry, J.R., Marengo, B.J., Rivkin, A.M., Foos, L.A. and Maleszewski, J.J. (2012) 'Less teaching, more learning: 10-yr study supports increasing student learning through less coverage and more inquiry', *Advances in Physiology Education*, 36, 325–35.
You may also like to read Luckie et al.'s (2012) 'Less teaching, more learning: 10-yr study supports increasing student learning through less coverage and more inquiry'. This long-term study has resulted in a fundamental change in the methods of teaching from a content-driven to a student inquiry-driven approach to improve student learning.

O'Loughlin, V.D. (2006) 'A "how to" guide for developing a publishable scholarship of teaching project', *Advances in Physiology Education*, 30, 83–88.
This paper provides a practical guide for science staff considering educational research. She writes about the importance of teachers participating in assessment and research into their teaching and then making their efforts visible and subject to appropriate peer scrutiny. The paper provides a step-by-step guide for developing and publishing an educational enquiry project.

CHAPTER 10

ENQUIRY INTO LEARNING AND TEACHING IN ARTS AND CREATIVE PRACTICE

Susan Orr and Julian McDougall

Learning outcomes

By the conclusion of this chapter it is anticipated that you will:

- Be able to identify the disciplinary research skills and expertise suitable to be adapted for educational enquiry within the fields of arts and creative practice;
- Understand the respective merits of these research approaches;
- Be able to link your own work and creative practice to the work of educational researchers; and
- Be able to reflect on the discourse and identity contexts that impact on educational enquiry.

Introduction: the making of the teacher

In this chapter we draw on our experiences as educational researchers and creative practitioners – activities we do not view as exclusive – who have taught on new lecturer initial teacher education courses (Postgraduate Certificates in Academic Practice) in mainstream higher education and in specialist arts universities. The key argument in this chapter is that there is now a relatively well rehearsed and understood discussion around arts practitioner and subject identity discourses and pedagogies. This can be built upon and extended to focus on a new area: educational enquiry for arts and creative practice disciplines. To develop this argument we will briefly explore the commonalities between *making, teaching* and *researching*, and will unpack issues of identity and discourse to trace a relationship between making, teaching and educational enquiry (as one type of research). These possibilities for exchange between the areas of teaching, making and educational enquiry offer rich and fertile opportunities to create new knowledge.

For the purposes of this chapter the term 'creative practices' refers specifically to a range of subject areas in higher education spanning art, design, media, performing arts and music. Whilst these subjects are all creative studio-based disciplines, they are also diverse and particular. However, for reasons of clarity, we draw together the key research and pedagogic characteristics of these subjects and refer to them as 'creative practices' throughout the chapter.

A review of literature in the field suggests to us that the broad characteristics such disciplines share are:

1. A commitment to *reflective practice*: planned and deliberate activities that engage the artist or designer in a critical manner with the relationship between conceptual, theoretical and practical concerns (de Freitas 2002);
2. A commitment to *process*: the process of the creation of the artefact as well as an interest in the final product (Cowdray and de Graaf, 2005; Orr, 2007);
3. A commitment to *creativity* (Cannatella, 2001): while the word creativity is highly contested and its parameters are elusive, a pursuit of creativity underpins all of these disciplines. In the Quality Assurance Agency (QAA, 2008a) *Subject Benchmark Statement for Art and Design* there are 46 references to the term creative. In the *Music QAA Subject Benchmark Statement* (QAA, 2008b) there are 41 references to the term, and in the *Communication, Film, Media and Cultural Studies Benchmark Statement* (QAA, 2008c) there are 34 references;

4. A commitment to *making*: as Elkins (2001) eloquently explains, making underpins practice. Thus the making of the 'work' is central to understanding the practice. Learning occurs in the production of work, or as Frayling puts it, playing with E.M. Forster's famous quotation, 'How can I tell what I think till I see what I make and do?' (cited in Wood and Biggs, 2004: 119).

These four characteristics are directly related to one another; a key site for reflection is the process of creative *making*. It is our contention that each of these four characteristics has their parallel within educational scholarship and research. Going further, the methods employed by creative practitioner-researchers – visual ethnographies (Pink, 2007), the visual/digital acquisition and representation of data, critical discourse analysis, aesthetic enquiry and interdisciplinary or *interdisciplined* enquiry (Rancière, 2012) – are intertwined with making and with the making of learning (through disciplinary pedagogies). Thus the power relationships between the artist and her representation of the world, the researcher and her construction of 'thick description' (Geertz, 1973) of social practice in the world and the teacher and her collaborative construction of knowledge with her students are consistent. Artefacts are made, as is knowledge; they are the outcomes of the same processes.

We are also able to draw out other clear connections between readers' interpretations of texts and researchers' interpretations of data. Arts-based educational research can be linked to Langer's notion (1957) of 'composed apparition' (cited in Barone and Eisner, 2006). Langer developed this term in relation to the way that a literary or other cultural text becomes a heuristic construction for the reader: an artificial textual world but 'composed' in relation to 'real' concerns. Research operates in the same way and thus researchers working in this way experiment with their research as text and its representational status. This kind of enquiry deliberately problematises categories of researcher, research subject, findings and reader of those findings (see for example Barone and Eisner, 2006; Bagley and Cancienne, 2001; Richardson, 1992).

Taking a similar approach, creative practitioner-pedagogues will seek to problematise the separation of teacher, student and knowledge (Bernstein, 1990). Elsewhere Andrews and McDougall (2012) call this 'curation pedagogy', informed by Rancière's (2009) story of the 'ignorant schoolmaster' and our own 'pedagogy of the inexpert' (Bennett et al., 2011; Kendall and McDougall, 2012). This approach asks students to 'show' creativity and critique in new spaces; not by recourse to skills, competences or analytical unmasking of the properties of a (contained) text, but by exhibiting and curating a moment in time of textual meaning-making and meaning-taking, and with a mindfulness to the potential artifice of such making and taking (Csikszentmihalyi, 1997). In short, we suggest that both research and pedagogy in creative practice can share and embrace this reflexive 'ignorance' and that 'curation' is a useful metaphor, not only for the exhibition of student work for assessment, but also as a way of thinking about what is happening when we undertake educational enquiry from within the context of creative practice.

Connecting creative practice research practices to educational enquiry

A commitment to reflective practice

Being reflective about the practice of teaching is a central tenet of new lecturer courses in higher education in the UK. On many such courses, reflective diaries, blogs and portfolios form a key part of the way that the course is delivered and assessed. The key imperative is for programme participants to utilise the concept of the reflective practitioner to heighten self-awareness of their own teaching styles and teaching approaches. Drawing from our experience of working with new lecturers from different disciplines, we note that lecturers coming from an arts background find that the reflective practice element of their Teacher Education course sits comfortably and aligns well with their own arts-based practice. This also relates to educational enquiry: the heightened self-awareness that sits at the heart of your disciplinary research practice will lend itself well to undertaking educational enquiry.

A commitment to process

Process may not be a term that you will often encounter in the field of educational enquiry but it can be very useful in this context as it can help you to focus attention on the lived and emergent experiences of teaching and learning. A focus on process and product can help you to enquire into teaching and learning as it unfolds in the studio (the process) and leads to the product of learning and teaching (students' achievements).

A commitment to creativity

Creative practice, as the term itself underlines, is associated with the development of creativity (Cannatella, 2001). While the word creativity is highly contested and its parameters are elusive, a pursuit of creativity underpins its constituent disciplines. Given that excellent teaching informed by educational enquiry is not a recipe, nor is it based on following a set formula, we would argue that creativity has a role to play. Excellent teaching is skilfully and carefully planned but when informed by enquiry it is also emergent, dynamic and serendipitous. As lecturers with a background in the arts you will doubtless be familiar with the emergent and contingent nature of both enquiry and practice. This will stand you in good stead when undertaking research into your own learning and teaching. From this perspective, the interweaving of enquiry and teaching can be viewed as 'intellectual bricolage' (Denscombe, 2008a: 27).

A commitment to making

In our engagement with new lecturers we work hard to encourage lecturers to go beyond the 'what will I teach?' question to move on to consider 'how will I teach?' This therefore relates to the 'making' of teaching, with the process of educational enquiry underpinning its development. In short, with a commitment to and understanding of 'making', creative practice lecturers are extremely well placed to explore and then subsequently craft the learning experience for their students. As in creative practice, this process of making in teaching can be multi-modal: the enquiry can relate to the room set up, the studio environment, the use of the space, the use of time and the whole sensory experience of the arts' learning environment. As such, through the process of educational enquiry, the diverse ways that a researcher explores and then, as a lecturer, makes informed use of such multi-modal understandings can be seen as the art of teaching practice or the 'making' of teaching (Loughran, 2002; Hall, 2010). Just as we require our students to document the process of their craft, we call on you in your educational enquiries to document the process of your teaching – itself a craft – to bring to bear a greater reflexivity on your enquiry/teaching/making: on your 'work'. In this way, we suggest that creative practices themselves are forms of enquiry.

Identity

If you are engaged in different types of creative arts (for example, film maker, designer, artist, musician) you will already see yourself as a practitioner. Here we ask you to negotiate your identity as a practitioner-researcher (Metz and Page, 2002). Practitioner research in education is partly a broad response to the problem of research in the field being perceived as overly abstract and theoretical and partly the domain of arts-based researchers who wish to experiment with the forms of both data and enquiry and to challenge the boundaries between research, theory and practice. For example, Hall (2010) who carried out interviews with artist teachers in schools, cites Prentice (1995: 11) who describes new teachers in art and design as having 'roots firmly embedded in their identity as person as artist, craft person or designer'. In another study of fine art lecturers' approaches to assessment, Orr noted that the lecturers' identities as artists imbued their assessment practices (2011). Similarly, in an interview-based study of part-time lecturers in a specialist arts university, Shreeve (2009) noted that for some of these lecturers being a practitioner was their central identity marker. The extent to which these lecturers viewed themselves as educators varied and the relationship between their identity as artists and their identity as educators was not always a comfortable one. All three of these studies suggest that many creative practice lecturers see their creative practitioner status as a key identity marker.

Bringing this research back to your own context we speculate that for some of you studio teaching is a tacit activity; mostly it happens and mostly it works. The aim of bringing greater reflexivity to your practice as an educator is to surface the tacit to move from what might be described as 'good enough' through to excellent practice. To date there has been a dearth of literature that explores the practices of studio-based higher education teaching (for notable exceptions see the *Journal of Art Design and Communication in Higher Education*; Swann, 2002; Shreeve et al., 2010; Drew, 2004). This is in sharp contrast to other teaching settings (for example the formal lecture) about which much has been written. For these reasons, we argue that your own practice can only develop if it is informed by your educational enquiry – using the tools and design instruments of your subject (visual methods, online exchanges, video, textual outcomes, observation of studio practice, performance, exhibition and critique) to explore and develop the spaces and interactions of learning and teaching in creative contexts.

The challenge of discourse

As explained in Chapter 2, each discipline, including creative practice disciplines, has its own particular ways of talking about itself which is a reflection of the discipline's epistemological and ontological positioning (Crotty, 1998). As such, confusion may occur when the same words are used in different contexts but they refer to different things. One example is the term 'ethics'. In relation to medical education the term ethics is associated with a very particular and prescribed code of ethics that will encompass medical care and scientific research requirements. In creative practice ethical discussions are likely to focus more on issues of representation and debates about censorship. So on the one hand the discourse around ethics in your field is more 'open', but on the other, it does not necessarily provide a clear code of practice to adhere to.

In our experience, this means that a generic institutional research ethics forms in universities, which may have been designed with the needs and understandings of other disciplines in mind, may appear alien and unhelpful in a creative practice setting. For example, in a university that one of the authors worked in, the ethics form for new lecturers carrying out educational enquiry had originated in a Faculty of Health and the form had to be re-imagined for use within an arts enquiry context. As stated in Chapter 4 of this text, it may therefore be helpful to ensure that you gain ethical consent in the context that is most appropriate for your enquiry project where those making a judgement will have a good understanding of the approach and type of enquiry you are undertaking.

You may also come across words with which you are familiar that are used differently in different disciplines and may require some translation. A good example of this is the project-centred learning (PCL) that is a mainstay of much creative practice education. In PCL the curriculum is not 'delivered' but is co-constructed with students who are given a fairly open brief and whose learning develops through their engagement with the project that they develop and respond to in individualised ways (Blair et al., 2012). This approach to PCL has its equivalent in Enquiry-Based Learning (EBL) which is introduced in Chapter 1 of this text. Thus the practice of EBL is familiar to many creative practice lecturers but the nomenclature may be unfamiliar. As this book recommends an enquiry-based approach to your teaching as well as to students' learning, this discursive framing is of key importance.

These two examples underline the need to map and translate across the fields of educational practice and creative practice. As lecturers who may be new to educational enquiry we encourage you to identify other examples where educational enquiry and creative practice need to be carefully mapped and translated and to share them with others in your discipline. You may be surprised by the number of similar ways of thinking and doing that you will encounter in educational enquiry that you were unaware of due to their different use of terminology.

Some alternative ways forward

In this section of the chapter we explore further the synergies and overlaps that we have already begun to discuss with regard to educational enquiry and enquiry within creative practice. As stated above, there are already many aspects of your existing approach to enquiry which can be used to undertake enquiry into your learning and teaching. However, you may wish also to adapt some of your known practices and adopt practices from education to create some 'hybrid' methods. This process is already underway, and the following discussion takes you on a brief journey through two existing exchanges of ideas and practices to help you to think through ways in which you could combine and extend your existing approaches to enquiry with new (to you) approaches from the social sciences. The first exchange that we discuss recounts how some arts researchers are increasingly using social science methodological approaches to research creative practice, while the second exchange shows how some social sciences researchers have begun to borrow artistic and creative research approaches.

Ethnography is a term usually associated with anthropological and sociological research, but here we suggest it is an approach that is equally resonant for creative arts and media teaching. The approach is particularly useful as it bears witness to the constructed and subjective nature of representation – of how we see and 'write' (in the broadest sense) the world. This is why it sits so well with educational enquiry, which is a composite approach drawing on a variety of methods (more traditionally those from the social sciences as discussed in the first chapters of this book). Ethnographic research is concerned with 'situation'; the researcher works from inside the social setting or social practice with which the research is concerned. A range of research methods can be used in combination with an emphasis on producing data which is grounded in the location or activity. We recognise also that the term 'data' can be viewed as a problematic term within the creative arts, but we feel it is important to deal with it, and to some extent embrace it, if you wish to avoid the pitfalls of marginalisation within the broader educational enquiry community. The key to the ethnographers' approach is the reflexive awareness of the way that data are constructed within complex situated social practices. As such, there can be no recourse to a positivist observation of data as being pre-existing and something to 'capture'. Ethnography, then, is:

> concerned not with presenting a distanced, scientific and objective account of the social world, but an account that recognizes the subject reality of the experiences of those people who constitute and construct the social world. (Pole and Morrison, 2003: 5)

Crucially, the specific and often complex nature of the location or activity is given prominence and broad generalisations are avoided in the analysis. The meaning of social action, from the perspective of research participants, is prioritised over the researcher's assumptions and claims of objective 'observation' are avoided. As such, this method is intended to be reflexive.

This approach sits extremely well with the approach taken by creative practitioners who additionally seek not to impose their 'world views' on texts and to give voice to, rather than speak for, the people represented by the artistic material. It is illustrated in Pink's video ethnography that explicitly explores the way that video frames researcher/subject dynamics as a representational medium, as opposed to being a mere way of 'capturing' data:

> Reflexivity entails more than simply an awareness of how participants' interactions are affected by their 'camera consciousness'. Rather, we need to firmly

situate their self-awareness within the cultural and media contexts in which they live out their everyday lives. (Pink, 2007: 99)

With this in mind, and with your own understandings of the processes underpinning creative practices to hand, you will be well placed to consider how to adopt aspects of an ethnographic approach for your own educational enquiry.

An example of this process in action can be found in an educational enquiry project in which one of the chapter author's explored the potential of video documentary making as a pedagogic tool for media students (McDougall, 2013). The focus of this learning activity was on digital video editing and online exchange of video as an ethnographic activity in itself. An ethnographic methodology (for pedagogy) enabled students to produce documentary films representing their communities' perceptions of local identities in relation to Europe and its future. In working ethnographically, students making the documentaries were at the same time the 'subjects' (agents) and 'objects' (the data) of the learning and the educational enquiry. One important aspect of the enquiry, though, was the extent to which students' own experiences would make them resistant to producing an ethnographic film 'against the grain' of mainstream documentary conventions. As the video medium is far from neutral, working ethnographically in documentary production requires a deliberate 'unknowing' of dominant modes of documentary construction, in order for the editing to be an act of 'thick description' of a social issue rather than an act of editorial selection and construction. The use of ethnographic documentary making was employed to engage students in a critical understanding of the act of editing and to 'come to know' how identity is constructed, negotiated and fluid. Students' thinking about the power of the edit as the representative act, mirroring the self-reflexive approach of ethnography, was central.

The second exchange focuses on the employment of artistic methods by those working within the social sciences (within which education is situated). Creative practice enquiry is sometimes positioned against the grain of social science traditions, insomuch as we are consistently remixing and resituating roles and identities – of artist, creative 'maker', student 'maker', teacher and 'researcher'. Yet, Hickman (2008a: 12) reminds us that there is a 'growing acceptance of arts based enquiry within education', going on to state:

> Visual art forms (and performance) can serve a useful purpose in educational research by conveying 'truths' about educational phenomena which are intuitively felt, expressed and communicated. (Hickman, 2008b: 21)

The social sciences are thus increasingly turning to new ways of working, gathering data, participating in inter-disciplinary spaces and presenting/representing data, findings and learning and that are heavily influenced by creative practices (particularly where new digital technologies are involved).

In the recent past there was a level of adherence to the orthodoxy that the written word (essay, paper or article) was both the standard and prioritised unit of knowledge transfer in the social sciences (Candlin, 2008). As such, any 'deviation' from this norm – for example, a practice-based research 'output' – has traditionally been expected to be equated to the written standard (i.e. the word–number equivalence that can be allocated to a website, art installation, musical performance or even videogame design). Furthermore, the social science orthodoxy has viewed with suspicion the common practice of assessing collaborative creative practice, so a written evaluation or commentary of some form is required in order for assessors to 'measure' individual learning within a group dynamic (Orr, 2010).

This is however changing. There is a growing community of practice around the use of visual, performative or more broadly 'creative' ways of sharing findings from research. For example, Marcalo (2009) challenged ontological assumptions about writing in her practice-based PhD research and used choreography *itself* (as opposed to documented writing *about* it) as a new 'documentation modality'. Marcalo's argument is simple: that conventional research does not require a commentary on itself – a further written supplement – it stands alone. Thus, although self-analysis will be evident within the written thesis, there is no requirement for a supplementary 'log' of it. So why then should dance performance require such a supplement in the form of dance notation? Why should the 'ontology of performance' not be accepted, regardless of its 'disappearance', or why should the written word be given such unquestioned status as a compensation for this 'lack'? The answer lies in shifting our way of thinking about documentation:

> As a choreographer, my encounters with writing are always uneasy, full of questions and ambivalences. These ambivalent encounters, however, have always been the source of fruitful 'poetic' and 'exegetic' creation, rather than a hindrance to it. I find that the contradictions that situating myself between writing and choreography brings to the fore, create a space of play (a dynamic space) that continuously keeps me interested in knowledge and meaning, that continuously sparks new thoughts, in new directions and for new purposes. (Marcalo, 2009: 114)

Disseminating your educational enquiry

Marcolo's discussion inevitably brings us on to the issue of research output. If 'artistic research [is] a form of knowledge production' (Borgdorff, 2011: 44) or as Dewey expresses it, knowledge 'gained in the creative act' (cited in Wood and Biggs, 2004: 119), then what form should the knowledge produced by your educational enquiry take? In creative practice there are diverse outputs that range from the ephemeral (a short performance) to the recorded (a film), through to installations and artefacts. Usefully, Denzin and Lincoln (2002) show existing examples of social science-based research which has been reported in the form of creative writing, performance and 'unofficial texts'. Here, then, we argue that creative outputs can and should carry educational knowledge and scholarship in a 'non text based reporting' format (Hickman, 2008b: 22).

This may seem awkward, as it goes against the grain of accepted dissemination methods in social science-based educational enquiry. However, we would argue that it ultimately provides very rich outputs. We therefore encourage you, as creative practitioners, to follow Marcalo's example and to embrace and develop these new directions for dissemination, as appropriate, in your own educational enquiry projects.

Making the familiar unfamiliar

Returning to our central theme in this chapter – that creative practice, teaching and educational enquiry overlap, intersect and resonate with one another – we now turn to a discussion of Adam Brown's (2010) teacher-researcher project. This offers a helpful example of both enquiry and pedagogy that deliberately sets out to engage with complicated 'in-between' spaces to explore the richness of such 'hybridity' for educational enquiry. In a practitioner-research project that clearly exemplifies the approach we are encouraging in this chapter, Brown experimented with strategies for photography and moving image learning using the 'drifting space of the street' as the workshop for this practice, with explicit attention to the interplay of written words and images. Brown's intervention is an example of the proliferation of creative arts and media educators wanting to 'play out' the relationship between students' formal education and technologically mediated 'prosumer' activities in the changing landscape of twenty-first century learning:

> The activities explored in this study were designed for Year 2 undergraduate students, with the aim of promoting critical discussion of many of the practices in which they already engage in the role of consumer or end-user, such as the online critique of images, or participation in discussion forums. Encouraging students to engage critically with the distribution technologies available to the contemporary image maker, such as blogging, online book production, and instantaneous distribution, demands that students confront and deconstruct the social and technical functions of these technologies. (Brown, 2010: 1)

Brown's students were taken out into the streets to produce and upload mobile, reproducible and multiple images to the web. Use was made of wi-fi access points across London to provide a fluid 'studio' with the Barbican Centre acting as a 'meeting point' and fixed location 'hub' for the foray. Here an overview of approaches is followed by an example of one student's responses:

> In a subversive activity, some participants downloaded images which others had posted to the blog, manipulated them digitally, and reposted the altered images. William Blake's tomb became Banksy's, and other images gained additional subjects. One student brought a one-shot analogue fisheye camera, and processed his film in a one-hour lab, uploading his images halfway through the day.

In Laura Nolan's project, her doctored 'tart cards' derive from conversations on social networking sites, and images taken in nightclubs in Maidstone, but language and image are combined and re-posted into material space. They return to the streets of the town, placing the language, the look and the attitude back where it came from. The use of Polaroid instant film deploys a technology that is designed for the creation of immediate, one-off productions, its spontaneity referencing the user-centred nature of web 2.0 technologies (Brown, 2010: 2).

In assessing the value of this intervention, Brown suggests that collaborative learning was 'revealed' in the spaces where individual students understood their work in the context of 'a stranger's gaze' and that there was a wholesale shift away from understanding creative practice as the work of the 'lone artist'. He relates how the unit has:

> succeeded in allowing students to engage with discursive and theoretically driven enquiry, in a way that other approaches have struggled with. By commencing with a piece of work made in a relational way – the blog – many discussions can be entered into relating to what is 'a work'? What is the influence of context to reception? Or – more pertinently at this stage – what is the relationship of maker to audience? Students are able to observe the pertinence of these questions due to the exploration of discursive forms in which they are already immersed, and by turning these on their head, perceive exciting new ways of conducting visual – and discursive – enquiry. (Brown, 2010: 2)

Researching your own practice is a key element of educational enquiry in creative practice. A key distinction between this way of working and other disciplines is that it is relatively unusual for the educational researcher to attempt to 'step outside' of her own practice in this field. Brown's experiment is another example of an educational researcher/creative practitioner designing a space for learning as an act of educational enquiry by re-negotiating and risk-taking – reconfiguring the 'space' where learning takes place, both physically and metaphorically. In doing this, the pedagogic design 'moment' becomes a process of taking a step back from being the one who 'knows' towards a more 'inexpert' curation of learning. We hope that these insights will encourage you to engage in such practices and to use your skills of creativity to undertake discipline-informed creative educational enquiry as Brown did.

Suggested activities

The following activities have been designed to help you map and translate your expertise and knowledge as a creative practice lecturer to the world of educational enquiry and should help you embark on educational enquiry from your own disciplinary setting with confidence.

Activity 10.1

If you are embarking on new research or practice in your discipline, what would you do? Where would you start? In what ways would you pursue your practice?

Write down the ways that lecturers in your discipline/arts context approach research and practice. How is new knowledge created?

Activity 10.2

Reflect on your creative practice. Do you view your own creative practice as something you would call research? Is your creative practice recognised as research within your university context? Practice-based research in the arts has a contested place in the academy and many universities are still hesitant about recognising creative practice as research. If you are interested in the debate that explores the ways that arts practice can be understood (or rejected) as a form of research see Candlin (2008) or Elkins (2004).

Activity 10.3

In the discussion above we explored how issues of identity relate to how you approach your teaching practice and your research into your teaching practice. Write down all the different ways you position yourself in relation to identity. It is our contention that it is useful to consider the plural identities you bring to teaching and educational enquiry to heighten your reflexivity.

Activity 10.4

In the discussion above we also explore the diverse creative outputs that students and practitioners in the creative arena exploit to communicate knowledge and learning. If you are currently studying on a Postgraduate Certificate course, it is likely that it will include a curriculum development or research project. This will provide you with opportunities to try out some of the ideas in this chapter. Are you able to use enquiry to adapt or remediate an assessment format? What output of enquiry will demonstrate your learning and development as a teacher? What findings from your enquiry might you be able to share more widely within your disciplinary community? You may feel that a website or a short film or a series of sketchbooks exemplifying your enquiry can be deployed to meet the learning objectives on your PG Cert course rather than a prescribed text-based submission format. However, please do discuss and agree this alternative format with your tutor before you submit!

Concluding thoughts: the benefits of exchange

When a creative practice lecturer encounters educational research and enquiry for the first time there can be a feeling that they are starting off as a novice in a new field. Our aim in drawing out the parallels and synergies between creative practice and teaching practice is to help you to bridge this gap and map your expertise to this new field. The expertise you bring in terms of methods of enquiry and creative output can only serve to widen the frame of existing learning and teaching enquiry which, as discussed above, primarily resides within a social sciences frame. You are an expert practitioner. You have much to offer the field of educational enquiry.

Suggested further reading: two annotated reading examples

The following two reading examples (reflecting useful interventions in themselves) are provided here with some accompanying discussion and application prompts for those working in arts and creative practice. They are examples of educational enquiry in practice where the researcher-practitioner-student relationships are collaborative and reflexive.

Orr, Richmond and Richmond 'Reflect on This!' (2010)
Orr et al. argue against the 'regime of truth' that has asserted a hegemonic discourse of reflection in education, suggesting an alternative view of reflexive pedagogy more appropriate for arts and media practice.

Discussion: The shift here is from reflecting on creativity to reflection being at one with, and integral to it. The article, the 'write up' of an enquiry into student experiences of studying on a Postgraduate Certificate in Education (PGCE) course, describes two performance modules that explicitly foreground reflexivity. When we merge theory and practice, enquiry and pedagogy, to implement action in the form, usually of change, we talk of 'praxis' and it is in the same sense that a 'reflexive' approach merges the reflection from the observable practice on which we reflect. Here the article describes the use of a 'catalogue document' as a medium for learning and assessment. Students are required, in this mode, to:

juxtapose fragments of journals written at the time of making with commentary concerned with the resolution of an idea. The result is a reverberation between what is known now and what was not known at the time of writing, which inevitably leads to another layer of reflection/commentary, thereby deepening learning. While we might learn and develop skills through practice (by trial and error), it is through active reflection on 'doing' that we become aware of, and empowered by, our own creative process. (Orr et al., 2010: 203)

Discussion: In your enquiry, what use can you make of journals, commentaries, sketchbooks, evaluations as modes for reflexive data collection about creative teaching and learning? How do they offer a space for this embrace of 'not knowing' in both your enquiry and subsequently your practice? What currency is given in your enquiry work to this movement within and upon the self? How might your design of assessment, informed by your enquiry, provide more space for such reflexion? As the authors have it, 'X marks the spot!' (2010: 206). In these ways you can progress from creative pedagogy to creative enquiry, or more productively, to weave the two together in all of your work.

McDougall and Sanders: 'The Conditions of Possibility' (2011)
This example tackles head on assumptions about 'digital natives' that we must be very careful to avoid in our work.[1] In a research project into enquiry-based learning in virtual worlds, the authors (one of whom was a PG Cert in Higher Education student) explored the relationship between aptitude for 'book learning' and 'virtual world learning' among Media undergraduates – the very people on whose behalf we might make such assumptions. Again, the boundaries between roles and practices are wilfully blurred. The researchers are both the teachers and one is a student-teacher. No attempt is made to 'step outside' of the social practices in the lens of the enquiry. In this enquiry-based module, the subject matter of the module is partly the experience itself – a self-reflexive set of learning outcomes. Students are engaging with a series of ontological questions about the nature of reality in relation to experience and so to do this in a virtual space like Second Life (where the residue of the 'real' remains – through the lecturer's spoken voice and resources) has a learning benefit in addition to its novelty. Students are required to complete a research journal based upon their experiences within virtual and gaming worlds. Rich educational enquiry, then, takes place within the module.

Discussion: We can see here a clear parallel with the previous examples – both reflection and reflexion are explicit intentions in the enquiry design. A key issue for the research was that any 'technological determinism' arising from unsubstantiated assumptions about the virtual reality context in itself fostering reflexivity might be seen as a contemporary form of a determinism that creative practitioners have been guilty of for decades. Do your art and performance students arrive with a disposition for rehearsal or studio work? How keenly aware are you of the 'currency conversion' from academic

---

[1]This refers to the oft-made assumption that current students (particularly those who have grown up using computers) will be 'digital natives' (a term originally coined by Prensky, 2001) and will be comfortable with, and competent in, the use of digital tools and materials.

'capital' (Bourdieu, 2004) in the orthodox sense to the domain of creative practice? How much attention is paid to such transition in your learning design? The answers to these questions can only be provided by your own practitioner-enquiry.

The researchers assert that 'literacy, in its critically reflexive mode, must be the outcome of virtual enquiry-based learning for students to move beyond "unreading"' (Gee, 2000) to critical reading. Just as we want our students to question the traditional curriculum (what is knowledge, what 'counts', how is power exercised, what is 'the Law' of assessment?) so we must afford them time and (virtual) space to be as critical in new digital environments'.

Discussion: This seems to offer an even clearer link to the frameworks constructed and negotiated by Orr et al. (2010). Critical literacy is a term that can embrace all of our practice – a kind of 'culture literacy' which amounts to a mindfulness of self as connected to culture. Risk and reflexion are prerequisites. And so the final key questions for your consideration must be – as a practitioner, let's say a photographer – how deeply are you thinking about risk and self-knowing, emotion and identity – not as being in the properties of 'the work' as the photography, from inception to the print and exhibition (or website) but in the context of 'the work' of the learning you design? And if you work in the convergence of 'old' and 'new' media, what space is created in your pedagogy for a sensitive playing out of the spaces 'in between' 'old school' book learning and virtual exploration? What kind of data might your enquiry yield to both answer some of these questions and inform your own practice in these domains? Crucially, how will the design of your enquiry (the methods, tools and instruments used – perhaps looking for a 'fit' between design and field – see Pink, 2007) relate to the design of your practice, and how will you account reflexively for these decisions?

CHAPTER 11

ENQUIRY INTO LEARNING AND TEACHING IN THE HUMANITIES

Rebecca O'Loughlin and Elaine Fulton

Learning outcomes

By the conclusion of this chapter it is anticipated that you will:

- Understand the reasons for the historical reluctance of many academics in the humanities to engage with educational enquiry and appreciate why it is important to reverse this trend;
- Grasp the importance and effectiveness of discipline-based educational enquiry in the humanities;
- Recognise the benefits of adapting and adopting some of the methods from the social sciences alongside your own disciplinary methods to conduct educational enquiry; and
- Have a number of practical ideas about how to conduct educational enquiry in your own discipline and be ready to implement them.

Introduction

We begin this chapter by briefly discussing the reasons why there has been some reluctance among academics in the humanities to engage in enquiry into learning and teaching in their disciplines, and we make a case for the reversal of this trend. In doing this, we challenge the assumption made by some, that one must become a 'social scientist' in order to conduct educational enquiry and we encourage you to utilise the research methods of your own disciplines to engage in this kind of research. We contend that as scholars in the humanities, you are in a unique position (perhaps, in fact, the *best* position) to undertake authentic, discipline-based educational enquiry, having acquired essential subject knowledge and skills, and a deep empathy with the culture of your disciplines and its methodological and epistemological standpoints.

After we have made a case for *why* you should conduct educational enquiry, we suggest *how* you may do so. We maintain that methods from the humanities disciplines may be the most effective way for such academics to engage with educational enquiry. This notwithstanding, we claim that it is a misrepresentation, and one which has restricted the flourishing of educational enquiry in the humanities, to conceive of research methods in the humanities and the social sciences as in opposition to each other, sharing little or no common ground. We assert that there is a greater degree of methodological affinity between the humanities and the social sciences than has historically been acknowledged, and that recognising their complementarity could lead to a fruitful exchange which would enhance and enrich both discipline-based and social scientist-led educational enquiry.

Working from our argument for hybrid methodologies, we identify qualitative methods as perhaps the most 'natural' choice for academics in the humanities, with a particular focus on documentary analysis, interviews and observed behaviour, and on feminist approaches. We present case studies from theology, religious studies and history to highlight practical examples of academics in the humanities contributing to educational enquiry, in the hope that you may be inspired by these to enrich your own practice.

Towards hybrid approaches to educational enquiry in the humanities

Those of you who work in a humanities discipline will no doubt have heard comments along the following lines from colleagues about the perceived irrelevance of educational enquiry to them: 'Isn't all that stuff just done by educationalists?'; 'I've tried reading pedagogic literature but it's all full of social science methods and jargon that mean nothing to me ... they don't even use proper references!'; 'My research takes place in a library, not a classroom'; 'I'm hardly going to get any research funding for that, am I?';

and: 'My department wouldn't value that: it won't give me a REF output'. Whilst we refer to 'educationalists' and 'social scientists' interchangeably in this chapter, we do of course appreciate that educationalists are only one type of 'social scientist'. They are well aware of the difficulties of developing crucial, discipline-based educational enquiry in branches of academia that sometimes regard their aims and methods as completely alien; this includes the humanities. Huber, for example, has noted that:

> The scholarship of teaching and learning is typically pursued as a kind of practitioner or action research by teachers in their own classrooms, not the circumstances or settings for which the investigative methods used in most disciplines … are well designed. Doing the scholarship of teaching and learning sits, therefore, at the edge of most disciplines. (2006: 72)

For another educationalist, Biesta (2007), educational enquiry is directed by the 'what works?' question, that is, by evidence-based practice; as a result, academics working in disciplines which are not grounded in evidence-based approaches can feel marginalised and alienated by unfamiliar methodologies and occasionally uncomfortable epistemological assumptions. And even at the most fundamental level, that of language, Yorke has aptly described educational enquiry as 'the research analogue of a second language' for non-educationalists (2003: 105).

However, Huber (2000), who is a cultural anthropologist by background, also throws out a challenge: 'do we *all* have to be social scientists?!'; a question which captures the very essence of this text. Huber's own negative response to her question is based on her belief that a variety of approaches should flourish: 'The challenge here is to reconceptualise relationships between the disciplines, so that the lessons flow in all directions rather than demanding the diffusion of one privileged way of knowing' (2000: 27). In this chapter, we will not only suggest reasons *why* we as academics in humanities should rise to meet this challenge, but will also suggest *how* we can make crucial contributions to educational enquiry without denying or departing from the methods and principles of our own disciplines.

So, why should academics in humanities not only engage with educational enquiry but also be active forces in its creation? First, social scientists do not 'own' educational enquiry, and nor do they claim to. Theirs may be the dominant mode of enquiry, which has served to discourage some academics from other disciplines joining in, but as Huber has noted, in their approach to educational enquiry they are simply drawing on their own disciplinary and methodological culture (2006). For those in the sciences and 'harder' social sciences such as economics, the first choice of research approach may be quasi-experimental design using instruments that yield numerical results about the efficacy of a teaching innovation. In comparison, academics in the 'softer' social sciences, such as anthropology, may be more comfortable with qualitative data, and may draw on approaches that perhaps more naturally tend towards focus groups and discourse analysis as a useful way of exploring, for example, the dynamics of seminar participation. As argued in Chapter 2 of this text, it makes most sense to start from what you know. Others – often in fields centred on textual interpretation, where material for analysis is not typically thought of as 'data' – have pursued systematic inquiry through strategically designed assignments and a close reading of student work (Huber, 2006).

Academics in humanities are just as much at liberty to employ their disciplinary research methods to educational enquiry as are social scientists. How this may best be done will be further explored below, but it is important to recognise that this practice is already taking place, and even a cursory look at humanities educational research journals provides a number of examples (see for example journals such as *Arts and Humanities in Higher Education, Research in the Teaching of English*, and *The History Teacher*). In theology and religious studies, there are at least two UK journals dedicated to educational enquiry in the field: *Teaching Theology and Religion* and *Discourse: Learning and Teaching in Philosophical and Religious Studies*. All of these journals provide a window into the nature and scope of educational enquiry in the humanities and into the different methods in use in this field, many of which come straight from the discipline. These approaches include humanities-friendly, non-empirical reflections on teaching situations and techniques (which may also be termed the 'case study' method), descriptive accounts of educational situations, documentary analysis via literature reviews, ethnographic research/participant observation, and qualitative surveys and autobiographies.

There is some evidence of quantitative research, but in both *Teaching Theology and Religion* and *Discourse*, this is at a minimum. Educational enquiry conducted by social scientists, although opting primarily for qualitative methods, makes far greater use of quantitative and empirical methods (O'Loughlin, 2008). And whilst a reluctance to embrace such methods is evidently no barrier to academics in the humanities publishing on educational enquiry, the differences between social science-based educational enquiry and existing educational enquiry in humanities disciplines should not be exaggerated. In fact, there is significant overlap between the two, with both using surveys/case studies, observation research (including ethnography/participant observation), documentary analysis (including literature reviews and secondary source analysis), phenomenography, comparative analysis and conceptual analysis. None of these are wholly alien to the academic in a humanities-based discipline; educational enquiry can use your knowledge and your existing skills without you having to unlearn all you know to become a reluctant social scientist. Familiarity with these methods can provide comfortable entry points to educational enquiry for the humanities scholar. As Gorard has noted (citing Mahoney, 2000):

> It is particularly important for the well-being of educational research that we
> do not waste time in methodological 'paradigm wars' ... in particular we need
> to overcome the false dualism of 'quantitative' and 'qualitative' approaches ...
> Words can be counted and numbers can be descriptive. (Gorard, 2001: 3)

Huber and Hutchings endorse this view:

> contemporary scholarship of all kinds is characterized by a growing per-
> meability of disciplinary boundaries, and ... the scholarship of teaching and
> learning is no exception. In the [teaching] commons, people from different
> disciplines come to find what their own discipline cannot or will not provide.
> (2005: 70)

The significant degree of methodological affinity across disciplines should
also act as a reminder that even within humanities research, itself a broad
field, there has never been anything approaching a methodological consen-
sus. It is this very diversity that produces the new knowledge and fresh
perspectives that keeps our disciplines alive.

If, then, you dare to go even further, and tap into the rich tradition of
social sciences-based educational enquiry whilst drawing on methods
from your own disciplines, you are likely to develop rounded and relevant educational research methods which your disciplinary colleagues
will be more likely to be disposed to using, but which will also add to
discourse in the field of educational enquiry as a whole. These hybrid
methods may also prove to be valuable to researchers from other disciplines, and your students will be the recipients of best practice from
social sciences-based educational enquiry which has been given added
value because it has been translated and adapted in ways which make
sense in a disciplinary context (see O'Loughlin, 2008). The point we want
to emphasise here is that there is an interdependence between educational enquiry undertaken by social scientists and educational enquiry
done by discipline-based academics. Social scientists have developed
modes of language and tried and tested tools which have been proven
to lead to successful innovations in learning and teaching. Discipline-
based academics not only provide the gateway through which these may
penetrate beyond the generic, but they also bring ways of thinking and
researching from their own disciplines to the table, and in doing so, help
to suggest ways in which the future of educational enquiry may develop
and become more widely accessible.

The harnessing of hybrid methodologies necessitates the development
of discipline-based educational enquiry in humanities subjects to complement educational research methodologies which are already well-established
in the social sciences. However, because the latter are so well developed,
there needs to be more focus on the former. It is not a case of allowing
discipline-based pedagogic models to monopolise educational enquiry, but

nor is it a case of academics in the humanities ceding 'the territory to vacuous technicist progressivism' (O'Loughlin, 2008: 12). This brings us to the second reason why, as an academic in the humanities, we would argue that you should feel free to use the tools you know best to engage in educational enquiry (albeit with an eye on the gains to be made from interdisciplinarity): you know your own disciplines better than anyone else, and are best placed to research the nature of teaching and learning within them. As Healey notes, 'the scholarship of teaching needs to be developed within the context of the culture of the disciplines in which it is applied' (2000: 169). He points out in a joint publication with Jenkins on discipline-based educational development, that some disciplines are characterised by distinctive forms of teaching (Healey and Jenkins, 2003). While the cases they give do not directly concern the humanities, some examples might include close reading of a text in literature, or primary source analysis ('gobbet' work) in history.

Building on the work of Wareing, it also seems that the values of discipline-based educational enquiry being carried out by those who are also practition-ers within the discipline can have manifold benefits. As discipline-based researchers you will, for example, tend to employ language, metaphors and epistemological assumptions familiar to others working in the discipline, you will be more inclined to address the aforementioned forms and styles of teaching specific to the discipline, and you will be more readily aware of particular skills requirements which affect student progression and achieve-ment in your discipline. You will also be more able to acknowledge existing habits of teaching and assessment than an 'outsider', and as an already-known member of a disciplinary community, perhaps find a more amenable audience for the resultant research findings (Wareing, 2005). You will ask questions and present ideas in a way that makes methodological and episte-mological sense to the disciplinary community whom the research is about and whose practice it is intended to enhance. The same research will in turn bring important new perspectives to educational enquiry as a whole; without discipline-specific content, educational enquiry is impoverished and of lim-ited interest to those operating outside the field of education.

It is also worth adding that at the time of writing this chapter, both the imperatives and incentives to enhance pedagogic practice in humanities disciplines have never been greater. In UK Higher Education we currently face a perfect storm: a severe economic downturn, coupled with a threefold rise in undergraduate degree tuition fees at most institutions. As a result, students are, understandably, becoming far more sensitive to the quantity and quality of their contact time with academic staff. In humanities subjects, where lab work and practicals rarely feature, this places even greater pres-sure on the pedagogic strategies employed in the classroom, and teaching practitioners in humanities subjects ignore the need to facilitate high-quality learning at their department and their discipline's peril. There has arguably never been a better, nor more important moment for humanities academics to start engaging in educational enquiry. Even institutions traditionally considered to be 'research-intensive' are starting to embrace excellence in learning and teaching, promoted in part by the UK's National Student Survey and national and international university league tables. Teaching excellence is increasingly being placed on a parallel with traditionally defined research excellence, with some universities instituting teaching-focused pathways to full professorships. In addition, bodies such as the UK's Higher Education Academy offer funding for small as well as larger discipline-based educational research projects at a time when funding for other forms of humanities research is dwindling.

So what does this mean in practice? In the remainder of this chapter, we will make some suggestions as to how methodologies and approaches common to many humanities subjects could be employed in developing educational enquiry in the humanities. The list we present does not pretend to be complete, or of equal value to every discipline; rather, the intention is to give you some initial ideas that you may wish to develop. We will proceed by dividing our reflections according to the two main types of source that researchers in the humanities most commonly use: written, or documentary, and non-written.

Written sources

Those of us engaged in humanities research can think of the many types of written or *documentary sources* that we analyse in our disciplinary studies. These include archival sources and primary sources (such as letters, diaries, poetry, songs or published material contemporary to whatever period we are studying), as well as relevant secondary sources (for example, books, articles and essays written by other academics) on whom our own research may draw and seek to refine, expand or refute. Similarly, educational enquiry within our disciplines can draw on documentary analysis of primary sources (for example, module handbooks, lecture and lesson plans, student written work, student module evaluation comments, and tutor reflections on the same) as well as secondary sources (such as studies of relevant pedagogical approaches and practices). As such, this route offers a clear potential link between educational research methods, humanities subject research and humanities educational research which could be exploited by humanities academics. Indeed, the fact that humanities academics spend so much of their time steeped in documents and engaged in documentary analysis, makes this approach an obvious choice of method for educational enquiry in humanities disciplines.

In terms of *how* written source material, once identified and resourced, may then be analysed with a pedagogical as opposed to traditional disciplinary research viewpoint, various humanities-friendly approaches spring to mind. At one level, much can be gained by using the very approach to primary source analysis that historians drum into their undergraduates at every possible moment: 'Who produced this source?', 'For whom was it produced?', 'Where? When? How? Why? To what effect?', 'How reliable is this source?', 'What are its biases and limitations?', 'What does it not tell us?' The application of such questioning to teaching-related sources will bring obvious insights; rather than looking at, say, a negative student module evaluation at face value, an appreciation of the wider socio-historical context in which the source was written, and a sharp sense of the potential limitations of the perspectives offered, will enable that evaluation to be more precisely analysed and its value appraised. The analysis of secondary literature can also work in exactly the same way for educational enquiry as for disciplinary work. In particular, the literature reviews which feature in many educational enquiry articles would resonate in the humanities, since a great deal of humanities subject research is based on the analysis and comparison of existing academic literature as a way of framing fresh research. As noted in Chapter 3 of this text, you should therefore find it a natural first step for educational enquiry in your discipline to engage in a literature review to contextualise the work that has been done before and consider fruitful developments of that work.

A further means of documentary analysis relevant to both the humanities and the social sciences is that of *conceptual analysis*, a form of documentary analysis which has a focus on ideas and their contested meanings, and with how this affects our understanding of the world. In conceptual analysis, the researcher examines terms, concepts and ideas which feature in documents, paying attention to the ways in which they are employed, their prevalence, and the adequacy and appropriateness (or otherwise) of their use, trying to understand what this connotes and what conclusions may be derived from it. This *close reading* of texts, this 'reading between the lines', so to speak, is ingrained in the approach to documents drawn upon by academics in the humanities.

Perhaps less prevalent in some humanities circles, but also worth including here, is the distinct yet related approach of *content analysis*. This method is quantitative, which some might regard as a reason to dismiss it. We include it in our chapter because we believe that quantitative research has a place in the humanities and that it could be a useful method for you to use in your educational enquiry. Content analysis has been defined as 'any technique for making inferences by objectively and systematically identifying specified characteristics of messages' (Holsti, 1969: 14, cited in Stemler, 2001). It can involve the counting of words and the identification of themes and dispositions or significant actors. In the humanities, it is most likely to take the form of textual analysis – it has been used to analyse printed texts, media documents, and song lyrics – but it is not limited to this, and may also be conducted on visual images and other materials.

Content analysis allows the researcher to identify patterns and themes in documents and other items; it is particularly useful for examining historical materials, because it allows for longitudinal analysis, enabling researchers to document trends over time. Of additional interest to humanities scholars will be its potential for determining authorship, because it allows researchers to compile a list of suspected authors, examine their prior writings, and correlate the frequency of words to help build a case for the probability of each person's authorship of the material under investigation (Stemler, 2001). Content analysis is also a transparent research method which has ease of replicability as one of its main advantages; the coding scheme and sampling procedure can be clearly set out, and the materials can normally be made available for others to use. Furthermore, it is an unobtrusive method which does not entail participants having to take the researcher into account, making it non-reactive, and it is a flexible approach which can be applied to a variety of different kinds of unstructured information. Finally, it allows information to be generated about social groups which are difficult to access.

However, content analysis is limited by the quality and the availability of material; it can only be as good as the documents on which the practitioner works (Bryman, 2012). This is true of any research method of course; the value of data is determined by the means by which the data are generated (for example, the way questions are written or the way the sample is selected) and by the way it is interpreted. Content analysis is also a descriptive method. It describes *what* is there, but it does not tell you *why* a particular term was used or *why* a particular pattern exists. Another potential pitfall of content analysis has been identified as faulty definitions of categories (Stemler, 2001) and the inevitability that researchers will determine categories and coding manuals that entail some interpretation and bias on their part. These factors can affect the reliability of the method. As Weber observes, problems with reliability are caused by the 'ambiguity of word meanings, category definitions, or other coding rules' (1990: 15, cited in Stemler, 2001). His recommendation is: 'To make valid inferences from the text, it is important that the classification procedure be reliable in the sense of being consistent: different people should code the same text in the same way' (1990: 12). This is echoed by Stemler's point that one of the most critical steps in content analysis is developing a set of explicit recording instructions for outside coders to follow (Stemler, 2001).

Scholars have urged particular caution when conducting content analysis by means of a word count. As an example, Stemler (2001; citing Weber, 1990) notes that synonyms may be used for stylistic reasons throughout a document and thus may lead the researchers to underestimate the importance of a concept. This relates to claims that content analytic studies have been accused of being atheoretical because the emphasis in content analysis on measurement can result in emphasis being placed on what is easy to measure rather than what is theoretically significant. Additional problems may arise when the aim is to impute latent rather than manifest content, since this increases the likelihood of mistaken assumptions (Bryman, 2012).

For these and other reasons, content analysis may be rejected out of hand by some humanities academics. We believe this is a mistake, because content analysis could valuably be used to underpin educational enquiry in your subject areas. For example, this method could be used to analyse module handbooks to assess, say the weight unconsciously placed by the writer upon certain learning outcomes over others. Insofar as content analysis deals with the identification of themes, dispositions, ideologies and beliefs, we believe its epistemological starting points correlate with many of the underlying aims of humanities research, making it an approach which has the potential to be both familiar and comfortable.

Non-written sources

A second major source accessible by academics in the humanities is that of non-written material; in disciplinary and social science-based educational enquiry alike this can include interviews, focus groups and observed behaviour. The idea that we can 'read' classroom performance and behaviour as a way of conducting educational enquiry is an interesting one. The 'Editor's Note' from a 2004 edition of *Teaching Theology and Religion* suggests also that there already exists among theology and religious studies academics the practice of reading one's own teaching career as a narrative, and it is not hard to see how the same could be applied to other disciplines where the concept of narrative is a significant one, such as history and English (Foster, 2004).

If behaviours, opinions and even careers can be 'read', how else might they be analysed? One approach, again not alien to most humanities disciplinary communities, is that of observation research. This falls into two types: structured/systematic observation, and unstructured observation, or ethnography. The former refers to the direct observation of behaviour and the recording of that behaviour in terms of predetermined categories devised prior to the start of data collection (Punch, 2009). There are various benefits to such an approach. For example, this method allows behaviour to be observed directly, unlike survey research, which only allows behaviour to be inferred (Bryman, 2012). Punch notes that structured observation 'breaks behaviour up into small parts'; although this can make it harder to grasp the bigger picture, it does facilitate the detailed recording and analysis of behaviours in a systematic manner (Punch, 2009: 155). Structured observation remains, though, an approach which works best when used alongside other methods since it rarely provides reasons for behaviour; it is of greater utility when accompanied with a method that can probe driving forces (Bryman, 2012). This can help obviate the risks of observers simply imputing intentions to what they see. There is also a danger of imposing an inadequate framework on the setting being observed; a solution to this can be for the period of structured observation to be preceded by a period of unstructured observation, so that appropriate variables and categories can be specified.

Unstructured observation, or ethnography, is the most prominent method of data collection alongside interviewing in qualitative research and is used to a greater or lesser extent in many humanities disciplines. The concept of 'ethnography' itself is derived from cultural anthropology and has been defined, pertinently for this chapter, as 'the art and science of describing a group or culture' (Punch, 2009: 124, citing Fetterman, 1989 and Neuman, 1994). It entails the prolonged participation of an individual, either covertly or overtly, in a particular social setting where they can observe the behaviour of members of that setting, ask questions and collect other relevant material, with an end goal of developing an understanding of that group within its own context (Punch, 2009).

The transferability of this approach to an educational context is not hard to imagine, and the advantages are numerous. The immersion in a given social setting enables the researcher to see through other people's eyes, to observe, confirm or counter what is taken for granted by interviewers, and to study deviant and covert activities (Bryman, 2004). Unstructured observation also allows for a naturalistic emphasis in which the world under scrutiny can be studied as far as possible in a 'natural' state undisturbed by the researcher: this can lead to telling encounters with the unexpected (known as 'rich points') as well as the expected (Punch, 2009; Green et al., 2012). The ethnographic approach does what other research approaches cannot, namely sensitise the researcher to cultural context and the symbolic significance of behaviours within that context (Punch, 2009). This allows some access to what could be described as 'insider meanings' (Green et al., 2012).

The classroom or similar learning environment provides you with the ideal opportunity to observe a particular group of people in a particular setting, and your ready access to it as a resource circumvents one of the potential disadvantages of unstructured observation: the difficulty of gaining access to a setting relevant to your research. Sometimes, this leaves researchers with covert research as the only option, but this has obvious disadvantages. Whilst it does guarantee that participants are less likely to adjust their behaviour because of the researcher's presence, it has ethical implications and comes with a fear of detection for the researcher (Bryman, 2012). Active and passive dilemmas are also a concern for the participant observer; they may feel that they have no choice but to get involved, even when the activities in which they participate are ones with which they are not comfortable. The observed may also feel unsettled by the shift in the classroom dynamic and by the effect this has on power relations between teacher and student. Naturally, students may behave differently if they know they are being observed. Finally, there is the problem of not knowing when to finish one's research; because of its unstructured nature and the absence of specific hypotheses to be tested, there is a tendency for participant observation to lack a sense of an obvious end point (Bryman, 2012). As Punch has noted, an ethnography 'is likely to be an unfolding and evolving sort of study, rather than prestructured' (2009: 127); as a result, flexibility and the ability to think on your feet are a must. Yet this approach remains very useful for humanities-based educational enquiry. It is interesting to note, for instance, that the QAA *Benchmark Statement* for Theology and Religious Studies lists the in-depth study of sacred practices, 'opportunities to consider the artistic, ethical, gendered, social, political and cultural char- acteristics of religion', and 'fostering empathetic engagement with both familiar and unfamiliar viewpoints' as being amongst the academic stand- ards for the subject (QAA, 2007b). Such standards may be particularly well (if not even best) met by means of participant observation. According to Patterson, who uses ethnography to teach theology and religious studies, fear is one of the most difficult hurdles to overcome when using this method: 'Fears about our right as non-experts to use ethnographic concepts and techniques, fears about the additional time and energy, fears about being too relationally and intellectually integrated with our students and Community Partners [the organisations in which Patterson's students were interned].' In her experience, only continual communication with her stu- dents, other staff and the participating organisations helped the class move through these fears and attain perspective (Patterson, 2003).

Alongside participation observation, interviews are a very widely employed method in qualitative research; again, here is an area in which many humanities researchers should not feel uncomfortable. Semi-structured or unstructured questionnaires and interviews would better suit the nature and purpose of most humanities disciplines than structured. As Becher and Trowler (2001) have written, in semi-structured interviews, the interviewer has a general list of points to be raised, but allows the respondent's interests and the resulting shape of the discussion to dictate the order and form in which these points are discussed and covered. Such interviews also have the potential for unprompted respondent-led points and ideas to arise in the interview in addition to those included in the pre-designed interview schedule and for additional questions and probes to be added as and when necessary. This approach clearly resonates with the kind of contextual questioning or close reading approaches that sit at the heart of many humanities subjects.

Related to this, but perhaps slightly less widely used in humanities research is the approach known as phenomenography. It does appear extensively in such disciplines as religious studies, however, and has been used to excellent effect in a recent article by Weller on 'Comparing Student and Lecturer and Student Accounts of Reading in the Humanities', where the focus was on students of theology, American studies, and comparative literature (Weller, 2010). Phenomenography is a form of ethnography which has been defined as 'the empirical study of the limited number of qualitatively different ways in which various phenomena in, and aspects of, the world around us are experienced, conceptualised, understood, perceived and apprehended' (Marton, 1994: 4424). The results of phenomenographic research are categories of description, in which different ways of understanding an entity or situation are logically and hierarchically interrelated to establish a typology. Ashworth and Lucas emphasise that 'a paramount requirement for phenomenography [is] to be sensitive to the individuality of conceptions of the world – it must be grounded in the lived reality of its research participants' (Ashworth and Lucas, 2000: 297, cited in Tight, 2003). This is achieved by 'bracketing' (Ashworth, 1999, cited in Tight, 2003). The objective of phenomenographic research is therefore to try to see the world from the subject's perspective as far as possible, meaning that the researcher has to set aside, or 'bracket', their own assumptions. It is as a result a particularly valuable method for researching student learning, and for coming to an awareness of the different ways in which students understand learning and approach studying.

Case Study 11.1   Empathetic engagement as a method for teaching religious history (McNary-Zak, 2002)

This useful case study recommends the phenomenological method of empathetic engagement as a method for teaching religious history, quoting the educational theorist Stephen Brookfield (1975):

> As with all phenomenological approaches, the purpose is to enter another's frame of reference so that the person's structures of understanding and interpretive filters can be experienced and understood by the educator, or a peer, as closely as possible to the way they are experienced and understood by the learner. (Cited in McNary-Zak, 2002: 104)

The study also cites Smart, who suggested a form of the phenomenological method as a complement to other methods of study and analysis which deals with the recurring problem of 'describing religious and secular worldviews as they actually are' (Smart, 1983, cited in McNary-Zak, 2002: 102). Smart refers to this method as structured empathy. Empathy 'helps us to better grasp the facts for the facts include the way [someone] feels and thinks about the world' (Smart, 1983, cited in McNary-Zak, 2002: 102–3).

McNary-Zak's own use of empathetic engagement to conduct educational enquiry was prompted by an African American student's claim that her family's story did not 'fit' with the material covered in a class on the history of American Catholicism. She recalls that the discernment of the student's worldview through a phenomenological process bracketed a particular moment and preserved her experience as legitimate without reducing it. Participation in this process required McNary-Zak to situate the student's remark in its appropriate context. She notes that her ability to 'feel in' enabled her to gain insight into the student's perspective and the source of her remark. Such empathy offered a non-threatening, non-confrontational way of seeing the student's worldview, and also diffused the traditional hierarchical power relation between teacher and student while still preserving otherness. This diffusion meant that the teacher became the learner and the student became a source of knowledge, and as such provided a unique opportunity to view and assess the course's operative assumptions. The result was a revised course and, one imagines, a deeper learning experience for both student and lecturer alike (McNary-Zak, 2002: 101–2).

The study outlines the advantages and disadvantages of empathetic engagement. One of the advantages is that this method cultivates an awareness of the multiculturalism and the need for deeper social interaction that characterises many classrooms. McNary-Zac also argues that:

> Empathetic engagement invites active participation in the ongoing process of interpretation of the past and present. When we encourage the unveiling of operative assumptions in ourselves and in our students we explore the realm of possibility for the study of religious history in the future. (2002: 104)

In terms of disadvantages, she points out that the method involves a risk which is often unfamiliar to students. It can lead them to realise that 'what [they] thought of as fixed ways of thinking and living are only options among a range of alternatives' (2002: 104). She reports that many students do not deem this risk a worthwhile one. In addition, for those students who choose to take this risk, the effects of empathetic engagement are initially personal and private. Only the individual can evaluate the dimensions of their empathetic engagement.

The final approach to which we would wish to draw attention is also one that can have a deep impact on students and practitioners, and is again one that is already used in humanities disciplines: a feminist approach. This is clearly more of a 'way of seeing' than methodology per se, yet has already been employed to creative effect in writing on the pedagogy of theology or, to be more specific, Thealogy (which unlike the term theology, relates to the study of the goddess).

Case Study 11.2   Using feminist approaches to the traditional seminar structure (Guest, 2008)

A key example here is an article by Guest entitled 'Because they're worth it: making room for female students and thealogy in higher education contexts', published in *Feminist Theology* in 2008. In this article, Guest employed her own critical self-reflection and her examination of student feedback to assess the value and discuss the difficulties of attempting to forge a women-only space within a traditional seminar structure. Her own particular agenda was explicit and unashamed:

> Partly then, the desire for a women-only class derives from the frustration that second wave feminist ideas seem to be being left behind when some women (certainly this woman) still thinks that some of those ideas and instincts were significant and durable, and the concomitant desire to try out something I never had the opportunity to take part in, but which always sounds as if it was a very positive experience for the women involved. (2008: 44)

Not only was Guest influenced by feminism in her intent, as she is in most of her academic output, but also in her subsequent analysis of the pedagogical situation she attempted to create. The result is a creative and provocative study that melds feminist criticism and educational enquiry together in a way that is innovative and an example of just how effectively discipline-based research techniques can contribute to educational enquiry.

Suggested activities

Activity 11.1

Run a focus group at the end of a module to ask your students about their views of the assessment methods you used and collate the data into a report for your colleagues.

Activity 11.2

Conduct a content analysis of your department's module handbooks from the past five years to identify any themes which have persisted, any changes of emphases which have occurred, and to help you redress any unintended biases (perhaps overemphasis on some modules at the expense of others which may lead to over- or under-recruitment for some modules; or undue emphasis on particular referencing systems).

 Activity 11.3

Introduce a group project into one of your modules (assessed or unassessed, as you choose) and explain to students that you will be silently observing their group meetings/activities. Share your observations with colleagues to generate a discussion about the pros and cons of using group work in your discipline; did group working give rise to any particular issues which suggest that it may be a particularly good fit for your discipline, or, which suggest that it conflicts with the culture of your discipline and is not a constructive method for educational research in your context?

Concluding thoughts

Our intention in this chapter has been to not only encourage you, as academics in the humanities, to engage in developing educational enquiry in your own disciplines, but to use the research methods of your disciplines to do so. Particular approaches have been highlighted, such as documentary analysis and observation research, but you are also encouraged to reflect on how you might apply research methods familiar to you in the analysis of teaching and learning in your own discipline. Hybrid methodologies, which encompass the best of disciplinary and the best of social sciences research approaches, can and should be embraced by academics in the humanities conducting educational enquiry. We encourage you, as discipline-based academics, to work with rather than against, methods from the social sciences. In our view, there is a symbiotic relationship between humanities-based and social sciences-based educational enquiry which has been under-exploited and which you are in a strong place to take forward.

Suggested further reading

Becher, T. and Trowler, P.R. (2001) *Academic Tribes and Territories: Intellectual Enquiry and the Cultures of Disciplines* (2nd edition). Buckingham: SRHE and Open University Press.

This is a classic text in the literature on higher education, which conceives of academic disciplines as distinct cultures. It explores the dynamics within disciplines and the relationships between different disciplines.

Rust, C. (ed.) (1999) *Proceedings of the 1999 7th International Symposium Improving Student Learning: Improving Student Learning Through the Disciplines*. Oxford: Oxford Centre for Staff and Learning Development, Oxford Brookes University.
This is a collection of essays which examine the role of disciplinary approaches to the scholarship of teaching and learning.

Healey, M. (2000) 'Developing the scholarship of teaching in higher education: a discipline-based approach', *Higher Education Research and Development*, 19(2), 169–89.
This article makes a strong case for discipline-based pedagogic research.

Bryman, A. (2012) *Social Research Methods* (4th edition). Oxford: Oxford University Press.
This is a comprehensive account of educational research methods and is a useful place to start for anyone embarking on educational research for the first time.

Some relevant journals:

- *Arts and Humanities in Higher Education*
- *Research in the Teaching of English*
- *Changing English: Studies in Culture and Education*
- *The History Teacher*
- *Studies in Medieval and Renaissance Teaching*
- *Journal of Music History Pedagogy*
- *Teaching Theology and Religion*
- *Discourse: Learning and Teaching in Philosophical and Religious Studies*

CHAPTER 12

ENQUIRY INTO LEARNING AND TEACHING IN THE HEALTH PROFESSIONS

Sharon Buckley and Patricia Fell

Learning outcomes

By the conclusion of this chapter it is anticipated you will:

- Have a greater awareness of the breadth of enquiry in health professions education;
- Recognise how your discipline expertise can inform your educational enquiry; and
- Feel confident about undertaking your own enquiry project.

Introduction

The importance of high-quality education for health professionals is well recognised by regulatory bodies such as the General Medical Council (GMC), the Nursing and Midwifery Council (NMC), the Health Care Professions Council (HCPC) and by international bodies such as the World Health Organisation (WHO). In recent years, the need for education and training to be underpinned by evidence has also been recognised (Ferguson and Day, 2005; Peterson, 1999). In 1999, Bligh and Parsell, writing in a medical context, clearly articulated the links between high-quality education, educational enquiry and subsequent clinical practice:

> Fundamentally, medical education is concerned with improving patient care. Ultimately, research into teaching and learning in medicine has its impact at the bedside, in the consulting room and in the wider community. (1999: 162)

Today, educational enquiry in the health professions is an increasingly well established and growing discipline, both in the UK and internationally, with professional organisations, peer-reviewed journals and active, engaged communities of educators who contribute to a growing evidence base for 'what works, for whom and in what circumstances' (Cook, 2012a).

The professional and academic backgrounds of those engaged in educational enquiry vary widely. They include not only the whole range of clinical professions, but also those trained in the life sciences, the social sciences or the humanities. An internet search of prominent figures in the field will quickly identify a radiographer who specialises in evidence-based education, a doctor developing the use of simulation in healthcare education, a sociologist working in interprofessional education (IPE) and an English graduate professor of clinical communication, among many others. The literature relating to the education of health professionals reflects this diversity, including both studies that draw on approaches from the positivist paradigm and those that reflect the interpretivist paradigm (Boet et al., 2011). For example, in 2010, the same issue of the *Journal of Research in Interprofessional Education and Practice* published both a randomised controlled trial that investigated the effects of interprofessional education on undergraduate students' behaviour in a simulated setting (Just et al., 2010), and a commentary on the value of ethnographic methods in health services and health professions education research (Gotleib-Conn, 2010).

This breadth of approach reflects the clinical arena, where the outcomes of experimental and observational methods drawn from the positivist paradigm influence practice (National Institute for Health and Clinical Excellence, 2012; Oxford Centre for Evidence Based Medicine, 2011) as, increasingly, do studies using methods drawn from the interpretive paradigm, which can often provide insight into areas that are not easily explored in other ways (Kuper et al., 2008). For example, between 2009 and 2011, as the 'Million women' cohort study was investigating the effect of different lifestyle factors, particularly hormone replacement therapy (HRT) on the health of middle-aged women in the UK (University of Oxford, 2013), others studies using semi-structured interviews and thematic analysis were shedding light on health professionals' experiences of discussing the place of death with terminally ill patients (Munday and Petrova, 2009) and on patient views about consultations with nurse prescribers (Stenner et al., 2011). As a health professional, depending on your own perspective, background and epistemological stance, you may have undertaken enquiry or used evidence drawn from studies based in either or both paradigms to inform your clinical practice.

When undertaking educational enquiry, or drawing on the healthcare education literature to inform your teaching, you will find yourself in a similar situation. In this chapter, we aim to provide you with a 'rough guide' to the breadth of health professions educational enquiry, to draw parallels between educational and clinical enquiry that illustrate how your professional skills can inform your educational investigations and to suggest some starting points for your own enquiry. We begin by considering the complexity of educational settings and the implications this has for the design and conduct of studies. We then outline the use of systematic reviews in health professions enquiry and how they can inform your educational work; explore issues relating to the use of one of the more controversial methods used in health professions enquiry – the randomised controlled trial (RCT) – and suggest that evaluation may be a fruitful starting point for your own investigations, allowing you to undertake relatively small-scale studies that can directly influence your own teaching practice. Along the way, we suggest parallels with the clinical setting that illustrate how your professional skills may inform your educational work. Finally, we draw on the experiences of individuals to offer insights into the reality of undertaking educational enquiry should you decide to engage in this exciting and fast-moving field.

The complexity of educational settings

The complexity of educational settings is well illustrated by an entertaining editorial in which Larry Gruppen, a psychologist working in the field of medical education, compares undertaking an educational RCT to investigating the spread of a virus using specifically bred, genetically identical laboratory rats. In education, as Gruppen observes, the 'rat' population,

> is happily running around the sewers, abandoned buildings or fields and may or may not be willing to cooperate for this study. Indeed, the researchers

may well be forced to lure the rats with bait. The rats are hardly genetically equivalent; there are Norway rats, pet rats, roof rats, and water rats. There may even be some hamsters, guinea pigs, and chipmunks mixed in. They have also come from various environments and have been exposed to a wide range of experiences and other pathogens before being caught for this research study. Once the researchers have gathered as many rats as they can (often less than what the power analysis might indicate), they attempt to randomise the rats into a control and intervention group, but, at this point, the SPCA steps in and declares that it is unethical to coerce the rats, so the researchers have to let the rats self-select to be exposed. (2008: 1–2)

This complexity, together with the varied backgrounds and perspectives of health professions educators, has led to vigorous discussion about both the types of evidence needed to inform educational development, and how enquiry should be undertaken. Contributors have considered the nature of evidence in clinical and educational settings (Patricio and Carneiro, 2012); the appropriateness or otherwise of RCTs and other experimental studies (Cook, 2012a; Baernstein et al., 2007; Norman, 2003); the similarities and differences between evaluation and research (Wall, 2010) and the utility of outcomes-based approaches to educational evaluation (Haji et al., 2013). Rejecting an *either/or* perspective, recent contributors have stressed the importance of choosing an investigative approach appropriate to the context being studied and to the question being asked. As David Cook, a prominent commentator on health professions education research has noted, 'We need carefully planned, theory-building, programmatic research, reflecting a variety of paradigms and approaches, as we accumulate evidence to change the art and science of education' (Cook, 2012a: 468).

Writing for those who are new to educational enquiry, Charlotte Ringsted and her colleagues (2011) have proposed a *research compass* model for educational enquiry that will help to clarify the purpose of a particular study, the questions it seeks to answer, and hence the most appropriate approach to use. The research compass model identifies four categories of study, each of which addresses a different purpose and type of question: explorative studies seek to describe phenomena and 'model' the relationships between them, experimental studies to justify an intervention, observational studies to predict outcomes and translational studies to consider the application of research findings to practice. The model builds on an earlier framework (Cook et al., 2008a), which suggested that educational enquiry may seek to describe a situation or intervention, justify an approach or clarify a situation, answering questions such as *What was done?*, *Did it work?*, *How or why did it work?*, respectively.

Whilst frameworks such as the 'research compass' can help to clarify the choice of approach and method, it is increasingly recognised that, for many questions, a 'mixed methods' approach that involves 'collecting, analysing and synthesising both quantitative and qualitative data in a single research project' (Halcomb et al., 2009: vi) is required. In their guide to using mixed methods in medical education research, Schifferdecker and Reed argue that 'the benefits of a mixed methods approach are particularly evident when studying new questions or complex initiatives and interactions' (2009: 637). These authors also argue that many health professionals will be familiar with such approaches from their clinical work as 'most patient care includes collecting and analysing both qualitative (patient history) and quantitative (physical examination and diagnostic test) data' (2009: 638). As such, it is likely that your professional approaches to data collection will serve you well as you undertake educational enquiry.

Reviewing the literature: systematic reviews in health professions education

Chapter 3 of this book discussed the importance of literature reviews for informing educational enquiry and commented that systematic reviews of the literature are relatively rare in higher education. In health professions education however, the preparation and use of systematic reviews is a well-recognised and growing trend. The Best Evidence Medical Education (BEME) collaboration is an important contributor to these developments, providing advice and support to groups reviewing a wide range of topics across many different branches of health professions education and publishing the outcomes of their work (BEME, 2013). At the time of writing, more than 20 BEME systematic reviews on topics as diverse as the use of simulation in clinical education (Issenberg et al., 2005) and the effects of using a portfolio on student learning (Buckley et al., 2009) have been published, and 16 more are in preparation (BEME, 2013). Developments such as these parallel the well-established use of systematic reviews to support clinical practice, and the ongoing work of organisations such as the Cochrane Collaboration whose systematic reviews provide sophisticated analysis and synthesis of primary research outcomes that can inform clinical decision making (Cochrane Collaboration, 2013).

As a health professional newly embarking on educational enquiry, the time and resource-intensive nature of a systematic review will most likely mean that you will be drawing on the insights of existing reviews to inform your work, rather than undertaking such a review yourself. In this regard, any experience you have of using the results of systematic review in your clinical practice will be very useful in helping you to navigate the world of educational systematic reviews. However, as you approach educational systematic reviews, it is important to be aware of the scope and nature of the systematic review in this field. From your clinical practice, your concept of systematic review may be one in which the results of studies that use experimental and possibly quasi-experimental methods, and which meet particular quality standards, are synthesised by statistical meta-analysis to give a sophisticated picture of the effectiveness or otherwise of a particular clinical intervention. As Case Study 12.1 illustrates, systematic reviews of this type have been undertaken in particular areas of health professions education.

 Case Study 12.1   A systematic review of internet-based learning in the health professions (Cook et al., 2008b)

In 2008, researchers from the Mayo Clinic, Minnesota and McMaster University in Canada published their review of the effectiveness of internet-based learning in health professions education. Two hundred and one out of nine hundred and thirty-one comparative studies retrieved for further consideration were included in the review. The authors undertook statistical meta-analyses comparing internet-based learning with no intervention and with non-internet based instructional methods. They found that, whilst internet-based learning was effective compared to no intervention, the differences between internet-based learning and other forms of learning were small, suggesting effectiveness similar to more traditional methods of instruction. They suggested that future studies should focus on 'how internet-based learning can be effectively implemented?' and 'when should internet-based learning be used?'

However, in health professions education, you will also find systematic reviews that adopt a very different approach. More recently, a second systematic review of internet-based health professions education used a realist approach which adopted a qualitative systematic review method 'to identify and explain the interactions between context, mechanism and outcome' (Wong et al., 2012: 93), as illustrated in Case Study 12.2.

 Case Study 12.2   Internet-based medical education: a realist review of what works, for whom and in what circumstances (Wong et al., 2012)

In 2010, Geoff Wong and his colleagues at University College London, UK, published their systematic review of the literature relating to internet-based education, this time considering only doctors and medical students. These authors undertook to extend the 2008 review by Cook and colleagues, investigating the questions left unanswered by the earlier work, including *how* internet-based learning can be implemented effectively and *when* such forms of learning should be used. Their review included studies of any design that used the internet to support learning involving medical students or doctors and containing evaluative data. Using a realist, qualitative approach to analysis of text and synthesis of data, they identified candidate theories that could explain the data they found in the 249 included studies. They concluded that learners are more likely to engage with internet-based learning if they perceive it to have greater benefits than non-internet alternatives, is easy to use and allows them to interact with a tutor or with their fellow students. However, like Cook and his colleagues before them, Wong and his colleagues found that their review was limited by the quality of reporting of published studies. They too exhorted educational researchers to report their work fully, in this case particularly to give rich descriptions of the intervention and context involved in their study that would facilitate future realist reviews of their work.

These two case studies illustrate the breadth of systematic reviews in health professions education. As both Wong and Cook have observed, education researchers wish to identify what works, for whom and in what circumstances and many systematic reviews in health professions education seek to investigate the evidence base for questions and topics for which experimental or quasi-experimental study designs are not appropriate. As such, you will find that the literature in health professions education includes different types of systematic review, again depending on the question being asked.

Experimental studies in health professions enquiry

The training and natural inclinations of many clinical educators may mean that they have a strong intellectual commitment to the use of experimental studies to support and inform clinical practice (Oxford Centre for Evidence-Based Medicine, 2011). It is not surprising, therefore, that examples of RCTs can be found in health professions educational enquiry as illustrated in Case Study 12.3.

Case Study 12.3   The effect of mindfulness practice on medical student stress levels (Warnecke et al., 2011)

This study investigated the effects of mindfulness meditation on the stress levels of medical students in the final two years of their programme. Over a period of eight weeks, students either undertook 30 minutes of guided mindfulness practice daily using an audio CD (intervention group) or were allocated to a 'usual care' control group that did not undertake any mindfulness practice. The study measured the effect of the intervention on students' stress levels using the Perceived Stress Scale (PSS) and the Depression, Anxiety and Stress Scale (DASS) and found that the practice of mindfulness could significantly lower students' levels of stress and anxiety. They recommended that such interventions be widely adopted within medical schools. The authors noted that whilst the trial supported the findings of other studies that had investigated the use of mindfulness, their study 'benefited from the superior study design of a single-blinded RCT' (2011: 382).

Recognising that study design should reflect the question being asked, acknowledges a place for experimental studies in health professions educational enquiry. However, the complexity of educational settings, so eloquently described by Gruppen (2008), means that designing and carrying out such studies is not a straightforward undertaking. This complexity is perhaps in part responsible for perceived limitations in the design and reporting of many published studies. David Cook who, together with colleagues, undertook the systematic review and meta-analysis of internet-based education illustrated in Case Study 12.1, has highlighted the limitations of studies that compare a teaching intervention with no teaching, commenting memorably that all such studies tend to show is that 'if you teach them, they will learn' (Cook, 2012b: 305). As such, Cook has argued cogently for study designs that compare different interventions (Cook, 2012b). Case Study 12.4 illustrates this approach, comparing two different interventions (in this case different forms of feedback on performance) against each other and against no teaching (no feedback on performance).

Case Study 12.4   The effect of feedback on learning of joint mobilisation skills (Chang et al., 2007)

The application of pressure to a joint in order to increase movement is an important skill for physiotherapists to learn. This study used an experimental study design to investigate whether giving students feedback about the degree of pressure they are applying to a joint aids their learning. A mechanical joint translation simulator simulated the tissue resistance students would feel when mobilising the joints of patients and gave them feedback about the degree of pressure being applied. Thirty-six undergraduate physical therapy students were randomly assigned to concurrent feedback, terminal feedback or control groups: being able to see the pressures they were applying during the training, after the training or not at all respectively. The study demonstrated that providing feedback helped students to learn the appropriate techniques, but that the timing of the feedback did not significantly affect their learning.

Case Study 12.4 illustrates that, whilst large effects are often seen when one form of teaching is compared with no teaching, differences between different types of intervention are often less easily observed. Since the effects of different interventions tend to be similar, detection of differences between them requires large sample sizes that are difficult for many studies to attain. Such difficulties are often exacerbated by incomplete reporting of experimental studies, particularly power calculations for RCTs (Baernstein et al., 2007), which can make it difficult for the reader to interpret the findings confidently. In this climate, health professionals who have experience of such approaches in clinical settings and who combine an experimental 'mindset' with sophisticated appreciation of the complexities of educational settings have much to contribute.

Evaluation in health professions educational enquiry

Evaluation of teaching and learning programmes is an essential part of educational practice that can inform curriculum development, assessment and educational policy (Frye and Hemmer, 2012; Tavakol et al., 2010; Wall, 2010) and, in consequence, is also an important part of health professions educational enquiry. In many ways, evaluation of educational programmes can be considered analogous to clinical audit or service review (Morrison, 2003). Both involve an ongoing cyclical model of reflection which seeks to ensure best practice through the continued review, analysis and implementation of change (Brain et al., 2011; Wall, 2010; Morrison, 2003) and both often address questions that require a mixed methods approach (Bowling, 2009; Goldie, 2006). If you have undertaken clinical audit or service review or used the results of such activities to inform your work, your familiarity and experience with these approaches may benefit your educational enquiry, particularly as limitations in the design of many educational evaluations have been recognised (Wall, 2010).

Educational evaluation can range 'from micro to macro, from the evaluation of individual teaching episodes to entire curricula, for the purposes of improving pedagogy or influencing national policy' (Wall, 2010: 336). As an academic new to the field, evaluation may offer a fruitful starting point for your educational enquiry, allowing you to undertake a relatively small-scale study that will benefit your educational practice, as Case Studies 12.5 and 12.6 illustrate.

 Case Study 12.5   Evaluating an undergraduate programme in mental health nursing (Yardley, 2011)

This study investigated how well a third-year mental health nursing curriculum equipped students to meet the physical health needs of adults with severe mental illness. The study used questionnaires and semi-structured interviews to explore students' knowledge and understanding of the factors that influence physical health in such patients and of the clinical skills needed to manage any problems that occur. Student perceptions of how the curriculum had prepared them for this aspect of practice were also explored. Yardley's findings highlighted deficits in students' knowledge and skills compared to the recommendations of professional bodies and led to curriculum change that helped the programme to address national concerns regarding the unmet physical health needs of adults with mental health problems.

 Case Study 12.6   Evaluating a peer-mentored hospital orientation day for medical students (Barker et al., 2012)

This recent evaluation of an educational initiative in which first-year medical students undertook a peer-mentored 'Hospital Orientation

Day' designed to provide insight into their future clinical training, used a mixed methods approach involving an online questionnaire survey and follow-up group interviews. Collecting mainly quantitative data, the questionnaire explored student perspectives on which aspects of the day were most beneficial to learning, whilst follow-up interviews provide a deeper understanding of its educational benefits. The findings showed that this initiative did foster students' insight into future clinical learning, highlighted the importance of student mentors in its success and suggested that the programme could be improved by introducing selection, training and appropriate rewards for student mentors.

Both of these case studies were undertaken by health professionals who were relatively new to educational enquiry. The next section considers their experiences of engaging in this new field and of bringing their disciplinary experience to bear on their educational work. For a fuller introduction to the area of educational evaluation, you may wish to explore the resources listed in the Further Reading section at the end of this chapter.

Some personal experiences of health professions educational enquiry

In deciding whether to get involved in educational enquiry, you may find it useful to hear from individuals who have already taken the step and who have found doing so beneficial on many levels. In 2012, we interviewed two health professionals in just this position: Lindsay Yardley and Tom Barker. Lindsay is a senior academic at Birmingham City University (BCU) who graduated as a nurse in 2003 and now teaches on a range of undergraduate nursing programmes. She undertook an evaluation of the mental health nursing curriculum at BCU as part of her Master of Education programme, which she completed in 2011. Tom is a trainee cardiac surgeon in the West Midlands who recently undertook a four-year clinical lecturer post at the University of Birmingham. In the second year of his lectureship, Tom enrolled on the first module of a Postgraduate Certificate in Learning and Teaching in Higher Education. Having enjoyed this more than he anticipated, he decided to complete the full qualification, which involved him undertaking the project to evaluate the hospitals orientation day for first-year medical students outlined in Case Study 12.6. Below is a digest of their perspectives on their engagement with health professions educational enquiry.

Both Lindsay and Tom are clear that their clinical background has informed their educational work. Tom reports that he: '*arranged for a couple of independent people to verify the thematic analysis ... I think it was because of my scientific background that I thought of that'*; whilst Lindsay comments that she: *'was able to use previously developed statistical analysis skills obtained through undertaking audits in clinical practice to help interpret the data obtained'*. In particular, skills used in their clinical work transferred well to the educational setting. Lindsay notes that: *'You need to be able to look at your research in an objective way … I think that is a skill that is transferable. Also the ability to analyse a situation and then apply problem solving skills … are transferable from the role of being a health professional to taking part in educational enquiry … although it may not initially feel like it … it's just applying them to a different context'*; whilst Tom found that: *'In essence, it [educational enquiry] wasn't different to doing scientific research. It wasn't a different thought process. It was just a case of trying to work it out'*.

However, both Tom and Lindsay found that it took some time to get used to working in a new area. For Lindsay, feelings of 'starting again' surfaced: *'I very much felt like a novice. One of the biggest barriers at first was understanding [the] language'*. For Tom, learning new skills was a gradual process: *'Methods such as thematic analysis are quite easy to learn and the more you do the better you become at it. At the beginning, you realise that you are asking a lot of leading questions; and then you listen to the transcripts and when you hear it back you try to improve'*.

In the end, for both Lindsay and Tom, the rewards of educational enquiry outweighed the difficulties. For Tom, reciprocity between his educational enquiry and his clinical work was an unexpected bonus: *'Undertaking the study definitely opened my eyes … in fact, I am now using the qualitative skills I developed in the postgraduate certificate in a study of tacit knowledge in cardiac theatres'*. For Lindsay, the rewards of working with students and influencing change were paramount: *'I think the rewards by far outweigh any of the barriers … for me, working with students in particular … to see the difference it is making to not only their learning but when we are out in the Trust … you just get a real sense of fulfilment … It's a real privilege'*.

Getting involved

We have found working with others involved in health professions education enquiry extremely valuable, indeed essential, to our work. While your institution will have its own communities of practice, there are many national and international organisations through which you can meet and work with other educators with similar interests.

The Royal College of Nursing (RCN) holds an annual education forum, and Networking for Education in Healthcare (NET) conferences provide excellent opportunities to meet and discuss issues of mutual interest. The UK Higher Education Academy discipline centre for Health and Social Care Education is devoted to practice and development of pedagogy in the health professions and holds regular events and workshops, including an annual conference. The Association for the Study of Medical Education (ASME) and the Association for Medical Education in Europe (AMEE) organise annual education conferences and publish peer-reviewed journals (*Medical Education* and *Medical Teacher* respectively); and AMEE has recently established *Med Ed World*, an extensive resource site through which regular webinars on topics of interest are held. Specialist groups are also active, for example the Society for Simulation in Health Care and the Centre for the Advancement of Interprofessional Education (CAIPE).

Concluding thoughts

In this chapter, we have attempted to illustrate the breadth of enquiry in health professions education, to suggest ways in which your clinical expertise can inform your educational work, and to offer ways of beginning to get involved. We recognise that the perspective that we have offered is influenced by our experience in medical and nursing education and that this discussion only 'scratches the surface' of a complex and dynamic field. However, we hope that our discussion has encouraged you to join us in learning more about 'what works, for whom and in what circumstances' for the benefit of our students and, ultimately, for the patients for whom they care.

Suggested further reading

The Association for Medical Education in Europe (AMEE) (available at: http://www. amee.org) produces a series of education guides that cover topical issues in medical and health professions education and are designed to inform teaching practice. The following two guides provide an excellent introduction to educational research and evaluation. Although written in a medical education context, both papers discuss issues of relevance to enquiry in any health profession education setting:

- Ringsted, C., Hodges, B. and Scherpbier, A. (2011) 'The research compass: an introduction to research in medical education: AMEE Guide No. 56', *Medical Teacher*, 33, 695–709.
- Frye, A. and Hemmer, P. (2012) 'Program evaluation models and related theories AMEE Guide no 67', *Medical Teacher*, 34, 288–99.

A good place to start in searching for systematic reviews in health professions is the Best Evidence Medical Education (BEME) website (http://www.bemecollaboration. org/Home/). This is an extensive site that includes links to published BEME systematic reviews, reviews in preparation and a wide range of resources relating to the nature of evidence in health professions education.

Further information about review methods and related issues can be found in:

- Cook, D.A. and West, C.P. (2012) 'Conducting systematic reviews in medical education: a stepwise approach', *Medical Education*, 46, 943–52; and
- Buckley, S. (2011) 'Case Study 6: reviewing evidence on the effects of an educational intervention', in K. Khan, R. Kunz, J. Kleijnen and G. Antes (eds) *Systematic Reviews to Support Evidence-Based Medicine* (2nd edition). London: Royal Society of Medicine, 139–148.

The National Foundation for Educational Research (NFER) has produced a useful guide to undertaking RCTs in education. Although not specific to health professions education, this guide includes a discussion of the differences between biomedical and educational RCTs and gives an in-depth consideration of design issues.

- Hutchinson, D. and Styles, B. (2010) *A Guide to Running Randomised Controlled Trials for Educational Researchers*. Slough: NFER.

For a practical guide to undertaking evaluation the following two resources will point you in the right direction:

- The evaluation cookbook available at: http://www.icbl.hw.ac.uk/ltdi/cookbook/cookbook.pdf. Although not specific to health professions education it provides an 'easy to read' overview of evaluation methods.
- Goldie, J. (2006) 'Evaluating educational programmes. AMEE Education Guide no 29', *Medical Teacher*, 28(3), 210–24. A guide to provide educators with a framework for undertaking evaluation. Although written in a medical education context it is relevant in any health profession education setting.

If you are thinking about including students as partners in your educational enquiry you will find the Higher Education Academy's 'Students as Partners' web page a useful starting point. This site contains links to evidence, resources and case studies. Available at: http://www.heacademy.ac.uk/students-as-partners.

Links for the associations mentioned in the above chapters are given below. All were accessed in July 2013.

- The Higher Education Academy discipline centre for health and social care education. Available at: http://www.heacademy.ac.uk/health-and-social-care
- Royal College of Nursing Education Forum Community. Available at: http://www.rcn.org.uk/development/communities/rcn_forum_communities/education
- Networking for Education in Healthcare (NET). Available at: http://www.jillrogersassociates.co.uk/net-conference-home.html
- The Association for the Study of Medical Education (ASME). Available at: http://www.asme.org.uk/
- The Association for Medical Education in Europe (AMEE). Available at: http://www.amee.org
- Academy of Medical Educators. Available at: http://www.medicaleducators.org/
- Society for Simulation in Health Care. Available at: http://ssih.org/
- Centre for the Advancement of Interprofessional Education (CAIPE). Available at: http://www.caipe.org.uk/

CHAPTER 13

ENQUIRY INTO LEARNING AND TEACHING IN THE PROFESSIONS: THE CASE OF LAW

Rob Clucas and Gerry Johnstone

Learning outcomes

By the conclusion of this chapter it is anticipated that you will:

- Be aware of the contested nature of 'law' as a discipline;
- Be able to appreciate the diversity of approaches to legal scholarship;
- Be able to understand the characteristic resources of legal scholarship; and
- Be ready to apply these resources to your own educational enquiry.

Introduction

Our goal in this chapter is to introduce and demonstrate some 'resources' that legal scholars might bring to the field of educational enquiry. Our chapter begins with a discussion of legal scholarship and its trajectory before discussing the results from a pilot study about the phenomenology of legal scholarship, and identifying the characteristic resources of a legal scholar. In the final two sections of this chapter, we employ these typically legal resources in our examination of two brief case studies, on assessment and widening access to higher education.

What is legal scholarship?

In order to explain to 'outsiders' or 'newcomers' what scholars within any discipline do, it is useful to elucidate two things: (i) the object of enquiry and (ii) how scholars approach the object of enquiry (the goals they pursue, the sort of questions they tend to ask, and the methods they typically use to answer them). In the case of law, it is relatively easy to explain the object of enquiry: law is something that most people are familiar with (Simpson, 1988: 1). Whereas those who study calculus, semiotics, or photonics might find it hard to explain what they study to newcomers, legal scholars should not find this difficult – they may provide a reminder that there is more to law than criminal law, and explain that law consists of rules and principles which regulate many aspects of our lives, creating entitlements and obligations, which are used to prevent and resolve disputes.[1] However, what is more difficult to get across is what legal scholars do when they study or research law.

What most legal scholars used to do, and what many still do, is often called 'black-letter' law or 'doctrinal' analysis. In order to explain the nature of doctrinal analysis it is useful to start by thinking about what practising lawyers or legal service providers do, since, as we shall see, a central purpose of doctrinal analysis is to enable law to function as a social practice.

Consider the following hypothetical scenario (which is the sort of scenario a first-year law student will cut their teeth on):

- I said to you: 'I'll sell you my bike for £200';
- You replied: 'That sounds like a good deal';
- The next day, you sold your own bike for £100, and turned up at my house with £200 in cash and asked for the bike;
- I then said: 'Sorry, X has offered me £250, so if you want it you'll have to match that';
- As you now have no bike and need one urgently, you reluctantly pay the extra £50 but indicate that you feel I was obliged to sell the bike for £200 as originally agreed.

---

[1]This is of course an oversimplification; for a discussion of the concept of law debate, see Clucas and O'Donnell (2002) and for the form/function debate, see Adams and Brownsword (2006).

If you subsequently decide you would like to recover your £50, and I refuse to refund it, you might consult a lawyer or legal adviser. You would be looking for two things:

1. A clear answer as to what the law says about this situation. Was I obliged to sell you the bike for £200? Are you now entitled to recovery of the £50 extra you unwillingly paid?; and
2. If you do have a legal entitlement, legal representation/assistance in the process you have to go through in order to recover your losses.

These are classic jobs of a lawyer, providing legal advice and assistance on a professional basis to resolve disputes. Lawyers might also advise and assist somebody to conduct their affairs in such a way that they meet their obligations and get what they are entitled to without getting involved in costly legal disputes, whether this involves contract, as above, or property (helping somebody to order the transferring of property on their death) or some other matter (and see Llewellyn, 1940, for an expansion of the 'law jobs').

However, one thing law students quickly learn is that the law governing many situations is not neatly defined and available in one location. In order to know the law relevant to the dispute set out above, it is necessary to understand and to be able to apply the principles of the law of contract. But, legal principles and rules have their source in a huge and complex variety of documents and practices. These include legislation emanating from the UK parliament and from Europe, delegated legislation (more detailed rules made by local authorities and a bewildering variety of agencies empowered by 'primary legislation'), and precedents (i.e. rules of law emerging from the way courts decide particular cases). Hence, it may be complex to find the sources of law on any particular matter (and one needs to know how to read that source), and it is also likely that the law is in many areas vague, unclear and incoherent.

This takes us to the task of the 'doctrinal' legal scholar which is to organise the law relating to a particular activity or issue into a coherent and workable body of legal doctrine. In order to do this, the doctrinal legal scholar must develop the knowledge and skills required to analyse a wide range of sources, using a variety of analytic techniques, such as 'finding' the *ratio decidendi* of a case (i.e. the legal principle on which an actual decision was based) or applying different rules of statutory interpretation, and to present the findings in an ordered and systematic manner.

One thing you might notice here is that in this doctrinal tradition of legal research, the legal scholar is basically servicing the legal profession. The legal scholar makes the law coherent and workable, so that legal professionals can better advise and assist their clients. A characteristic of legal scholars who work in this doctrinal tradition is that they have quite close ties to the legal profession, and many are actually qualified as legal professionals. Concomitantly, many have quite loose or even barely existing ties to scholars in cognate academic disciplines.

For complex reasons, this entire paradigm of legal scholar as assistant to the legal professions began to be transformed a few decades ago. Although doctrinal legal research still exists, and may still be the hub of many legal scholars' work, it has been challenged and to some extent displaced by a variety of different conceptions of the role of the legal scholar. The story of this change is a complex one, and here we have space only for an extremely brief sketch, but it is crucial to relate this if we are to think about what legal scholars can bring to educational enquiry.

Part of the origins of this change was the adoption by some doctrinal scholars of a more evaluative approach to particular judicial decisions and areas of law. In doing so, most appealed to values which some of the law-creators (mainly judges, and to a lesser extent parliamentarians) themselves proclaimed. One such value is *fairness*. Many judges, in deciding a particular case, claim not to be blindly following existing rules and precedents, but interpreting and applying these in a manner designed to produce a fair outcome. Another such value is *reason*. Again, judges often claim that reason points them to a certain outcome. Using these 'internal legal values' as their cues, some legal scholars began evaluating particular decisions and areas of law, using as a critical standard some sense of fairness and rationality. In textbooks, a trend started whereby straightforward exposition of the law began to be followed by appraisal and, to the extent that the law fell short of the standards of fairness and rationality applied by legal scholars, by proposals for legal reform.

This trend opened a small gap between legal scholars and legal professionals, who, on the whole, preferred a 'plain fact' view of law as the rules-in-the-books, uncomplicated by demands for essential fairness or rationality. As such, some legal scholars who were particularly keen on evaluative legal scholarship began to show more interest in other disciplines which could provide important conceptual and methodological resources that they could draw upon. Rather than appeal simply to intuitive but rough notions of fairness and reason, and often in parallel with an understanding of law as intrinsically intertwined with moral values, many began to draw upon works in other disciplines which could make their evaluative scholarship sharper and better informed. For example, theories of justice developed by philosophers might be drawn upon in order to give content to the idea of 'fairness'.

As they became more exposed to other disciplines, many legal scholars began to work in a manner that was methodologically more sophisticated. First, social and political science and theory were drawn upon in order to pose interesting questions about the ideology of law: about how law was shaped less by neutral application of objective and universal standards of justice and fairness, more by socio-economic structures and interests and the social values of particular classes, races and genders. Secondly, an interest emerged in evaluating law not just by looking at 'law in the books', but at 'law in action': if the fairness of a particular rule is in question, it is crucial not simply to examine the rule as an abstract entity, but to examine how the rule is applied and with what sorts of effects in the 'real world'. This requires different means of working, with traditional techniques of legal analysis being supplemented by empirical methods from the social scientists. In result, it is now much harder to draw sharp distinction between what legal scholars do and what empirical social sciences or analytical philosophers, or social and political theorists, do.

The characteristic features or resources of legal scholarship and what they might bring to educational enquiry

What, then, is legal scholarship? In this second section of our chapter, we discuss what constitutes the 'characteristic features' or 'characteristic resources' of legal scholarship, despite its varied nature, and what these features or resources might bring to educational enquiry.

In order to identify these, we have carried out a small (pilot) empirical study, which is being expanded and written up fully elsewhere (Clucas, in progress). Our study was an exercise in descriptive phenomenology using the methodology of Giorgi (1992), to discover the lived experience – the 'what' and 'how' – of legal scholarship. This study focused on first-person written accounts of a recent experience of doing legal scholarship by three legal academics at the University of Hull (which we believe is typical of types of legal scholarship in the UK). In our analysis, we sought to discern the underlying structure of the experience, describing both the essence of the experience of doing legal scholarship, and individual/sub-specialist specific meanings also. The common features of legal scholarship that underpin all these experiences are the following.

Responsiveness to real-world issues

All participants saw their work as being in some way a response to real-world problems that have (or could have) an important impact on individuals and organisations. These 'real-world problems' were as varied as proposals put forward by policy makers; the identification and analysis of types of decision making made in a particular area of bureaucratic practice; and the exercise of power within a particular legal area, examined over time through case studies. It is characteristic that legal scholars are interested in the impact of legal rules and power and the regulation of the lives of individuals and organisations. It is this type of focus on the effect of rules and power on real people that is likely to make our application of legal scholarship to educational enquiry so distinctive. As we hope you will see from the case studies below, legal academics tend to ask particular types of questions about the framing of a debate or issue, and have a characteristic sensitivity to questions of (a) workability or means–end rationality of certain systems of rules, and (b) the fairness, both substantive and procedural, of those rules.

Law as an analytical discipline

Legal scholarship is very analytical, in a way that has parallels with, but is not identical to, philosophy. The participants shared a common understanding of conventional (doctrinal) legal scholarship as being concerned with close analysis of primary legal materials (legislation and case law), though they did not all claim to engage (exclusively or at all) with doctrinal methods. When we apply this practice to the study of education, we see its utility in a focus on the primary materials at hand (often rules of some kind), and a careful evaluation of their coherence and values.

The rigorous evaluation of arguments

Closely related to these first two points is the legal scholar's rigorous evaluation of arguments. When considering the impact of rules or power on individuals or organisations, legal scholars are not content to take claims about efficacy or justice at face value. They also have a watchful eye on the coherence of a set of associated arguments on an issue: two or more claims may be sound in isolation, but do they contradict each other when taken as part of a connected whole? The value of this habit to other disciplines will be obvious to you.

A legal sense of authority

To provide 'authority' is a technical legal practice in which a scholar might cite a statute or a case in support for a proposition of law, that is, as having a sense of right, weight, evidence, and authorisation. This is a custom that probably has its roots in the advocacy of legal practitioners, but it is also a useful scholarly habit. In our study, questions of authority took the following form: why ought you to recognise the competence of a particular person to comment on such-and-such an area, or the appropriateness of a particular topic for *legal* enquiry, or why should you regard a particular person as having reliable standards of scholarship? All of these questions are variations on a repeated and penetrating 'Why?' This sceptical attitude insists on some demonstration of the reasons for following a particular rule, practice, or pronouncement, and acts as a safeguard against the blind following of practices or persons.

Legal scholarship as a persuasive practice

In their writing of what could have been a purely descriptive account, our participants shaped their narratives in a characteristically clear, ordered and persuasive way that seemed to have an eye on the influencing of the reader. We suspect that the roots of this attribute are in the technical training of constructing an argument for advancing one's client's interests. Persuasion is, of course, not a trait that is limited to law as a discipline, but the participants' accounts do seem to display a very distinct style of writing when compared to the observations of a scientist, or even social scientist, for example. You may gauge the worth of this distinctively legal scholarship practice to educational enquiry by the success of our persuasive endeavours, explicit and less so, in this chapter.

There were clear variations in the experiences of our participants, and so only the elements above can be described as universal. However, there is one particularly significant, non-universal, yet also very typical feature of legal scholarship that we believe it is worth drawing attention to here, and that is *interdisciplinarity*. One of our participants described research that is predominantly doctrinal in style; the other two participants were concerned with clearly interdisciplinary work that transcended and even disregarded the traditional doctrinal 'legal' boundaries.

As stated above, these divergent experiences of legal scholarship have their roots in the theoretical divisions within the discipline, between predominantly doctrinal scholars who service some branch of the legal professions or institutions, and between scholars who contest the boundaries of law as being limited to formal legal institutions, and/or who regard the questions of values such as justice and equality as central to law, rather than as necessarily external values. Because of these fundamental disagreements about the nature of law itself, it seems unlikely that an interdisciplinary approach to law will ever be universal to legal scholars.

Nonetheless, interdisciplinarity is significant to law in the same way that having two legs is significant to human beings: not all human beings possess two legs, so this cannot be said to be a *universal* experience, but having two legs is an important and frequently occurring aspect of the experience of being human! This type of approach is pragmatic, seeking to employ methods that further our understanding whether or not they are regarded as 'orthodox' for the area being studied. Our participants were also keen to stress the need for ensuring rigour and avoiding dilettantism, by working with scholars in different fields, and by expanding their own scholarship competencies. This characteristic of legal scholarship may therefore be said to be a willingness to engage at a deep level with methods that work for whatever area is being studied, without feeling hamstrung by disciplinary boundaries.

What conclusions can we draw from this enquiry into the *what* and *how* of legal scholarship? We can see that if we wish to think about what legal scholars can bring to educational enquiry, we need to grasp that much of this is not so much highly technical legal analysis, or a distinctive legal technique that is divorced from other disciplines. Rather, its contribution is likely to be something broader but less precise. The key offerings, we suggest, are a highly analytical and rigorous approach that is responsive to the real-world problems of individuals or groups, combined with a keen focus on issues of fairness, rationality and justification. Being a legal scholar also seems to inculcate a disposition to typically persuasive writing. In addition to this, many varieties of legal scholarship will offer a well-honed interdisciplinarity gleaned from engaging with a range of cognate disciplines which are drawn upon as sources of concepts and methods that might be employed in evaluative legal scholarship. In the sections that follow, we engage with these resources of legal scholarship to illuminate our two case studies.

 ### Case Study 13.1   Assessment in law – procedural fairness

How might a characteristically legal approach to assessment aid educational enquiry? Here, we suggest that even the questions asked by a legal scholar are likely to be different to most other disciplinary approaches to this issue. In this short case study, we do not examine how (best) to assess students in general, or how best to assess the substantive content of a particular module. Rather, we are interested in the administrative rules and procedures that surround the assessment process, and the exercise of power involved.

In recent decades there has been an increased emphasis on robust marking procedures that ensure reliable and fair examining of students, at a standard commensurate with the rest of the higher education sector. Moreover, these procedures need to be tough enough to ensure consistency across academics and within an academic's own practice, during high-intensity marking periods with urgent externally imposed deadlines. The fact that we now have marking criteria and outline answers encourages the sense of objectivity and scientific methods, as does argument between colleagues about whether to award a 58 or 60 to a particular piece of work (see Shepherd, 2000, for a discussion of the philosophical paradigm that these teaching assumptions are rooted in).

Objectivity and consistency are key components of a particular type of fairness concerned with universal administration, or procedural justice. For example, if essay X has characteristics a, b and c, and you award it 65 per cent, then you ought to do likewise to essay Y that has relevantly similar characteristics. Procedural justice is not the only academic concern: there is an implicit concern for substantive justice, or individual merit, also. If you were to choose some other method of grading assessments than those specified in the published marking criteria – perhaps, in times of marking overload, you are tempted to 'process' your exam scripts by throwing them from the top of a flight of stairs and assigning grade according to the step each script lands on – you would be aware of the unfairness of doing so, as well as the dereliction of professional standards this would entail.

Yet, for all our concerns about assessing our students justly, academics seem, as a class, slightly casual about questions of procedural and substantive justice throughout the assessment process as a whole. Anecdotally, we have heard reports of boards of examiners at some HE institutions where procedural requirements – the rules of progression and degree classifications – have been ignored wholesale in the interests of doing what one person in one meeting feels is right for one particular student. Here, there is a conflict between what is arguably fair to the individual student (substantive justice) and the issue of (a) applying rules that are published and are applicable to a particular case, and (b) consistently applying rules to relevantly similar students (two aspects of procedural justice), without recognition or explicit discussion of the tensions between these values.

At a less idiosyncratic level, we might also consider the rules of degree classification themselves, and not merely their application. As you will be aware, if you have lived through institutional changes in classification rules, or moved institutions, changing weighting of the final year, or the borderline boundary between degree classes, and the rules that are applied to these borderline situations, has a material impact on the degree classifications of individual students, as does 'dropping' the student's worst results. As Yorke et al. (2004) note, in an article in which the impact that another institution's algorithm would have on the degree classifications of students considered, the variable results were shown to be 'disturbing' and significant. A student who was awarded a 2:1 at one institution, would, elsewhere, achieve only a 2:2 (see also Yorke et al., 2002, for consideration of grading methods and equity, and Stowell, 2004, for discussion of equity, justice and standards in assessment decision making in higher education in the UK).

As legal scholars, we are interested in the exercise of power – here, specifically, the power of individual institutions to determine their individual degree classification rules, and the impact this has on individual students. To the best of our knowledge, there is no league table available that compares these rules, and no general awareness among prospective students of their importance – despite there being a keen interest in a student's

(Continued)

(Continued)

chances of graduating with a 2:1 from a particular institution. This seems strange to us. If you were negotiating a contract and had a choice of legal jurisdiction, you would be well advised to choose that which was most favourable to your interests; likewise if you were electing whether to deal with the end of your marriage or civil partnership in secular courts, secular mediation, or religious forms of alternative dispute resolution.

In the field of the sociology of human rights, discussing the unevenness of the applicability of supposedly universal rights, Woodiwiss observes that:

> inequalities intrinsic to even 'good societies' also, to varying degrees, affect the coverage, value content and legal form of their domestic rights discourses ... each society will tend to produce a human rights regime that suits itself, especially in the sense that it interferes as little as possible with the prevailing disposition of power. Thus, although human rights regimes provide protections for the weaker parties in sets of social relations, there are always modes of protection available that are less disruptive of the status quo than others, and these less disruptive regimes are those that tend to become established. (2005: 5)

Woodiwiss is referring here to the tendency of human rights regimes to prefer the (hetero) normative person as rights holder: the land-owning, white, male subject rather than the landless, non-white, female subject. A similar process is observed by do Mar Pereira (2012) concerning feminist theory, in the way that non-feminist scholars draw epistemic boundaries and relate feminist scholarship to these, enabling and legitimating a selective engagement with feminist work that corresponds conveniently with mainstream frameworks of knowledge.

As legal scholars we are well positioned to ask whether a similar pattern of preference is operating in the institutional rules of degree classification. Might there be normativities in higher education that are being obscured by our general failure to enquire into the schemes adopted by particular types of institution? Are there particular types of students that are favoured or disadvantaged by certain classificatory patterns? Which institutional interests are supported by minimal tinkering with classification rules, rather than wholesale review? Which types of accommodation, results or circumstances are 'proper' in relation to degree classification, and which are discarded as being unworthy of notice (and by which standards)?

In sum, in this brief (and necessarily limited) consideration of assessment, we hope to have exemplified, at least in outline, the characteristically legal resources of analytical rigour, a focus on the real-world issue of the impact of classification rules on individual students, a concern with justice, and an engagement with interdisciplinary scholarship that may shed light on this area. As a legal scholar, we argue that you are extremely well placed to draw on your disciplinary skills to ask these questions of your own institution or to extend your questioning powers to other areas of your teaching and students' learning.

Case Study 13.2   Widening access to higher education

Our second case study focuses on policies of widening access to higher education. We take 'widening access policies' to be any policy, whether initiated by government or pursued by institutions themselves, designed to enable people from disadvantaged backgrounds to participate in higher education and to attend the top universities should they have the ability to do so. Such policies could, of course, extend to different types of groups, but the emphasis, in Britain at least, has tended to be on those suffering from 'socio-economic disadvantage'. Such policies are also the subject of more systematic enquiry by specialists in educational research and social scientists (Brennan and Naidoo, 2008; Kettley, 2007). One legal scholar, Lois Bibbings (2006) analyses such policies, although she draws as much upon her experience in widening participation work as upon her legal knowledge and skills.

Why did we select this topic as a case study? We believe that it showcases how our distinctively legal resources not only provide us with a different 'take' on issues in educational enquiry, but also an interest in topics that might be neglected by other education scholars.

As legal scholars, our almost inevitable starting point is the identification and analysis of the arguments proffered respectively by advocates and critics of widening access. Just as in a law case, arguments are presented by those advocating and those opposing a particular outcome to a dispute (say, that X should give Y £50), and these arguments are then weighed in terms of their persuasiveness (are they evidenced; are they well-reasoned; are they presented well?), we might do the same for the debate over a public policy. In what follows, we draw upon various sources but especially the survey in Taylor et al. (no date).

(Continued)

(Continued)

Key arguments in favour of widening access policies include:

- they are needed in order to tackle social disadvantage and exclusion – which is a product (as well as a cause) of lack of participation in higher education;
- they can benefit universities in that they break down barriers between universities and the communities in which they are located and hence help universities to become and to be regarded as more socially relevant;
- they can improve the educational experience of all students in university since a more diverse student body is likely to lead to a richer range of perspectives being brought to bear on various subject matters;
- they can improve society, since participation in higher education tends to make people better citizens;
- they can be implemented without any sacrifice of educational standards.

On the other side, those against widening access policies may argue that they:

- dilute the value of a university education and degree, which *should* be a mark of distinction;
- are discriminatory, with middle-class students and students from private schools being pushed out of top universities to make way for increasing numbers from deprived backgrounds;
- are based on speculation and even wishful thinking – there is no evidence to support various claims made about the social benefits of widening access, especially its supposed potential to reduce social exclusion;
- are very expensive – retention and completion rates for students recruited through widening access policies have been low and overcoming this requires huge resources to be directed towards pastoral care, extra support, and so on (which is most likely to be allocated by diversion of resources from other, more traditional, HE activities);
- lead to a general decline of standards and the proliferation of 'Mickey Mouse degrees' which do not immerse students in an academic discipline but rather seek (with limited success) to impart knowledge and skills traditionally transmitted through apprenticeships and in-house training.

As legal scholars we are extremely well placed to subject these and other positions to critical scrutiny, using various methods. We could simply assess the merits of each individual argument. For example, with regard to the (critics') claim that widening access polices are expensive and divert resources away from more traditional higher education activities, as lawyers we would want to examine whether there was any evidence to support such a claim. In addition, however, we could examine the *force* of such claims, even if they could be established. For example, if we did find evidence of extra costs associated with widening access, and some transfer of resources, we would ask why that, in itself, amounted to a fatal criticism of policies of widening access: why is extra cost assumed to be more important than the benefits? One could acknowledge that widening access will be expensive but still regard it as desirable, and/or one could consider whether resource implications could be addressed in some other way.

Taking this analysis of the arguments deeper, as legal scholars we would be able to *distil* the argument between advocates and critics of widening access, and tease out the differences that really matter (a core legal skill), as follows. On one side, advocates believe that widening access is required by demands of social justice, *and* this would on the whole be beneficial to universities and society. Hence, there is the 'justice' argument and the 'social benefits' argument, and these need to be analysed separately (and given relative weight). Critics, on the other hand, oppose widening access policies because they believe them to be unjust (operate with a different notion of justice to the advocates) and because they regard them as undermining all that is valuable about (traditional) university education.

Our guess is that, as legal scholars, we might be wary about reaching a firm conclusion on the desirability, or not, of widening access. We would be content to provide an analysis that enables readers to make up their own minds, but in full awareness of the range and complexity of the issues involved, including the genuinely competing values at stake. What is important from the legal perspective is that there is informed and nuanced debate about the matter rather than the more common trading of rival slogans.

Suggested activities

Activity 13.1

Undertake a review of assessment policies, procedures and practices in your department, indicating what reforms, if any, you would introduce.

Activity 13.2

Analyse the range of attitudes towards widening access in your department and institution. How would you seek to influence policies and attitudes in your setting?

Concluding thoughts

We hope to have explained, and exemplified in our case studies, some of the distinctive qualities of legal scholarship: analytical rigour, a focus on real-world issues, a concern with justice, rationality and justification, and an engagement with interdisciplinary scholarship. Constraints of space mean that we have been unable to develop our analyses (and persuasive writing) in a manner that would be available elsewhere, but nonetheless we hope that you will have some appreciation of not only *what* our specific toolbox of skills can add to educational enquiry, but *how* our particular legal perspective shapes the topics we find interesting, and our focus on particular aspects of these topics.

As a concluding observation, we note that education as a practice is situated within educational institutions, and is thus a paradigmatic example of law understood in the broad functional sense as 'the enterprise of subjecting human conduct to the governance of rules' (Fuller, 1969: 96). It seems to us that enquiry into these aspects of education in particular, would be likely to bear fruit for the legal scholar.

Suggested further reading

Feintuck, M. and Stevens, R. (2013) *School Admissions and Accountability: Planning, Choice or Chance*. Bristol: Policy Press.

Sedley, S. (2011) *Ashes and Sparks: Essays on Law and Justice*. Cambridge: Cambridge University Press.

Wacks, R. (2008) *Law: A Very Short Introduction*. Oxford: Oxford University Press.

REFERENCES

AARE (2013) *Code of Ethics* [online] http://www1.aare.edu.au/pages/page72.asp [Accessed 10 August 2013].

Adams, J. and Brownsword, R. (2006) *Understanding Law* (4th edition). London: Sweet and Maxwell.

AERA (2011) *Code of Ethics* [online] http://www.aera.net/Portals/38/docs/About_AERA/CodeOfEthics(1).pdf [Accessed 10 August 2013].

AHRQ (2013) *Dissemination Planning Tool: Exhibit A Advances in Patient Safety: From Research to Implementation* [online] http://www.ahrq.gov/pinofessionals/quality-patient-safety/patient-safety-resources/resources/advances-in-patient-safety/planning-tool.html [Accessed 24 July 2013].

Allen, D. and Tanner, K. (2005) 'Approaches to biology teaching and learning: from a scholarly approach to teaching to the scholarship of teaching', *Cell Biology Education*, 4, 1–6.

American Society for Plant Biology (2012) *ASPB Education Foundation Grants* [online] http://my.aspb.org/?EF_Grant [Accessed 26 July 2013].

Andrews, B. and McDougall, J. (2012) 'Curation pedagogy: further towards the inexpert', *Media Studies*, 3(6), 152–66.

APA (2013) *Ethical Principles of Psychologists and Code of Conduct* [online] http://www.apa.org/ethics/code/index.aspx [Accessed 8 July 2013].

Ashworth, P. (1999) 'Bracketing in phenomenology: renouncing assumptions in hearing about student cheating', *International Journal of Qualitative Studies in Education*, 12, 707–22.

Ashworth, P. and Lucas, U. (2000) 'Achieving empathy and engagement: a practical approach to the design, conduct and reporting of phenomenographic research', *Studies in Higher Education*. 25(3), 295–308.

Baernstein, A., Liss, H.K., Carney, P.A. and Elmore, J.G. (2007) 'Trends in study methods used in undergraduate medical education research, 1969–2007', *Journal of the American Medical Association*, 298, 1038–45.

Bagley, C. and Cancienne, M.B. (2001) 'Educational research and intertextual forms of (re)presentation: the case for dancing the data', *Qualitative Inquiry*, 7(2), 221–37.

Barefoot, H.C. and Russell, M.B. (2012) 'Effecting sustainable change to assessment practice and experience in the biosciences', in *STEM Annual Conference Proceedings, Higher Education Academy* [online] http://www.heacademy.ac.uk/assets/documents/stem-conference/STEMLearningandTeachingIssues1/Helen_Barefoot_Mark_Russell.pdf [Accessed 26 July 2013].

Barefoot, H.C., Lou, F. and Russell, M.B. (2011) 'Peer assessment: educationally effective and resource efficient', *Blended Learning in Practice*, 5, 21–35.

Barker, T.A., Ngwenya, N., Morley, D., Jones, E., Thomas, C.P. and Coleman, J.J. (2012) 'Hidden benefits of a peer-mentored "Hospital Orientation Day": first-year medical students' perspectives', *Medical Teacher*, 34, 229–35.

Barnett, R. (2005) *Reshaping the University: New Relationships Between Research, Scholarship and Teaching*. Maidenhead, UK: McGraw-Hill/Open University Press.

Barone, T. and Eisner, E.W. (2006) 'Arts-based educational research', in J.L. Green, G. Camilli and P.B. Elmore (eds), *Handbook of Complementary Methods in Education Research*. Mahwah, NJ: American Educational Research Association.

Bassey, M. (1981) 'Pedagogic research: on the relative merits of search for generalisation and study of single events', *Oxford Review of Education*, 7(1), 73–94.

Becher, T. and Trowler, P.R. (2001) *Academic Tribes and Territories* (2nd edition). Buckingham: SRHE and Open University Press.

BEME (2013) *The Best Evidence Medical Education (BEME) Collaboration* [online] http://www.bemecollaboration.org/ [Accessed 6 August 2013].

Bennet, C. and Dewar, J. (2013) 'SoTL and interdisciplinary encounters in the study of students' understanding of mathematical proof', in K. McKinney (ed.), *The Scholarship of Teaching and Learning in and across the Disciplines*. Bloomington, IN: Indiana University Press, 54–73.

Bennett, P., Kendall, A. and McDougall, J. (2011) *After the Media: Culture and Identity in the 21st Century*. Abingdon: Routledge.

BERA (2011) *Ethical Guidelines for Educational Research* [online] http://www.bera.ac.uk/guidelines [Accessed 13 June 2013].

Bernstein, B. (1990) *The Structuring of Pedagogic Discourse*. Oxford: Blackwell.

Bibbings, L. (2006) 'Widening participation and higher education', *Journal of Law and Society*, 33(1), 74–91.

Biesta, G. (2007) 'Why "what works" won't work: evidence-based practice and the democratic deficit in educational research', *Educational Theory*, 57(1), 1–22.

Biggs, J and Tang, C (2011) *Teaching for Quality Learning at University* (4th edition). Maidenhead: Open University Press.

Blair, B., Orr, S. and Yorke, M. (2012) '*Erm, that question ... I think I probably would've just put something in the middle and sort of moved on to the next one, because I think it's really unclear*': How art and design students understand and interpret the National Student Survey. [online] http://www.heacademy.ac.uk/

resources/detail/disciplines/Art%20and%20design/GLAD_report_April2012 [Accessed 27 July 2013].

Bleakley, A. (2012) 'The curriculum is dead! Long live the curriculum! Designing an undergraduate medicine and surgery curriculum for the future', *Medical Teacher*, 34, 543–47.

Bligh, J. and Parsell, G. (1999) 'Research in medical education: finding its place', *Medical Education*, 33, 162–63.

BMA (2011) *Requests for the Disclosure of Data for Secondary Purposes* [online] http://bma.org.uk/practical-support-at-work/ethics/confidentiality-and-health-records [Accessed 8 July 2013].

Boet, S., Sharm, S., Goldman, J. and Reeves, S. (2011) 'Medical education research: an overview of methods', *Canadian Journal of Anaesthesia*, 59, 159–70.

Borgdorff, H. (2011) 'The production of knowledge in artistic research', in M. Biggs and H. Karlsson (eds), *The Routledge Companion to Research in the Arts*. Abingdon: Routledge.

Bourdieu, P. (2004) 'The forms of capital', in S. Ball (ed.), *The Routledge Reader in Sociology of Education*. Abingdon: Routledge.

Bovill, C. (2013) 'An investigation of co-created curricula within higher education in the UK, Ireland and the USA', *Innovations in Education and Teaching International*. [online] http://dx.doi.org/10.1080/14703297.2013.770264 [Accessed 24 July 2013].

Bowling, A. (2009) *Research Methods in Health: Investigating Health and Health Services* (2nd edition). Buckingham: Open University Press.

Boyer Commission on Educating Undergraduates in the Research University (1998) *Reinventing Undergraduate Education: A Blueprint for America's Research Universities* [online] http://www.niu.edu/engagedlearning/research/pdfs/Boyer_Report.pdf [Accessed 13 June 2013].

Boyer, E. (1990) *Scholarship Reconsidered: Priorities of the Professoriate*. San Francisco, CA: Jossey Bass.

Boyle, A. (2003) 'Reflection, alignment and mineralogy', *Planet*, Special Edition No. 5, 62–5 [online] http://www.gees.ac.uk/pubs/planet/pse5back.pdf [Accessed 25 July 2013].

Brain, J., Scholfield, J., Gerrish, K., Mawson, S., Mabbott, I., Patel, D. and Gerrish, P. (2011) *Healthcare Quality Improvement Partnership. A Guide for Clinical Audit and Service Review* [online] http://hqip.org.uk/assets/LQIT-uploads/Guidance-0212/HQIP-CA-PD-009-220212-A-Guide-for-Clinical-Audit-Research-and-Service-Review.pdf [Accessed 6 August 2013].

Brannen, J. (1988) 'Research note: the study of sensitive subjects', *The Sociological Review*, 36(3), 552–63.

Brennan, J. and Naidoo, R. (2008) 'Higher education and the achievement (and/or prevention) of equity and social justice', *Higher Education*, 56(3), 287–302.

Brew, A. (2001) *The Nature of Research: Inquiry in Academic Contexts*. London: Routledge/Falmer.

Brew, A. (2006) *Research and Teaching: Beyond the Divide*. Basingstoke, UK: PalgraveMacmillan.

Brew, A. (2011) 'Higher education research and the scholarship of teaching and learning: the pursuit of excellence', *International Journal for the Scholarship of Teaching and Learning*, 5(2) [online] http://dspaceprod.georgiasouthern.edu:8080/xmlui/bitstream/handle/10518/3642/IJ-SoTL_v5n2_Brew.pdf?sequence=1 [Accessed 23 July 2013].

Brew, A. and Boud, D. (1995) 'Teaching and research: establishing the vital link with learning', *Higher Education*, 29(3), 261–73.

Brewer, C.A. (2004) 'Near real-time assessment of student learning and understanding in biology courses', *Bioscience*, 54(11), 1034–39.

Brewer, C.A. and Smith, D. (eds) (2011) *Vision and Change in Undergraduate Biology Education: a Call to Action*. Washington, DC: American Association for the Advancement of Science.

Brookfield, S. (1975) 'Using critical incidents to explore assumptions', in T. H. Buxton and K.W. Prichard (eds) *Excellence in University Teaching: New Essays*. Columbia, SC: University of South Carolina Press.

Brown, A. (2010) 'City reflection, street text: using mobile networking technologies to facilitate reflective workshop practice on location', *ADM / HEA Bulletin*, January 2010 [online] http://www.adm.heacademy.ac.uk/resources/case-studies/city-reflection-street-text-using-mobile-networking-technologies-to-facilitate-reflective-workshop-practice-on-location [Accessed 27 July 2013].

Bryman, A. (2004) *Social Research Methods* (2nd edition). Oxford: Oxford University Press.

Bryman, A. (2012) *Social Research Methods* (4th edition). Oxford: Oxford University Press.

Buckley, S. (2011) 'Case Study 6: reviewing evidence on the effects of an educational intervention', in K. Khan, R. Kunz, J. Kleijnen and G. Antes (eds), *Systematic Reviews to Support Evidence-Based Medicine* (2nd edition). London: Royal Society of Medicine.

Buckley, S., Coleman, J., Davison, I., Khan, K.S., Zamora, Z., Malick, S., Morley, D., Pollard, D., Ashcroft, T., Popovic, C. and Sayers, J. (2009) 'The educational effects of portfolios on undergraduate student learning: a Best Evidence Medical Education (BEME) systematic review. BEME Guide no 11', *Medical Teacher*, 31(4), 282–98.

Burrell, G. and Morgan, G. (1979) *Sociological Paradigms and Organisational Analysis*. London: Heinemann Educational.

Burton, N., Brundrett, M. and Jones. M. (2008) *Doing your Education Research Project*. London: Sage.

Candlin, F. (2008) 'A dual inheritance: the politics of educational reform and PhDs in art and design', in R. Hickman (ed.), *Research in Art and Design Education*. Bristol: Intellect, 99–108.

Cannatella, H. (2001) 'Art assessment', *Assessment and Evaluation in Higher Education*, 26(4), 319–26.

Chalmers, D. (2011) 'Progress and challenges to the recognition and reward of the Scholarship of Teaching in higher education', *Higher Education Research and Development*, 30(1), 25–38.

Chang, J.-Y., Chang, G.-L., Chang, C.-J., Chung, K.-C. and Hsu, A.-T. (2007) 'Effectiveness of two forms of feedback on training of a joint mobilisation skills by using a joint translation simulator', *Physical Therapy*, 87(4), 418–30.

Chick, N.L (2013) 'Difference, privilege and power in the Scholarship of Teaching and Learning: the value of humanities SoTL', in K. McKinney (ed.), *The Scholarship of Teaching and Learning in and across the Disciplines*. Bloomington, IN: Indiana University Press, 15–33.

Chick, N.L., Haynie, A. and Gurung, R.A.R (eds) (2012) *Exploring More Signature Pedagogies: Approaches to Teaching Disciplinary Habits of Mind*. Sterling, VA: Stylus.

Chickering, A.W. and Gamson, Z.F. (1987) 'Seven principles for good practice in undergraduate education', *American Association for Higher Education Bulletin*, 39(7), 3–7.

Cleaver, E., Supple, C. and Kerr, D. (2007) *Participation Under the Spotlight: Interrogating Policy and Practice and Defining Future Directions*. A position paper on the future of children and young people's participation. Slough: NFER [online] http://www.nfer.ac.uk/about-nfer/events/participation-under-the-spotlight/LPIpositionpaper.pdf [Accessed 8 July 2013].

Clucas, B. and O'Donnell, K. (2002) 'Conjoined twins: the cutting edge', *Web JCLI*, 5 [online] http://webjcli.ncl.ac.uk/2002/issue5/clucas5.html [Accessed 17 July 2013].

Clucas, R. (in progress) 'A phenomenological study of legal scholarship'.

Cochrane Collaboration (2013) *Cochrane Reviews* [online] http://www.cochrane.org/cochrane-reviews [Accessed 27 June 2013].

Coghlan, D. and Brannick, T. (2010) *Researching Your Own Organisation* (3rd edition). London: Sage.

Cohen, L., Manion, L. and Morrison, K. (2011) *Research Methods in Education* (7th edition). Abingdon: Routledge.

Cook, D.A. (2012a) 'Randomised controlled trials and meta-analysis in medical education: what role do they play?', *Medical Teacher*, 34, 468–73.

Cook, D.A. (2012b) 'If you teach them, they will learn: why medical education needs comparative effectiveness research', *Advances in Health Science Education*, 17, 305–10.

Cook, D.A. and West, C.P. (2012) 'Conducting systematic reviews in medical education: a stepwise approach', *Medical Education*, 46, 943–52.

Cook, D.A., Bordage, G. and Schmidt, H.G. (2008a) 'Description, justification and clarification: a framework for classifying the purposes of research in medical education', *Medical Education*, 42, 128–33.

Cook, D.A., Levinson, A.J., Garside, S., Dupras, D.M., Erwin, P.J. and Montori, V.M. (2008b) 'Internet-based learning in the health professions: a meta-analysis', *Journal of the American Medical Association*, 300(10), 1181–96.

Courant, R. and Robbins, H. (1941) *What is Mathematics? An Elementary to Ideas and Methods*. London: Oxford University Press.

Coursera (2013) *29 New Schools, 92 New Courses, 5 Languages, 4 Continents and 2.7 Million Courserians* [online] http://blog.coursera.org/post/43625628117/29-new-schools-92-new-courses-5-languages-4 [Accessed 24 July 2013].

Cousin, G. (2009) *Researching Learning in Higher Education: an Introduction to Contemporary Methods and Approaches*. Abingdon: Routledge.

Cowdray, R. and de Graff, E. (2005) 'Assessing highly-creative ability', *Assessment and Evaluation in Higher Education*, 30(5), 507–18.

Creative Commons (2013) *About The Licenses: What our Licences Do* [online] http://creativecommons.org/licenses/ [Accessed 24 July 2013].

Creswell, J.W. (2008) *Research Design: Qualitative, Quantitative, and Mixed Methods Approaches*. London: Sage.

Cronin P., Ryan, F. and Coughlan, M. (2008) 'Undertaking a literature review: a step-by-step approach', *British Journal of Nursing*, 17(1), 38–43.

Crotty, M. (1998) *The Foundations of Social Research: Meaning and Perspective in the Research Process*. London: Sage.

Csikszentmihalyi, M. (1997) *Creativity: Flow and the Psychology of Discovery and Invention*. New York: Harper Perennial.

de Freitas, N. (2002) 'Towards a definition of studio documentation: working tool and transparent record', *Working Papers in Art and Design 2* [online] http://sitem.herts.ac.uk/artdes_research/papers/wpades/vol2/freitasfull.html [Accessed 27 July 2013].

Deignan, T. (2009) 'Enquiry-based learning: perspectives on practice', *Teaching in Higher Education*, 14(1),13–28.

Denscombe, M. (2008a) 'The art of research: art teachers' affinity with ethnography', in R. Hickman (ed.), *Research in Art and Design Education: Issues and Exemplars*, Readings in Art and Design Education Series. Bristol: Intellect, 25–34.

Denscombe, M. (2008b) 'Communities of practice: a research paradigm for the mixed-method approach', *Journal of Mixed Methods Research*, 2(3), 270–83.

Denscombe, M. (2010) *The Good Research Guide: for Small-scale Social Research Projects* (4th edition). Maidenhead: Open University Press.

Denzin, N. and Lincoln, Y. (2002) *The Qualitative Inquiry Reader*. London: Sage.

Department for Education and Skills (2003) *The Future of Higher Education*. Cm 5735. London: HMSO [online] http://www.bis.gov.uk/assets/BISCore/corporate/MigratedD/publications/F/future_of_he.pdf [Accessed 13 June 2013].

Devine, F. and Heath, S. (1999) *Sociological Research Methods in Context*. Basingstoke: Macmillan.

Dickson-Swift, V., James, E., Kippen, S. and Liamputtong, P. (2009) 'Researching sensitive topics: qualitative research as emotion work', *Qualitative Research*, 9(1), 61–79.

Dolan, E.L. (2007) 'Grappling with the literature of education research and practice', *CBE-Life Sciences Education*, 6, 289–96.

do Mar Pereira, M. (2012) '"Feminist theory is proper knowledge, but…" : the status of feminist scholarship in the academy', *Feminist Theory*, 13(3), 283–303.

Donald, J.G. (2002) *Learning to Think: Disciplinary Perspectives*. San Francisco, CA: Jossey Bass.

Drew, L. (2004) 'The experience of teaching creative practices: conceptions and approaches to teaching in the community of practice dimensions', in A. Davies (ed.), *Enhancing Curricula: Towards the Scholarship of Teaching in Art, Design and Communication in Higher Education*. London: Centre for Learning and Teaching (CLTAD), 106–23.

Elgie, S., Childs, R., Fenton, N., Levy, B.A., Lopes, V., Szala-Meneok, K. and Wiggers, R.D. (2012) *Researching Teaching and Student Outcomes in Postsecondary Education. A Guide*. Toronto: Higher Education Quality Council of Ontario.

Elicker, J., McConnell, N. and Hall, R. (2010) 'Research participation for course credit in introduction to psychology: why don't people participate?', *Teaching of Psychology*, 37(3), 183–85.

Elkins, J. (2001) *Why Art Cannot Be Taught: A Handbook for Art Students*. Chicago, IL: University of Illinois Press.

Elkins, J. (2004) 'Theoretical remarks on combined creative and scholarly PhD degrees in the visual arts', *Journal of Aesthetic Education*, 38(4), 22–31.

Elton, L. (2005) 'Scholarship and the research and teaching nexus', in R. Barnett (ed.), *Reshaping the University: New Relationships Between Research, Scholarship and Teaching*. Maidenhead: McGraw-Hill/Open University Press, 108–18.

Elton, L. (2009) 'Guiding students into a discipline: the significance of the student's view', in C. Kreber (ed.), *The University and its Disciplines. Teaching and Learning Within and Beyond Disciplinary Boundaries*. Abingdon: Routledge, 129–39.

Falchikov, N. and Goldfinch, J. (2000) 'Student peer assessment in higher education: a meta-analysis comparing peer and teacher marks', *Review of Educational Research*, 70, 287–322.

Feldman, S. (2012) 'Questions, questions: students are suffering from survey fatigue – as are we all', *Times Higher Education* [online] http://www.timeshighereducation.co.uk/story.asp?storyCode=418606&sectioncode=26 [Accessed 13 June 2013].

Ferguson, L. and Day, R.A. (2005) 'Evidence-based nursing education: myth or reality?', *Journal of Nursing Education*, 44(3), 107–15.

Fetterman, D. (1989) *Ethnography: Step-by-Step*. Thousand Oaks, CA: Sage.

Foreman-Peck, L. and Winch, C. (2010) *Using Educational Research to Inform Practice: a Practical Guide to Practitioner Research in Universities and Colleges*. Abingdon: Routledge.

Foster, C.R. (2004) 'Editor's note', *Teaching Theology and Religion*, 7(4), 179–80.

Franke, R.H. and Kaul, J.D. (1978) 'The Hawthorne experiments: first statistical interpretation', *American Sociological Review*, 43, 623–43.

Frye, A. and Hemmer, P. (2012) 'Program evaluation models and related theories AMEE Guide no 67', *Medical Teacher*, 34, 288–99.

Fuller, I.C., Gaskin, S. and Scott, I. (2003) 'Student perceptions of Geography and Environmental Science fieldwork in the light of restricted access to the field, caused by Foot and Mouth Disease in the UK in 2001', *Journal of Geography in Higher Education*, 27(1): 79–102.

Fuller, L.L. (1969) *The Morality of Law* (revised edition). New Haven, CT and London: Yale University Press.

Gee, J.P. (2000) 'Discourse and sociocultural studies in reading', in M.L. Kamil, P.B. Mosenthal, P.D. Pearson, and R. Barr (eds), *Handbook of Reading Research* (Volume III). Mahwah, NJ: Lawrence Erlbaum Associates, 195–207.

Geertz, C, (1973) *The Interpretation of Cultures*. New York: Basic Books.

Giorgi, A. (1992) 'Description versus interpretation: competing alternative strategies for qualitative research', *Journal of Phenomenological Psychology*, 23(2), 119–35.

Glassick, C., Huber, M. and Maeroff, G. (1997) *Scholarship Assessed: Evaluation of the Professoriate*. The Carnegie Foundation for the Advancement of Teaching. San Francisco, CA: Jossey-Bass.

Gliddon, C.M. and Rosengren, R.J. (2012) 'A laboratory course for teaching laboratory techniques, experimental design, statistical analysis, and peer review process to undergraduate science students', *Biochemistry and Molecular Biology Education*, 40(6), 364–71.

Goldie, J. (2006) 'Evaluating educational programmes. AMEE Education Guide no 29', *Medical Teacher*, 28 (3), 210–24.

Gorard, S. (2001) 'A changing climate for educational research? The role of research capacity building', Cardiff: Cardiff School of Social Science, Occasional Paper Series, Paper 45.

Gotleib-Conn, L. (2010) 'Using ethnographic methods to understand change in interprofessional practice', *Journal of Research in Interprofessional Education and Practice*, 1(3), 301–3.

Gough, D., Oliver, S. and Thomas, J. (2012) *An Introduction to Systematic Reviews*. London: Sage.

Graham-Matheson, L. (2010) 'Research informed teaching', in L. Graham-Matheson, (ed.), *Research Informed Teaching: Exploring the Concept*. Canterbury Christ Church University: UK, 6–9 [online] http://www.canterbury.ac.uk/Support/learning-teaching-enhancement-unit/Documents/RIT/00-RIT-All.pdf [Accessed 23 July 2013].

Grauerholz, L. and Main, E. (2013) 'Fallacies of SoTL: rethinking how we conduct our research', in K. McKinney (ed.), *The Scholarship of Teaching and Learning in and across the Disciplines*. Bloomington, IN: Indiana University Press, 152–68.

Green, J.L., Skukauskaite, A. and Baker, W D. (2012) 'Ethnography as epistemology', in J. Arthur, M. Waring, R. Coe and L.V. Hedges (eds), *Research Methods and Methodologies in Education*. London: Sage.

Griffiths, R. (2004) 'Knowledge production and the research–teaching nexus: the case of the built environment disciplines', *Studies in Higher Education*, 29(6), 709–26.

Gross, N (2007) 'Pragmatism, phenomenology and twentieth century American sociology', in C. Calhoun (ed.), *Sociology in America: a History*. Chicago, IL: University of Chicago Press, 183–224.

Gruppen, L. (2008) 'Is medical education research "hard" or "soft" research?', *Advances in Health Sciences Education*, 13(1), 1–2.

Guest, D. (2008) 'Because they're worth it: making room for female students and thealogy in higher education contexts', *Feminist Theology*, 17(1), 43–71.

Gurung, R.A.R., Chick, N.L. and Haynie, A. (eds) (2009) *Exploring Signature Pedagogies: Approaches to Teaching Disciplinary Habits of Mind*. Sterling, VA: Stylus.

Haji, F., Morin, M.-P. and Parker, K. (2013) 'Rethinking programme evaluation in health professions education: beyond "did it work?"', *Medical Education*, 47, 342–51.

Hake, R.R. (1998) 'Interactive-engagement versus traditional methods: a six-thousand-student survey of mechanics test data for introductory physics courses', *American Journal of Physics*, 66(1), 64–74.

Halcomb, E.J., Andrew, S. and Brannen, J. (2009) 'Introduction to mixed methods research for nursing and the health sciences', in S. Andrew and E. Halcomb (eds) *Mixed Methods Research for Nursing and the Health Sciences*. Chichester: Blackwell Publishing Ltd (John Wiley and Sons).

Hall, J. (2010) 'Making art, teaching art, learning art: exploring the concept of the artist teacher', *International Journal of Art & Design Education*, 29(2), 103–10.

Hammersley, M. (2000) *Taking Sides in Social Research. Essays on Partisanship and Bias*. London: Routledge.

Hammersley, M. (2012) *Methodological Paradigms in Educational Research*, British Educational Research Association online resource [online] http://www.bera.ac.uk/resources/methodological-paradigms-educational-research. [Accessed 13 June 2013].

Harmsworth, S., Turpin, S., TQEF National Co-ordination Team (2000) with Rees, A. and Pell, G. (2001) *Creating an Effective Dissemination Strategy: an Expanded Interactive Workbook for Educational Development Projects* [online] http://www.innovations.ac.uk/btg/resources/publications/dissemination.pdf [Accessed 24 July 2013].

Harrison, J. (2011) *Smarter Assessment = Smarter Students! Using Assessment for Learning in Children's Nurse Education*. Paper presented at the Higher Education Academy E-learning in Health Conference, Birmingham, UK, 27–28 June.

Hart, C. (1998) *Doing a Literature Review*. London: Sage.

Hawking, S.W. and Penrose, R. (1970) 'The singularities of gravitational collapse and cosmology', *Proceedings of the Royal Society A, Mathematical, Physical and Engineering Sciences*, 314(1514), 529–48.

HEA (2011) *UK Professional Standards Framework for Teaching and Supporting Learning in Higher Education* [online] http://www.heacademy.ac.uk/ukpsf [Accessed 13 June 2013].

HEA (2013a) *Your Discipline* [online] http://www.heacademy.ac.uk/disciplines [Accessed 13 June 2013].

HEA (2013b) *Funding Opportunities: Teaching Development Grants* [online] http://www.heacademy.ac.uk/funding [Accessed 26 July 2013].

HEA and Genetics Education Networking for Innovation and Excellence (2009) *Reward and Recognition in Higher Education. Institutional Policies and their Implementation*. York: Higher Education Academy.

HEA STEM (2012) *HEA STEM Funding Opportunity: Departmental Bids* [online] http://www.heacademy.ac.uk/stem [Accessed 24 February 2013].

Healey, M. (2000) 'Developing the scholarship of teaching in higher education: a discipline-based approach', *Higher Education Research and Development*, 19(2), 169–89.

Healey, M. (2003) 'The scholarship of teaching: issues around an evolving concept', *Journal of Excellence in College Teaching*, 14(2/3), 5–26.

Healey, M. (2005) 'Linking research and teaching: disciplinary spaces', in R. Barnett (ed.), *Reshaping the University: New Relationships between Research, Scholarship and Teaching*. Maidenhead: McGraw-Hill/Open University Press, 30–42.

Healey, M. and Jenkins, A. (2003) 'Discipline-based educational development', in H. Eggins and R. Macdonald (eds), *The Scholarship of Academic Development*. Buckingham: SRHE and Open University Press, 47–57.

Heath, S., Brooks, R., Cleaver, E. and Ireland, E. (2009) *Researching Young People's Lives*. London: Sage.

HEFCE (2011) *Assessment Framework and Guidance on Submissions* [online] http://www.ref.ac.uk/pubs/2011-02/ [Accessed 13 June 2013].

HESA (2013) *Destination of Leavers from Higher Education Institutions* [online] http://www.hesa.ac.uk/index.php?option=com_content&task=view&id=1899&Itemid=239 [Accessed 13 June 2013].

Hestenes, D. and Wells, M. (1992) 'The Force Concept Inventory', *Physics Teacher*, 30, 141–58.

Hickman, R. (2008a) 'Introduction', in R. Hickman (ed.), *Research in Art and Design Education: Issues and Exemplars*, Readings in Art and Design Education Series. Bristol: Intellect, 11–14.

Hickman, R. (2008b) 'The nature of research in arts education', in R. Hickman (ed.), *Research in Art and Design Education: Issues and Exemplars*, Readings in Art and Design Education Series. Bristol: Intellect, 15–24.

Hilbert, D. (1902) 'Mathematical problems', *Bulletin of the American Mathematical Society*, 8(10), 437–79.

Hinton, T., Gannaway, D., Berry, B. and Moore, K. (2011) *The D-Cubed Guide: Planning for Effective Dissemination*. Sydney: Australian Teaching and Learning Council [online] http://www.olt.gov.au/system/files/The%20D-Cubed%20guide%20-%20web%20and%20email%20version.pdf [Accessed 24 July 2013].

HM Government (1998) Education Reform Act. London: HMSO [online] http://www.legislation.gov.uk/ukpga/1988/40/contents [Accessed 13 June 2013].

HM Government (2000) Freedom of Information Act. London HMSO [online] http://www.legislation.gov.uk/ukpga/2000/36/contents [Accessed 7 July 2013].

Holsti, O.R. (1969) *Content Analysis for the Social Sciences and Humanities*. Reading, MA: Addison-Wesley.

Huber, M.T. (2000) 'Disciplinary styles in the scholarship of teaching: reflections on The Carnegie Academy for the Scholarship of Teaching and Learning', in C. Rust (ed.), *Proceedings of the 1999 7th International Symposium Improving Student Learning: Improving Student Learning Through the Disciplines*. Oxford: Oxford Centre for Staff and Learning Development, Oxford Brookes University, 20–31.

Huber, M.T. (2006) 'Disciplines, pedagogy, and inquiry-based learning about teaching', *New Directions for Teaching and Learning (Special Issue: Exploring Research-Based Teaching)*, 107, 63–72.

Huber, M.T. (2013) 'Foreword', in K. McKinney (ed.), *The Scholarship of Teaching and Learning in and across the Disciplines*. Bloomington, IN: Indiana University Press, ix–xv.

Huber, M.T. and Hutchings, P. (2005) *The Advancement of Teaching and Learning: Building the Teaching Commons*, The Carnegie Foundation for the Advancement of Teaching/A Carnegie Foundation Report on the Scholarship of Teaching and Learning in Higher Education. San Francisco, CA: Jossey-Bass.

Huber, M.T. and Morreale, S. (eds) (2002) *Disciplinary Styles in the Scholarship of Teaching and Learning: Exploring Common Ground*. Washington, DC: American Association for HE and the Carnegie Foundation.

Huffman, D. and Heller, P. (1995) 'What does the Force Concept Inventory actually measure?', *Physics Teacher*, 33(3), 138–43.

Hutchings, P. (2002) *Ethics of Inquiry: Issues in the Scholarship of Teaching and Learning*. Menlo Park, CA: The Carnegie Foundation for the Advancement of Teaching.

Hutchings, P. (2003) 'Competing goods: ethical issues in the scholarship of teaching and learning', *Change*, 35(5), 26–33.

Hutchings, P. and Shulman, L.S. (1999) 'The scholarship of teaching: new elaborations, new developments', *Change*, 31(5), 10–15 [online] http://www.carnegie

foundation.org/elibrary/scholarship-teaching-new-elaborations-new-developments [Accessed 13 June 2013].

Hutchings, W. (2007) *Enquiry-Based Learning: Definitions and Rationale*. Centre for Excellence in Enquiry Based Learning, University of Manchester [online] http://www.ceebl.manchester.ac.uk/resources/papers/hutchings2007_definingebl.pdf [Accessed 13 June 2013].

Hutchinson, D. and Styles, B. (2010) *A Guide to Running Randomised Controlled Trials for Educational Researchers*. Slough: NFER.

Issenberg, S.B., Mcgaghie, W.C., Petrusa, E.R., Gordon, D.L. and Scalese, R.J. (2005) 'Features and uses of high-fidelity medical simulations that lead to effective learning: a BEME systematic review', *Medical Teacher*, 27(1), 10–28.

Jackson, N. (2003) *A Personal Perspective on Enquiry-Based Learning*, LTSN Generic Centre [online] http://www.heacademy.ac.uk/resources/detail/id328_a_personal_perspective_on_ebl [Accessed 13 June 2013].

Jenkins, A. and Healey, M. (2005) *Institutional Strategies for Linking Teaching and Research*. York: The Higher Education Academy [online] www.heacademy.ac.uk/assets/York/documents/resources/resourcedatabase/id585_institutional_strategies_to_link_teaching_and_research.pdf [Accessed 13 June 2013].

JISC (2011) *JISC Grant Funding 06/11: JISC eContent Capital Programme: Call for Projects* [online] http://www.jisc.ac.uk/fundingopportunities/funding_calls/2011/06/econtentcapital.aspx [Accessed 26 July 2013].

Just, M., Schnell, M.W., Bongartz, M. and Schulz, C. (2010) 'Exploring effects of interprofessional education on undergraduate students' behaviour: a randomised controlled trial', *Journal of Research in Interprofessional Education and Practice*, 1(3), 182–99.

Kahn, P. and O'Rourke, K. (2004) *Guide to Enquiry-Based Learning*. University of Manchester [online] http://www.ceebl.manchester.ac.uk/resources/guides/kahn_2004.pdf [Accessed 23 July 2013].

Kelly, O. and Lovatt. J. (2012) 'A case study exploring students' problem-solving strategies in a PBL chemistry task', *New Directions in Teaching and Learning in Physical Sciences*, 8, 38–42.

Kendall, A. and McDougall, J. (2012) 'Critical media literacy after the media: can we see clearly now?', in K. Tyner, and A. Gutiérrez (eds), *Alfabetización mediática en contextos digitales múltiples, Revista Communicar, 38*. Andalucia, Spain: Grupo Communicar.

Kenyon, E. and Hawker, S. (1999) 'Once would be enough: some reflections on the issue of safety for lone researchers', *The International Journal of Social Research Methodology: Theory and Practice*, 2(4), 313–27.

Kettley, N. (2007) 'The past, present and future of widening participation research', *British Journal of Sociology of Education*, 28(3), 333–47.

Kim, S., Phillips, W., Pinsky, L., Brock, D., Phillips, K. and Keary, J. (2006) 'A conceptual framework for developing teaching cases: a review and synthesis of the literature across disciplines', *Medical Education*, 40(9), 867–76.

King, H. (2008) 'The state of evidence in geoscience education research', *Workshop on Linking Evidence and Promising Practices in STEM Undergraduate Education*. The National Academies Board on Science Education [online] http://www7.nationalacademies.org/bose/HelenKing_Report.pdf [Accessed 25 July 2013].

King, H., McKenna, C., Hughes, J. and Bremner, E. (2012) *Disciplinary Thinking* [online] http://disciplinarythinking.wordpress.com/about/background/ [Accessed 7 August 2013].

Kreber, C. (ed.) (2009) *The University and its Disciplines: Teaching and Learning Within and Beyond Disciplinary Boundaries*. Abingdon: Routledge.

Kuhn, T.S. (1996) *The Structure of Scientific Revolutions* (3rd edition). Chicago, IL: University of Chicago Press.

Kuper, A., Reeves, S. and Levinson, W. (2008) 'An introduction to reading and appraising qualitative research', *British Medical Journal*, 337, 404–7.

Langer, S. (1957) *Problems of Art*. New York: Scribner.

Letherby, G., Scott, J. and Williams, M. (2013) *Objectivity and Subjectivity in Social Research*. London: Sage.

Libarkin, J. (2009) 'Geocognition research: an international discipline'. Invited address to the American Geophysical Union Fall Meeting, 2009.

Linsemneier, R.A., Olds, S.A. and Kolikant, Y.B.D. (2006) 'Instructor and course changes resulting from an HPL-inspired use of personal response systems', in *36th Annual Frontiers in Education, Conference Program, Vols 1–4 Border: Internal, Social and Cultural*, 1485–9.

Llewellyn, K.N. (1940) 'The normative, the legal, and the law-jobs: the problem of juristic method', *Yale Law Journal*, 49(8), 1355–400.

Loughran, J. (2002) 'In search of meaning in learning about teaching of teacher education', *Journal Effective Reflective Practice*, 53(1), 33–43.

Luckie, D.B., Aubry, J.R., Marengo, B.J., Rivkin, A.M., Foos, L.A. and Maleszewski, J.J. (2012) 'Less teaching, more learning: 10-yr study supports increasing student learning through less coverage and more inquiry', *Advances in Physiology Education*, 36, 325–35.

McCarthy, M. (2008) 'The scholarship of teaching and learning in higher education: an overview', in R. Murray (ed.), *The Scholarship of Teaching and Learning in Higher Education*. Maidenhead: SRHE/Open University Press, 6–15.

MacDonald-Ross, G. (2005) 'Research into teaching philosophy', *Academy Exchange*, 2, 16–18.

McDougall, J. (2013) '"It's hard not to be a teacher sometimes": citizen ethnography in schools', *Citizenship, Teaching and Learning*.

McDougall, J. and Sanders, R. (2011) 'What our students have taught us about virtual learning', *Networks*, Spring [online] http://www.adm.heacademy.ac.uk/networks/networks-spring-2011/features/what-our-students-have-taught-us-about-virtual-learning/ [Accessed 14 August 2013].

MacFarlane, B. (2007) *The Academic Citizen: the Virtue of Service in University Life*. Abingdon: Routledge.

McKenzie, J. and Alexander, S. (2006) 'Variation in ways of experiencing dissemination: implications for the adoption and adaptation of teaching and learning innovation projects', in *Critical Visions, Proceedings of the 29th HERDSA Annual Conference*, Western Australia, 10–12 July 2006, 222–228 [online] http://www.herdsa.org.au/wp-content/uploads/conference/2006/papers/McKenzie.pdf [Accessed 24 July 2013].

McKinney, K. (2007) *Enhancing Learning through the Scholarship of Teaching and Learning: the Challenges and Joys of Juggling*. San Francisco, CA: Jossey Bass.

McKinney, K. (ed.) (2013) *The Scholarship of Teaching and Learning in and across the Disciplines*. Bloomington, IN: Indiana University Press.

McKinney, P. and Levy, P. (2006) *Inquiry-based Learning and Information Literacy Development: a CETL Approach* [online] http://www.ics.heacademy.ac.uk/downloads//italics/vol5iss2/strategic%20IL%20(4).htm [Accessed 15 June 2013].

McLinden, M. and Edwards, C. (2011) 'Developing a culture of enquiry-based, independent learning in a research-led institution: findings from a survey of pedagogic practice', *International Journal for Academic Development*, 16(2), 147–62.

McNary-Zak, B. (2002) 'Wading through the quagmire of religious history', *Teaching Theology and Religion*, 5(2), 101–4.

McVitty, D (2012) 'How much do students need to know about pedagogy?', *Educational Developments*, 13(4), 16.

Mahoney, J. (2000) 'Strategies of causal inference in small-N analysis', *Sociological Methods and Research*, 28(4), 387–424.

Marcalo, R. (2009) 'Failing to do without: writing as classical documentation of post-classical choreographic documentation', *Journal of Writing in Creative Practice*, 2(1), 105–16.

Marton, F. (1994) 'Phenomenography', in T. Husén and T.N. Postlethwaite (eds), *International Encyclopaedia of Education*, Vol. 8 (2nd edition). London: Pergamon, 4424.

Marton, F. and Saljo, R. (1976) 'On qualitative differences in learning – 1: outcome and process', *British Journal of Educational Psychology*, 46(1), 4–11.

Medawar, P.B. (1977) 'Unnatural science', *New York Review of Books*, 13–18.

Mendes, P., Thomas, C. and Cleaver, E. (2011) 'The meaning of prompt feedback and other student perceptions of feedback: should National Student Survey scores be taken at face value?', *Engineering Education*, 6(1), 31–9 [online] http://84.22.166.132/journal/index.php/ee/issue/view/43.html [Accessed 25 July 2013].

Merton, R.K. (1948) 'The self fulfilling prophecy'. *The Antioch Review*, 8(2), 193–210.

Metz, M. and Page, R. (2002) 'The uses of practitioner research and status issues in educational research: reply to Gary Anderson', *Educational Researcher*, October (31): 26–7.

Michael, J. (2006) 'Doing and reporting educational research', *Advances in Physiology Education*, 30(3), 99 [online] http://advan.physiology.org/content/30/3/99.full [Accessed 26 July 2013].

Molleman, A. and Barefoot, H. (2009) 'Motivating reluctant students to go on placement', *Proceedings of the 2009 ASET Placement and Employability Professionals' Conference, 8–10 September, Lancaster University Conference Centre*, 59–61.

Moran, L. (2011) 'Mission to Mars: a one-week introductory project for new physics students', *New Directions in Teaching and Learning in Physical Sciences*, 7, 1–4.

Morrison, J. (2003) 'ABC of learning and teaching in medicine: evaluation', *British Medical Journal*, 326, 385–7.

Mosteller, F., Nave, B. and Miech, E. (2004) 'Why we need a structured abstract in education research', *Educational Research*, 33, 29–34.

Munday, D. and Petrova, M. (2009) 'Exploring preferences for place of death with terminally ill patients: qualitative study of experiences of general practitioners and community nurses in England', *British Medical Journal*, 338, b2391.

Mura, R. (1993) 'Images of mathematics held by university teachers of mathematical sciences', *Educational Studies in Mathematics*, 25(4), 375–85.

National Committee of Enquiry into Higher Education (1997) *Higher Education in the Learning Society* [online] http://www.leeds.ac.uk/educol/ncihe/ [Accessed 13 June 2013].

National Institute for Health and Clinical Excellence (2012) 'About us' [online] http://www.nice.org.uk/aboutnice/ [Accessed 6 August 2013].

Nelson, R.A. and Olsson, M.G. (1986) 'The pendulum: rich physics from a simple system', *American Journal of Physics*, 54(2), 112–21.

Neuman, R. (1994) 'The research-teaching nexus: applying a framework to university students' learning experiences', *European Journal of Education*, 29(3), p323–339.

New York Academy of Medicine Library (2013) *What is Grey Literature?* [online] http://www.greylit.org/about [Accessed 27 June 2013].

Newman, M. (2003) *A Pilot Systematic Review and Meta-analysis on the Effectiveness of Problem Based Learning*, Special Report 2, on behalf of the Campbell Collaboration Systematic Review Group on the Effectiveness of Problem Based Learning [online] http://www.heacademy.ac.uk/assets/documents/subjects/medev/pbl_report.pdf [Accessed 27 June 2013].

Norman, G. (2003) 'RCT = results confounded and trivial: the perils of grand educational experiments', *Medical Education*, 37(7), 582–84.

Norton, L. (2009) *Action Research in Teaching and Learning. A Practical Guide to Conducting Pedagogical Research in Universities*. Abingdon: Routledge.

Novak, J.D. and Musonda, D. (1991) 'A twelve-year longitudinal study of science concept learning', *American Education Research Journal*, 28(1), 117–153.

O'Loughlin, R. (2008) 'The relationship between pedagogical and discipline-specific research methods: critical perspectives', *Discourse*, 7(2), 67–120.

O'Loughlin, V.D. (2006) 'A "how to" guide for developing a publishable scholarship of teaching project', *Advances in Physiology Education*, 30, 83–88.

Opie, C. (ed.) (2004) *Doing Educational Research. A Guide to First-time Researchers*. London: Sage.

Orr, S. (2007) 'Assessment moderation: constructing the marks and constructing the students', *Assessment & Evaluation in Higher Education*, 32(6), 64–56.

Orr, S. (2010) 'Collaborating or fighting for the marks? Students' experiences of group work assessment in the performing arts', *Assessment and Evaluation in Higher Education*, 35(3), 301–14.

Orr, S. (2011) '"Being an artist you kind of, I mean, you get used to excellence": identity, values and fine art assessment practices', *International Journal of Art and Design Education*, 30(1), 37–44.

Orr, S., Richmond, J.D. and Richmond, D. (2010) 'Reflect on this!', *Journal of Writing in Creative Practice*, 3(3), 197–210.

Oxford Centre for Evidence-Based Medicine (2011) *Levels of Evidence* (revised) [online] http://www.cebm.net/index.aspx?o=5653 [Accessed 6 August 2013].

Pace, D. and Middendorf, J. (eds) (2004) *New Directions for Teaching and Learning (Special Issue: Decoding the Disciplines: Helping Students Learn Disciplinary Ways of Thinking)*, 98.

Padilla-Walker, L., Thompson, R., Zamboanga, B. and Schmersal, L. (2005) 'Extra credit as incentive for voluntary research participation', *Teaching of Psychology*, 32(3), 150–53.

Pampaka, M. and Williams, J. (2012) *Mathematical Modelling and Problem Solving* [online] http://www.transmaths.org/mmps/ [Accessed 24 June 2013].

Parker, J. (2008) 'Comparing research and teaching in university promotion criteria', *Higher Education Quarterly*, 62(3), 237–51.

Paterson, B., Gregory, D. and Thorne, S. (1999) 'A protocol for researcher safety', *Qualitative Health Research*, 9(2), 259–69.

Patricio, M. and Carneiro, A.V. (2012) 'Systematic reviews of evidence in medical education and clinical medicine: is the nature of evidence similar?', *Medical Teacher*, 34, 474–82.

Patterson, B.A.B. (2003) 'Ethnography as pedagogy: learning and teaching in a religion department internship class', *Teaching Theology & Religion*, 6(1), 224–34.

Perkins, D. (1999) 'The many faces of constructivism', *Educational Leadership*, 57(3), 6–11.

Perkins, D. (2006) 'Constructivism and troublesome knowledge', in J.H.F. Meyer and R. Land (eds), *Overcoming Barriers to Student Understanding: Threshold Concepts and Troublesome Knowledge*. Abingdon: Routledge, 33–47.

Petcovic, H.L., Libarkin, J.C. and Baker, K.M. (2009) 'An empirical methodology for investigating geocognition in the field', *Journal of Geoscience Education*, 57(4), 316–28 [online] http://www.nagt-jge.org/doi/pdf/10.5408/1.3544284 [Accessed 25 July 2013].

Peterson, S. (1999) 'Time for evidence-based medical education', *British Medical Journal*, 318, 1223–4.

Pink, S. (2007) *Doing Visual Ethnography*. London: Sage.

Pole, C. and Morrison, M. (2003) *Ethnography for Education*. Maidenhead: Open University Press.

Pólya, G. (1945) *How to Solve It*. Princeton, NJ: Princeton University Press.

Poole, G. (2013) 'Square one: what is research?', in K. McKinney (ed.), *The Scholarship of Teaching and Learning in and Across the Disciplines*. Bloomington, IN: Indiana University Press, 135–51.

Porter, S., Whitcomb, M. and Weitzer, E. (2004) 'Multiple surveys of students and survey fatigue', *New Directions for Institutional Research*, (121), 63–73.

Potter, J. (2008) 'Starting with the discipline', in R. Murray (ed.), *The Scholarship of Teaching and Learning in Higher Education*. Maidenhead: SRHE/Open University Press, 58–68.

Prensky, M. (2001) 'Digital natives, digital immigrants', *On the Horizon*, 9(5), 1–6.

Prentice, R. (ed.) (1995) *Teaching Art & Design: Addressing Issues and Identifying Directions*. London: Cassell.

Prosser, M., Rickinson, M., Bence, V., Hanbury, A. and Kulej, M. (2006) *Formative Evaluation of Accredited Programmes*. The Higher Education Academy [online] http://www.heacademy.ac.uk/assets/documents/research/formative_evaluation_of_accredited_programmes_may_2006.pdf [Accessed 13 June 2013].

Punch, K.F. (2009) *Introduction to Research Methods in Education*. London: Sage.

QAA (2007a) *Subject Benchmark Statement: Biosciences* [online] http://www.qaa.ac.uk/Publications/InformationAndGuidance/Pages/Subject-benchmark-statement-Biosciences.aspx [Accessed 26 July 2013].

QAA (2007b) *Subject Benchmark Statement: Theology and Religious Studies* (2nd edition) [online] http://www.qaa.ac.uk/Publications/InformationAndGuidance/Pages/Subject-benchmark-statement-Theology-and-religious-studies.aspx [Accessed 5 August 2013].

QAA (2008a) *Subject Benchmark Statement: Art and Design* [online] http://www.qaa.ac.uk/Publications/InformationAndGuidance/Pages/Subject-benchmark-statement---Art-and-design-.aspx [Accessed 27 July 2013].

QAA (2008b) *Subject Benchmark Statement: Music* [online] http://www.qaa.ac.uk/Publications/InformationAndGuidance/Pages/Subject-benchmark-statement-Music-.aspx [Accessed 27 July 2013].

QAA (2008c) *Subject Benchmark Statement: Communication, Media, Film and Cultural Studies* [online] http://www.qaa.ac.uk/Publications/InformationAndGuidance/Pages/Subject-benchmark-statement-Communication-media-film-and-cultural-studies.aspx [Accessed 27 July 2013].

Rabin, B.A., Brownson, R.C., Haire-Joshu, D., Creuter, M.W. and Weaver, N.L. (2008) 'A glossary for dissemination and implementation research in health', *Journal of Public Health Management and Practices*, 14(2), 117–23.

Ramsden, P. and Martin, E. (1996) 'Recognition of good university teaching: policies from an Australian study', *Studies in Higher Education*, 21(3), 299–315.

Rancière, J. (2009) *The Emancipated Spectator*. London: Verso.

Rancière, J. (2012) Keynote Speech at *Crossroads in Cultural Studies* conference. Paris: UNESCO/Sorbonne, July.

Reid, C. (1996) *Hilbert*. New York: Springer-Verlag.

Richardson, L. (1992) 'The consequences of poetic representation: writing the Other, rewriting the Self', in C. Ellis and M.G. Flaherty (eds), *Investigating Subjectivity. Research on Lived Experience*. London: Sage, 125–40.

Ringsted, C., Hodges, B. and Scherpbier, A. (2011) 'The research compass: an introduction to research in medical education: AMEE Guide No. 56', *Medical Teacher*, 33, 695–709.

Robertson, J. (2007) 'Beyond the "research/teaching nexus": exploring the complexity of academic experience', *Studies in Higher Education*, 32(5), 541–56.

Robson, C. (2002) *Real World Research* (2nd edition). Oxford: Blackwell.

Robson, C. (2011) *Real World Research* (3rd edition). Chichester: Wiley.

Rowland, S. (2006) *The Enquiring University Compliance and Contestation in Higher Education*. Milton Keynes: Open University Press.

Royal Academy of Engineering (2013a) *Statement of Ethical Principles* [online] http://www.raeng.org.uk/societygov/engineeringethics/pdf/Statement_of_Ethical_Principles.pdf [Accessed 8 July 2013].

Royal Academy of Engineering (2013b) *The Engineering Message* [online] http://www.raeng.org.uk/education/eenp/engineering_resources/pdf/club/2_The_Engineering_Message.pdf [Accessed 25 July 2013].

Rust, C. (ed.) (1999) *Proceedings of the 1999 7th International Symposium Improving Student Learning: Improving Student Learning Through the Disciplines*. Oxford: Oxford Centre for Staff and Learning Development, Oxford Brookes University.

Samarapungavan, A., Westby, E.L. and Bodner G.M. (2006) 'Contextual epistemic development in science: a comparison of chemistry students and research chemists', *Science Education*, 90(3), 468–95.

Savage, M. and Williams, J. (1990) *Mechanics in Action-modelling and Practical Investigations*. Cambridge: Cambridge University Press.

Savinainen, A. and Scott, P. (2002) 'The Force Concept Inventory', *Physics Education*, 37, 45–52.

Savin-Baden, M. (2008) 'Liquid learning and troublesome spaces: journeys from the threshold?', in R. Land, J. Meyer and J. Smith (eds), *Threshold Concepts within Disciplines*. Rotterdam: Sense Publishers, 75–88.

Schifferdecker, K.E. and Reed, V.A. (2009) 'Using mixed methods research in medical education: basic guidelines for researchers', *Medical Education*, 43(7), 637–44.

Science and Technology Committee (2012) *Second Report. Higher Education in Science, Technology, Engineering and Mathematics (STEM) Subjects*. House of Lords Science and Technology Committee. London: HMSO [online] http://www.publications.parliament.uk/pa/ld201213/ldselect/ldsctech/37/3702.htm [Accessed 26 July 2013].

Shapiro, C., Ayon, C., Moberg-Parker, J., Levis-Fitzgerald, M. and Sanders, E.R. (2013) 'Strategies for using peer-assisted learning effectively in an undergraduate bioinformatics course', *Biochemistry Molecular Biology Education*, 41, 24–33.

Shepherd, L.A. (2000) 'The role of assessment in a learning culture', *Educational Researcher*, 29(7), 4–14.

Shreeve, A. (2009) '"I'd rather be seen as a practitioner, come in to teach my subject": identity work in part-time art and design tutors', *International Journal of Art & Design Education*, 28(2), 151–59.

Shreeve, A., Sims, E. and Trowler, P. (2010) 'A kind of exchange: learning from art and design teaching', *Higher Education Research & Development*, 29(2), 125–38.

Shulman, L.S. (1993) 'Teaching as community property: putting an end to pedagogical solitude', *Change*, 25(6), 6–7.

Shulman, L.S. (2004) *The Wisdom of Practice: Essays on Teaching, Learning, and Learning to Teach*. S. Wilson (ed.), San Francisco, CA: Jossey-Bass.

Shulman, L.S. (2005) 'Signature pedagogies in the professions', *Daudalus*, 134(3), 52–59.

Simpson, A. (1988) *Invitation to Law*. Oxford: Blackwell.

Smart, N. (1983) *Worldviews: Crosscultural Explorations of Human Beliefs*. New York: Scribner's.

Spronken-Smith, R. and Walker, R. (2010) 'Can inquiry-based learning strengthen the links between teaching and disciplinary research?', *Studies in Higher Education*, 35(6), 723–40.

SRA (2013) *A Code of Practice for the Safety of Social Researchers* [online] http://the-sra.org.uk/wp-content/uploads/safety_code_of_practice.pdf [Accessed 8 July 2013].

Stemler, S. (2001) 'An overview of content analysis', *Practical Assessment, Research & Evaluation*, 7(17) [online] http://PAREonline.net/getvn.asp?v=7&n=17 [Accessed 5 August 2013].

Stenner, K.L., Courtenay, M. and Carey, N. (2011) 'Consultations between nurse prescribers and patients with diabetes in primary care: a qualitative study of patient views', *International Journal of Nursing Studies*, 48(1), 37–46.

Stierer, B. (2008) 'Learning to write about teaching: understanding the writing demands of lecturer development programmes in higher education', in R. Murray (ed.), *The Scholarship of Teaching and Learning in Higher Education*. Maidenhead: SRHE/Open University Press, 34–45.

Stokes, A. (2011a) 'Geocognition: a new research discipline for the 21st century?', *Geological Society of London, Higher Education Network launch event* [online] http://www.geolsoc.org.uk/page9929.html [Accessed 25 July 2013].

Stokes, A. (2011b) 'A phenomenographic approach to investigating students' conceptions of geoscience as an academic discipline', in A. Feig and A. Stokes (eds), *Qualitative Inquiry in Geoscience Education Research*. Geological Society of America, Special Paper No. 474, 23–35.

Stowell, M. (2004) 'Equity, justice and standards: assessment decision-making in higher education', *Assessment and Evaluation in Higher Education*, 29(4), 495–510.

Sturgis, P., Smith, P. and Hughes, G. (2005) *A Study of Suitable Methods for Raising Response Rates in School Surveys*. Research Report RR721. London: Department for Educational Skills [online] http://webarchive.nationalarchives.gov.uk/20130401151715/https://www.education.gov.uk/publications/eOrderingDownload/RR721.pdf [Accessed 8 July 2013].

Swann, C. (2002) 'Nellie is dead', *Art Design and Communication in Higher Education*, 1, 50–53 (reproduced without change from *Designer*, April, 1986).

Takacs, G. (2003) 'How does your positionality bias your epistemology?', *Thought & Action*, Summer, 27–38.

Tannery, P. and Henry, C. (eds) (1894) *Oeuvres de Fermat, Volume 2*. Paris: Gauthier-Villars et fils [online] http://archive.org/details/oeuvresdefermat942ferm [Accessed 25 July 2013].

Tavakol, M., Gruppen, L.D. and Torabi S. (2010) 'Using evaluation research to improve medical education', *The Clinical Teacher*, 7, 192–96.

Taylor, G., Mellor, L. and Walton, L. (no date) *The Politics of Widening Participation* [online] http://www.c-sap.bham.ac.uk/CSAP/ALAC/CommunityInvolvement/wideningparticipation.html [Accessed 17 July 2013].

TESTA (2013) *Transforming the Experience of Students Through Assessment* [online] http://www.testa.ac.uk/ [Accessed 24 July 2013].

Thomas, G. (2009) *How to Do your Research Project*. London: Sage.

Thomas W.I. and Thomas, D.S. (1928) *The Child in America: Behavior Problems and Programs*. New York: Knopf.

Tight, M. (2003) *Researching in Higher Education*. Buckingham: SRHE and Open University Press.

Titus, S. and Horsman, E. (2009) 'Characterizing and improving spatial visualization skills', *Journal of Geoscience Education*, 57(4), 242–54.

Trigwell, K., Martin, E., Benjamin, J. and Prosser, M. (2000) 'Scholarship of teaching: a model', *Higher Education Research and Development*, 19, 155–68.

Trowler, P. (2009) 'Beyond epistemological essentialism: academic tribes in the twenty-first century', in C. Kreber (ed.), *The University and its Disciplines*. New York: Routledge, 181–95.

Trowler, V. (2010) *Student Engagement Literature Review*. York: Higher Education Academy [online] http://www.heacademy.ac.uk/assets/documents/studentengagement/StudentEngagementLiteratureReview.pdf [Accessed 25 July 2013].

UNESCO (2012) *OER Paris Declaration* [online] http://www.unesco.org/new/fileadmin/MULTIMEDIA/HQ/CI/CI/pdf/Events/Paris%20OER%20Declaration_01.pdf [Accessed 24 July 2013].

United Nations (2013) *The Universal Declaration of Human Rights* [online] http://www.un.org/en/documents/udhr/ [Accessed 8 July 2013].

Universities Safety and Health Association and Universities and Colleges Employers Association (2011) *Guidance on Health and Safety in Fieldwork* [online] http://www.ucea.ac.uk/en/publications/index.cfm/guidance-on-health-and-safety-in-fieldwork [Accessed 8 July 2013].

University of Leeds (2013) *Definition of Scholarship* [online] hr.leeds.ac.uk/download/downloads/id/267/definition_of_scholarship [Accessed 10 August 2013].

University of Oxford (2013) *Cancer Research UK Million Women Study 2013* [online] http://www.millionwomenstudy.org/introduction/ [Accessed 3 July 2013].

Usher, K.J. and Arthur, D. (1998) 'Process consent: a model for enhancing informed consent in mental health nursing', *Journal of Advanced Nursing*, 27(4), 692–97.

Vardi, I. and Quin, R. (2011) 'Promotion and the scholarship of teaching and learning', *Higher Education Research and Development*, 30(1), 39–49.

Walford, G. (2001) *Doing Qualitative Educational Research: a Personal Guide to the Research Process*. London: Continuum.

Wall, D. (2010) 'Evaluation: improving practice, influencing policy', in T. Swanwick (ed.), *Understanding Medical Education: Evidence, Theory and Practice*. Oxford: Wiley-Blackwell.

Wareing, S. (2005) 'Discipline-specific professional development: just branding?', *Educational Developments*, 6(1), 12–14 [online] http://www.seda.ac.uk/?p=5_4_1&pID=6.1 [Accessed 5 August 2013].

Warnecke, E., Quinn, S., Ogden, K., Towle, N. and Nelson, M.R. (2011) 'A randomised controlled trial of the effects of mindfulness practice on medical student stress levels', *Medical Education*, 45, 381–88.

Weber, R.P. (1990). *Basic Content Analysis* (2nd edition). Newbury Park, CA: Sage.

Weller, S. (2010) 'Comparing student and lecturer and student accounts of reading in the humanities', *Arts and Humanities in Higher Education*, 9(1), 87–106.

Wenger, E. (1998) *Communities of Practice: Learning, Meaning and Identity*. Cambridge: Cambridge University Press.

Wiles, A. (1995) 'Modular elliptic curves and Fermat's Last Theorem', *Annals of Mathematics*, 141(3), 443–551.

Wiles, R., Crow, G., Charles, V. and Health, S. (2007) 'Informed consent and the research process: following rules or striking balances?', *Sociological Research Online*, 12(2) [online] http://www.socresonline.org.uk/12/2/wiles.html [Accessed 8 July 2013].

Williams, P. (2010) *Special Agents: The Nature and Role of Boundary Spanners*. Paper to the ESRC Research Seminar Series – Collaborative Futures: New Insights from Intra and Inter-Sectoral Collaborations, University of Birmingham, February 2010 [online] http://www.download.bham.ac.uk/govsoc/pdfs/special-agents-paper.pdf [Accessed 23 July 2013].

Williams, T., Dunlap, E., Johnson, B. and Hamid, A. (1992) 'Personal safety in dangerous places', *Journal of Contemporary Ethnography*, 21(3), 343–74.

Willmott, C. (2011) 'Here's one we prepared earlier: involving former students in careers advice', *Bioscience Education*, 18 [online] http://journals.heacademy.ac.uk/doi/abs/10.3108/beej.18.1SE [Accessed 26 July 2013].

Wong, G., Greenhalgh, T. and Pawson, R. (2010) 'Internet-based medical education: a realist review of what works, for whom and in what circumstances', *BMC Medical Education*, 10(12) [online] http://www.biomedcentral.com/1472-6920/10/12 [Accessed 6 August 2013].

Wong, G., Greenhalgh, T., Westhorp, G. and Pawson, R. (2012) 'Realist methods in medical education research: what are they and what can they contribute?', *Medical Education*, 46, 89–96.

Wood, A. and Biggs, I. (2004) 'Creative practices and the "Stigma of the Therapeutic": an issue for post graduate pedagogy?', in M. Miles (ed.), *New Practices – New Pedagogies: A Reader (Innovations in Art and Design)*. Swets & Zeitlinger [online] http://www.elia-artschools.org/images/products/25/new_pedagogies.pdf [Accessed 22 October 2013].

Woodiwiss, A. (2005) *Human Rights*. London: Routledge.

Yardley, L. (2011) *Have we been caught napping; the physical health and well-being of adult clients with severe mental illness*. MA Education Dissertation. Birmingham City University.

Yorke, M. (2003) 'Pedagogical research in higher education: an emerging policy framework', in H. Eggins and R. Macdonald (eds), *The Scholarship of Academic Development*. Buckingham: SRHE and Open University Press, 104–16.

Yorke, M., Barnett, G., Bridges, P., Evanson, P., Haines, C., Jenkins, D., Knight, P., Scurry, D., Stowell, M. and Woolf, H. (2002) 'Does grading method influence honours degree classification?', *Assessment and Evaluation in Higher Education*, 27(3), 269–79.

Yorke, M., Barnett, G., Evanson, P., Haines, C., Jenkins, D., Knight, P., Scurry, D., Stowell, M. and Woolf, H. (2004) 'Some effects of the award algorithm on honours degree classifications in UK higher education', *Assessment and Evaluation in Higher Education*, 29(4), 401–13.

Zeegers, P. (2001) 'Approaches to learning in science: a longitudinal study', *British Journal of Educational Psychology*, 71(1), 115–32.

INDEX